EVERYMAN'S LIBRARY

259

ROMANCE

Everyman, I will go with thee, and be thy guide,
In thy most need to go by thy side

ELIAS LÖNNROT. Born 1802. Finnish philologist, poet, and folklorist. Practised medicine in country districts, where he transcribed traditional ballads, among them the *Kalevala* cycle, which he published from 1838 to 1849. Became professor of Finnish literature at Helsinki, and died 1884.

KALEVALA

THE LAND OF THE HEROES

IN TWO VOLUMES · VOLUME ONE

TRANSLATED BY
W. F. KIRBY

INTRODUCTION BY
J. B. C. GRUNDY, M.A., PH.D.

LONDON J. M. DENT & SONS LTD
NEW YORK E. P. DUTTON & CO INC

KALEVALA

RUNO I.—BIRTH OF VÄINÄMÖINEN

Argument

Prelude (1-102). The Virgin of the Air descends into the sea, where she is fertilized by the winds and waves and becomes the Water-Mother (103-176). A teal builds its nest on her knee, and lays eggs (177-212). The eggs fall from the nest and break, but the fragments form the earth, sky, sun, moon and clouds (213-244). The Water-Mother creates capes, bays, sea-shores, and the depths and shallows of the ocean (245-280). Väinämöinen is born from the Water-Mother, and is tossed about by the waves for a long time until he reaches the shore (281-344).

I AM driven by my longing,
And my understanding urges
That I should commence my singing,
And begin my recitation.
I will sing the people's legends,
And the ballads of the nation.
To my mouth the words are flowing,
And the words are gently falling,
Quickly as my tongue can shape them,
And between my teeth emerging.   10

Dearest friend, and much-loved brother,
Best beloved of all companions,
Come and let us sing together,
Let us now begin our converse,
Since at length we meet together,
From two widely sundered regions.
Rarely can we meet together,
Rarely one can meet the other,
In these dismal Northern regions,
In the dreary land of Pohja.   20
Let us clasp our hands together,
Let us interlock our fingers ;
Let us sing a cheerful measure,
Let us use our best endeavours,

While our dear ones hearken to us,
And our loved ones are instructed,
While the young are standing round us,
Of the rising generation,
Let them learn the words of magic,
And recall our songs and legends,   30
Of the belt of Väinämöinen,
Of the forge of Ilmarinen,
And of Kaukomieli's sword-point,
And of Joukahainen's crossbow :
Of the utmost bounds of Pohja,
And of Kalevala's wide heathlands.

These my father sang aforetime,
As he carved his hatchet's handle,
And my mother taught me likewise,
As she turned around her spindle,
When upon the floor, an infant,
At her knees she saw me tumbling,   40
As a helpless child, milk-bearded,
As a babe with mouth all milky.
Tales about the Sampo failed not,
Nor the magic spells of Louhi.
Old at length became the Sampo ;
Louhi vanished with her magic ;
Vipunen while singing perished ;
Lemminkainen in his follies.   50

There are many other legends ;
Songs I learned of magic import ;
Some beside the pathway gathered ;
Others broken from the heather ;
Others wrested from the bushes ;
Others taken from the saplings,
Gathered from the springing verdure,
Or collected from the by-ways,
As I passed along as herd-boy,
As a child in cattle-pastures,   60
On the hillocks, rich in honey,
On the hills, for ever golden,
After Muurikki, the black one,
By the side of dappled Kimmo.

Then the Frost his songs recited,
And the rain its legends taught me;
Other songs the winds have wafted,
Or the ocean waves have drifted;
And their songs the birds have added,
And the magic spells the tree-tops.   70

In a ball I bound them tightly;
And arranged them in a bundle;
On my little sledge I laid it,
On my sleigh I laid the bundle;
Home upon the sledge I brought it,
Then into the barn conveyed it;
In the storehouse loft I placed it,
In a little box of copper.

In the cold my song was resting,
Long remained in darkness hidden.   80
I must draw the songs from Coldness,
From the Frost must I withdraw them,
Bring my box into the chamber,
On the bench-end lay the casket,
Underneath this noble gable,
Underneath this roof of beauty.
Shall I ope my box of legends,
And my chest where lays are treasured?
Is the ball to be unravelled,
And the bundle's knot unfastened?   90
Then I'll sing so grand a ballad,
That it wondrously shall echo,
While the rye-bread I am eating,
And the beer of barley drinking.
But though ale should not be brought me,
And though beer should not be offered,
I will sing, though dry my throttle,
Or will sing, with water only,
To enhance our evening's pleasure,
Celebrate the daylight's beauty,   100
Or the beauty of the daybreak,
When another day is dawning.

I have often heard related,
And have heard the song recited,

How the nights closed ever lonely,
And the days were shining lonely.
Only born was Väinämöinen,
And revealed the bard immortal,
Sprung from the divine Creatrix,
Born of Ilmatar, his mother.   110
 Air's young daughter was a virgin,
Fairest daughter of Creation.
Long did she abide a virgin,
All the long days of her girlhood,
In the Air's own spacious mansions,
In those far extending regions.
 Wearily the time passed ever,
And her life became a burden,
Dwelling evermore so lonely,
Always living as a maiden,   120
In the Air's own spacious mansions,
In those far-extending deserts.
 After this the maid descending,
Sank upon the tossing billows,
On the open ocean's surface,
On the wide expanse of water.
 Then a storm arose in fury,
From the East a mighty tempest,
And the sea was wildly foaming,
And the waves dashed ever higher.   130
 Thus the tempest rocked the virgin,
And the billows drove the maiden,
O'er the ocean's azure surface,
On the crest of foaming billows,
Till the wind that blew around her,
And the sea woke life within her.
 Then she bore her heavy burden,
And the pain it brought upon her,
Seven long centuries together,
Nine times longer than a lifetime.   140
Yet no child was fashioned from her,
And no offspring was perfected.
 Thus she swam, the Water-Mother,
East she swam, and westward swam she,

Swam to north-west and to south-west,
And around in all directions,
In the sharpness of her torment,
In her body's fearful anguish ;
Yet no child was fashioned from her,
And no offspring was perfected.   150

Then she fell to weeping gently,
And in words like these expressed her :
" O how wretched is my fortune,
Wandering thus, a child unhappy !
I have wandered far already,
And I dwell beneath the heaven,
By the tempest tossed for ever,
While the billows drive me onward,
O'er this wide expanse of water,
On the far-extending billows.   160

" Better were it had I tarried,
Virgin in aërial regions,
Then I should not drift for ever,
As the Mother of the Waters.
Here my life is cold and dreary,
Every moment now is painful,
Ever tossing on the billows,
Ever floating on the water.

" Ukko, thou of Gods the highest,
Ruler of the whole of heaven,   170
Hasten here, for thou art needed ;
Hasten here at my entreaty.
Free the damsel from her burden,
And release her from her tortures.
Quickly haste, and yet more quickly,
Where I long for thee so sorely."

Short the time that passed thereafter,
Scarce a moment had passed over,
Ere a beauteous teal came flying
Lightly hovering o'er the water,   180
Seeking for a spot to rest in,
Searching for a home to dwell in.

Eastward flew she, westward flew she,
Flew to north-west and to southward,

But the place she sought she found not,
Not a spot, however barren,
Where her nest she could establish,
Or a resting-place could light on.
    Then she hovered, slowly moving,
And she pondered and reflected, 190
"If my nest in wind I 'stablish
Or should rest it on the billows,
Then the winds will overturn it,
Or the waves will drift it from me."
    Then the Mother of the Waters,
Water-Mother, maid aërial,
From the waves her knee uplifted,
Raised her shoulder from the billows,
That the teal her nest might 'stablish,
And might find a peaceful dwelling. 200
Then the teal, the bird so beauteous,
Hovered slow, and gazed around her,
And she saw the knee uplifted
From the blue waves of the ocean,
And she thought she saw a hillock,
Freshly green with springing verdure.
There she flew, and hovered slowly,
Gently on the knee alighting,
And her nest she there established,
And she laid her eggs all golden, 210
Six gold eggs she laid within it,
And a seventh she laid of iron.
    O'er her eggs the teal sat brooding,
And the knee grew warm beneath her ;
And she sat one day, a second,
Brooded also on the third day ;
Then the Mother of the Waters,
Water-Mother, maid aërial,
Felt it hot, and felt it hotter,
And she felt her skin was heated, 220
Till she thought her knee was burning,
And that all her veins were melting.
Then she jerked her knee with quickness,
And her limbs convulsive shaking,

Rolled the eggs into the water,
Down amid the waves of ocean,
And to splinters they were broken,
And to fragments they were shattered.

In the ooze they were not wasted,
Nor the fragments in the water,   230
But a wondrous change came o'er them,
And the fragments all grew lovely.
From the cracked egg's lower fragment,
Now the solid earth was fashioned,
From the cracked egg's upper fragment,
Rose the lofty arch of heaven,
From the yolk, the upper portion,
Now became the sun's bright lustre;
From the white, the upper portion,
Rose the moon that shines so brightly;   240
Whatso in the egg was mottled,
Now became the stars in heaven,
Whatso in the egg was blackish,
In the air as cloudlets floated.

Now the time passed quickly over,
And the years rolled quickly onward,
In the new sun's shining lustre,
In the new moon's softer beaming.
Still the Water-Mother floated,
Water-Mother, maid aërial,   250
Ever on the peaceful waters,
On the billows' foamy surface,
With the moving waves before her,
And the heaven serene behind her.

When the ninth year had passed over,
And the summer tenth was passing,
From the sea her head she lifted,
And her forehead she uplifted,
And she then began Creation,
And she brought the world to order,   260
On the open ocean's surface,
On the far extending waters.

Wheresoe'er her hand she pointed,
There she formed the jutting headlands;

Wheresoe'er her feet she rested,
There she formed the caves for fishes;
When she dived beneath the water,
There she formed the depths of ocean;
When towards the land she turned her,
There the level shores extended,   270
Where her feet to land extended,
Spots were formed for salmon-netting;
Where her head the land touched lightly,
There the curving bays extended.
Further from the land she floated,
And abode in open water,
And created rocks in ocean,
And the reefs that eyes behold not,
Where the ships are often shattered,
And the sailors' lives are ended.   280
Now the isles were formed already,
In the sea the rocks were planted;
Pillars of the sky established,
Lands and continents created;
Rocks engraved as though with figures,
And the hills were cleft with fissures.
Still unborn was Väinämöinen;
Still unborn, the bard immortal.
Väinämöinen, old and steadfast,
Rested in his mother's body   290
For the space of thirty summers,
And the sum of thirty winters,
Ever on the placid waters,
And upon the foaming billows.
So he pondered and reflected
How he could continue living
In a resting-place so gloomy,
In a dwelling far too narrow,
Where he could not see the moonlight,
Neither could behold the sunlight.   300
Then he spake the words which follow,
And expressed his thoughts in this wise:
"Aid me Moon, and Sun release me,
And the Great Bear lend his counsel,

Through the portal that I know not,
Through the unaccustomed passage.
From the little nest that holds me,
From a dwelling-place so narrow,
To the land conduct the roamer,
To the open air conduct me,   310
To behold the moon in heaven,
And the splendour of the sunlight;
See the Great Bear's stars above me,
And the shining stars in heaven."

When the moon no freedom gave him,
Neither did the sun release him,
Then he wearied of existence,
And his life became a burden.
Thereupon he moved the portal,
With his finger, fourth in number,   320
Opened quick the bony gateway,
With the toes upon his left foot,
With his nails beyond the threshold,
With his knees beyond the gateway.

Headlong in the water falling,
With his hands the waves repelling,
Thus the man remained in ocean,
And the hero on the billows.

In the sea five years he sojourned,
Waited five years, waited six years,   330
Seven years also, even eight years,
On the surface of the ocean,
By a nameless promontory,
Near a barren, treeless country.

On the land his knees he planted,
And upon his arms he rested,
Rose that he might view the moonbeams,
And enjoy the pleasant sunlight,
See the Great Bear's stars above him,
And the shining stars in heaven.   340

Thus was ancient Väinämöinen,
He, the ever famous minstrel.
Born of the divine Creatrix,
Born of Ilmatar, his mother.

RUNO II.—VÄINÄMÖINEN'S SOWING

Argument

Väinämöinen lands on a treeless country and directs Sampsa
Pellervoinen to sow trees (1–42). At first the oak will not grow, but
after repeated sowings it springs up, overshadows the whole country,
and hides the sun and moon (43–110). A little man rises from the
sea, who fells the oak, and permits the sun and moon to shine again
(111–224). Birds sing in the trees ; herbs, flowers and berries grow on the
ground ; only the barley will not spring up (225–256). Väinämöinen
finds some barleycorns in the sand on the shore, and fells the forest,
leaving only a birch-tree as a resting-place for the birds (257–264). The
eagle, grateful for this, strikes fire, and the felled trees are consumed
(265–284). Väinämöinen sows the barley, prays to Ukko for its increase,
and it grows and flourishes (285–378).

THEN did Väinämöinen, rising,
Set his feet upon the surface
Of a sea-encircled island,
In a region bare of forest.
　　There he dwelt, while years passed over,
And his dwelling he established
On the silent, voiceless island,
In a barren, treeless country.
　　Then he pondered and reflected,
In his mind he turned it over,　　　　　　　　10
" Who shall sow this barren country,
Thickly scattering seeds around him ? "
　　Pellervoinen, earth-begotten,
Sampsa, youth of smallest stature,
Came to sow the barren country,
Thickly scattering seeds around him.
　　Down he stooped the seeds to scatter,
On the land and in the marshes,
Both in flat and sandy regions,
And in hard and rocky places.　　　　　　　　20
On the hills he sowed the pine-trees,
On the knolls he sowed the fir-trees,

And in sandy places heather ;
Leafy saplings in the valleys.
    In the dales he sowed the birch-trees,
In the loose earth sowed the alders,
Where the ground was damp the cherries,
Likewise in the marshes, sallows.
Rowan-trees in holy places,
Willows in the fenny regions,   30
Juniper in stony districts,
Oaks upon the banks of rivers.
    Now the trees sprang up and flourished,
And the saplings sprouted bravely.
With their bloom the firs were loaded,
And the pines their boughs extended.
In the dales the birch was sprouting,
In the loose earth rose the alders,
Where the ground was damp the cherries,
Juniper in stony districts,   40
Loaded with its lovely berries ;
And the cherries likewise fruited.
    Väinämöinen, old and steadfast,
Came to view the work in progress,
Where the land was sown by Sampsa,
And where Pellervoinen laboured.
While he saw the trees had flourished,
And the saplings sprouted bravely,
Yet had Jumala's tree, the oak-tree,
Not struck down its root and sprouted.   50
    Therefore to its fate he left it,
Left it to enjoy its freedom,
And he waited three nights longer,
And as many days he waited.
Then he went and gazed around him,
When the week was quite completed.
Yet had Jumala's tree, the oak-tree,
Not struck down its root and sprouted.
    Then he saw four lovely maidens ;
Five, like brides, from water rising ;   60
And they mowed the grassy meadow,
Down they cut the dewy herbage,

On the cloud-encompassed headland,
On the peaceful island's summit,
What they mowed, they raked together,
And in heaps the hay collected.

From the ocean rose up Tursas,
From the waves arose the hero,
And the heaps of hay he kindled,
And the flames arose in fury.   70
All was soon consumed to ashes,
Till the sparks were quite extinguished.

Then among the heaps of ashes,
In the dryness of the ashes,
There a tender germ he planted,
Tender germ, of oak an acorn
Whence the beauteous plant sprang upward,
And the sapling grew and flourished,
As from earth a strawberry rises,
And it forked in both directions.   80
Then the branches wide extended,
And the leaves were thickly scattered,
And the summit rose to heaven,
And its leaves in air expanded.

In their course the clouds it hindered,
And the driving clouds impeded,
And it hid the shining sunlight,
And the gleaming of the moonlight.

Then the aged Väinämöinen,
Pondered deeply and reflected,   90
" Is there none to fell the oak-tree,
And o'erthrow the tree majestic?
Sad is now the life of mortals,
And for fish to swim is dismal,
Since the air is void of sunlight,
And the gleaming of the moonlight."

But they could not find a hero,
Nowhere find a man so mighty,
Who could fell the giant oak-tree,
With its hundred spreading branches.   100
Then the aged Väinämöinen,
Spoke the very words which follow :

"Noble mother, who hast borne me,
Luonnotar, who me hast nurtured ;
Send me powers from out the ocean :
(Numerous are the powers of ocean)
So that they may fell the oak-tree,
And destroy the tree so baneful,
That the sun may shine upon us,
And the pleasant moonlight glimmer."　110

Then a man arose from ocean,
From the waves a hero started,
Not the hugest of the hugest,
Nor the smallest of the smallest.
As a man's thumb was his stature ;
Lofty as the span of woman.

Decked his head a helm of copper,
On his feet were boots of copper,
On his hands were copper gauntlets,
Gloves adorned with copper tracings ;　120
Round his waist his belt was copper ;
In his belt his axe was copper ;
And the haft thereof was thumb-long,
And the blade thereof was nail-long.

Väinämöinen, old and steadfast,
Deeply pondered and reflected :
"While he seems a man in semblance,
And a hero in appearance,
Yet his height is but a thumb-length,
Scarce as lofty as an ox-hoof."　130

Then he spoke the words which follow,
And expressed himself in this wise :
"Who are you, my little fellow,
Most contemptible of heroes,
Than a dead man scarcely stronger ;
And your beauty all has vanished."

Then the puny man from ocean,
Hero of the floods, made answer :
"I'm a man as you behold me,
Small, but mighty water-hero,　140
I have come to fell the oak-tree,
And to splinter it to fragments."

Väinämöinen, old and steadfast,
Answered in the words which follow:
"You have hardly been created,
Neither made, nor so proportioned,
As to fell this mighty oak-tree,
Overthrow the tree stupendous."

Scarcely had the words been spoken,
While his gaze was fixed upon him,   150
When the man transformed before him,
And became a mighty hero.
While his feet the earth were stamping,
To the clouds his head he lifted,
To his knees his beard was flowing,
To his spurs his locks descended.
Fathom-wide his eyes were parted,
Fathom-wide his trousers measured;
Round his knee the girth was greater,
And around his hip 'twas doubled.   160
Then he sharpened keen the axe-blade,
Brought the polished blade to sharpness;
Six the stones on which he ground it,
Seven the stones on which he whet it.

Then the man stepped forward lightly,
Hastened on to do his mission;
Wide his trousers, and they fluttered
Round his legs as onward strode he,
And the first step taken, brought him
To the shore so soft and sandy;   170
With the second stride he landed
On the dun ground further inland,
And the third step brought him quickly,
Where the oak itself was rooted.

With his axe he smote the oak-tree,
With his sharpened blade he hewed it;
Once he smote it, twice he smote it,
And the third stroke wholly cleft it.
From the axe the flame was flashing,
Flame was bursting from the oak-tree,   180
As he strove to fell the oak-tree,
Overthrow the tree stupendous.

Thus the third blow was delivered,
And the oak-tree fell before him,
For the mighty tree was shattered,
And the hundred boughs had fallen,
And the trunk extended eastward,
And the summit to the north-west,
And the leaves were scattered southward,
And the branches to the northward.   190

He who took a branch from off it,
Took prosperity unceasing,
What was broken from the summit,
Gave unending skill in magic ;
He who broke a leafy branchlet,
Gathered with it love unending.
What remained of fragments scattered,
Chips of wood, and broken splinters,
On the bright expanse of ocean,
On the far-extending billows,   200
In the breeze were gently rocking,
On the waves were lightly drifted,
Like the boats on ocean's surface,
Like the ships amid the sea-waves.

Northward drove the wind the fragments,
Where the little maid of Pohja,
Stood on beach, and washed her head-dress,
And she washed her clothes and rinsed them,
On the shingle by the ocean,
On a tongue of land projecting.   210

On the waves she saw the fragments,
Put them in her birch-bark wallet,
In her wallet took them homeward ;
In the well-closed yard she stored them,
For the arrows of the sorcerer,
For the chase to furnish weapons.

When the oak at last had fallen,
And the evil tree was levelled,
Once again the sun shone brightly,
And the pleasant moonlight glimmered,   220
And the clouds extended widely,
And the rainbow spanned the heavens,

O'er the cloud-encompassed headland,
And the island's misty summit.
Then the wastes were clothed with verdure,
And the woods grew up and flourished;
Leaves on trees and grass in meadows.
In the trees the birds were singing,
Loudly sang the cheery throstle;
In the tree-tops called the cuckoo.   230
Then the earth brought forth her berries;
Shone the fields with golden blossoms;
Herbs of every species flourished;
Plants and trees of all descriptions;
But the barley would not flourish,
Nor the precious seed would ripen.
Then the aged Väinämöinen,
Walked around, and deeply pondered,
By the blue waves' sandy margin,
On the mighty ocean's border,   240
And six grains of corn he found there,
Seven fine seeds of corn he found there,
On the borders of the ocean,
On the yielding sandy margin.
In a marten's skin he placed them,
From the leg of summer squirrel.
Then he went to sow the fallows;
On the ground the seeds to scatter,
Near to Kaleva's own fountain,
And upon the field of Osmo.   250
From a tree there chirped the titmouse:
" Osmo's barley will not flourish,
Nor will Kaleva's oats prosper,
While untilled remains the country,
And uncleared remains the forest,
Nor the fire has burned it over."
Väinämöinen, old and steadfast,
Ground his axe-blade edge to sharpness
And began to fell the forest,
Toiling hard to clear the country.   260
All the lovely trees he levelled,
Sparing but a single birch-tree,

That the birds might rest upon it,
And from thence might call the cuckoo.
    In the sky there soared an eagle,
Of the birds of air the greatest,
And he came and gazed around him.
"Wherefore is the work unfinished,
And the birch-tree still unfallen?
Wherefore spare the beauteous birch-tree?"   270
    Said the aged Väinämöinen,
"Therefore is the birch left standing,
That the birds may perch upon it;
All the birds of air may rest there."
    Said the bird of air, the eagle,
"Very wisely hast thou acted,
Thus to leave the birch-tree standing
And the lovely tree unfallen,
That the birds may perch upon it,
And that I myself may rest there."   280
    Then the bird of air struck fire,
And the flames rose up in brightness,
While the north wind fanned the forest,
And the north-east wind blew fiercely.
All the trees were burned to ashes,
Till the sparks were quite extinguished.
    Then the aged Väinämöinen,
Took the six seeds from his satchel,
And he took the seven small kernels,
From the marten's skin he took them,   290
From the leg of summer squirrel,
From the leg of summer ermine.
    Then he went to sow the country,
And to scatter seeds around him,
And he spoke the words which follow:
"Now I stoop the seeds to scatter,
As from the Creator's fingers,
From the hand of Him Almighty,
That the country may be fertile,
And the corn may grow and flourish.   300
    "Patroness of lowland country,
Old one of the plains; Earth-Mother,

Let the tender blade spring upward,
Let the earth support and cherish.
Might of earth will never fail us,
Never while the earth existeth,
When the Givers are propitious,
And Creation's daughters aid us.
  " Rise, O earth, from out thy slumber,
Field of the Creator, rouse thee,   310
Make the blade arise and flourish,
Let the stalks grow up and lengthen,
That the ears may grow by thousands,
Yet a hundredfold increasing,
By my ploughing and my sowing,
In return for all my labour.
  " Ukko, thou of Gods the highest,
Father, thou in heaven abiding,
Thou to whom the clouds are subject,
Of the scattered clouds the ruler,   320
All thy clouds do thou assemble,
In the light make clear thy counsel,
Send thou forth a cloud from eastward,
In the north-west let one gather,
Send thou others from the westward,
Let them drive along from southward,
Send the light rain forth from heaven,
Let the clouds distil with honey,
That the corn may sprout up strongly,
And the stalks may wave and rustle."   330
  Ukko, then, of Gods the highest,
Father of the highest heaven,
Heard, and all the clouds assembled,
In the light made clear his counsel,
And he sent a cloud from eastward,
In the north-west let one gather,
Others, too, he sent from westward,
Let them drive along from southward,
Linked them edge to edge together,
And he closed the rifts between them.   340
Then he sent the rain from heaven,
And the clouds distilled sweet honey,

That the corn might sprout up stronger,
And the stalks might wave and rustle.
Thus the sprouting germ was nourished,
And the rustling stalks grew upward,
From the soft earth of the cornfield,
Through the toil of Väinämöinen.

After this, two days passed over,
After two nights, after three nights,   350
When the week was full completed,
Väinämöinen, old and steadfast,
Wandered forth to see the progress ;
How his ploughing and his sowing
And his labours had resulted.
There he found the barley growing,
And the ears were all six-cornered,
And the stalks were all three-knotted.

Then the aged Väinämöinen
Wandered on and gazed around him,   360
And the cuckoo, bird of springtime,
Came and saw the birch-tree growing.
" Wherefore is the birch left standing,
And unfelled the slender birch-tree ? "

Said the aged Väinämöinen,
" Therefore is the birch left standing,
And unfelled the slender birch-tree,
As a perch for thee, O Cuckoo ;
Whence the cuckoo's cry may echo.
From thy sand-hued throat cry sweetly,   370
With thy silver voice call loudly,
With thy tin-like voice cry clearly,
Call at morning, call at evening,
And at noontide call thou likewise,
To rejoice my plains surrounding,
That my woods may grow more cheerful,
That my coast may grow more wealthy,
And my region grow more fruitful."

RUNO III.—VÄINÄMÖINEN AND JOUKAHAINEN

Argument

Väinämöinen increases in wisdom and composes songs (1–20). Joukahainen sets out to contend with him in wisdom ; but as he cannot overcome him, he challenges him to a duel, whereupon Väinämöinen grows angry, and sinks him in a swamp by his magic songs (21–330). Joukahainen, in great distress, finally offers his sister Aino in marriage to Väinämöinen, who accepts the offer and releases him (331–476). Joukahainen returns home discomfited, and relates his misfortunes to his mother (477–524). The mother rejoices at the prospect of such an alliance, but the daughter laments and weeps (525–580).

VÄINÄMÖINEN, old and steadfast
Passed the days of his existence
Where lie Väinölä's sweet meadows,
Kalevala's extended heathlands :
There he sang his songs of sweetness
Sang his songs and proved his wisdom
    Day by day he sang unwearied,
Night by night discoursed unceasing,
Sang the songs of by-gone ages,
Hidden words of ancient wisdom,   10
Songs which all the children sing not,
All beyond men's comprehension,
In these ages of misfortune,
When the race is near its ending.
    Far away the news was carried,
Far abroad was spread the tidings
Of the songs of Väinämöinen,
Of the wisdom of the hero ;
In the south was spread the rumoui ,
Reached to Pohjola the tidings.   20
    Here dwelt youthful Joukahainen,
He, the meagre youth of Lapland ;
And, when visiting the village,
Wondrous tales he heard related,

How there dwelt another minstrel,
And that better songs were carolled,
Far in Väinölä's sweet meadows,
Kalevala's extended heathlands ;
Better songs than he could compass ;
Better than his father taught him.   30
    This he heard with great displeasure,
And his heart was filled with envy
That the songs of Väinämöinen
Better than his own were reckoned.
Then he went to seek his mother ;
Sought her out, the aged woman,
And declared that he would journey,
And was eager to betake him,
Unto Väinölä's far dwellings,
That he might contend with Väinö.   40
    But his father straight forbade him,
Both his father and his mother,
Thence to Väinölä to journey,
That he might contend with Väinö.
" He will surely sing against you,
Sing against you, and will ban you,
Sink your mouth and head in snow-drifts,
And your hands in bitter tempest :
Till your hands and feet are stiffened,
And incapable of motion."   50
    Said the youthful Joukahainen,
" Good the counsel of my father,
And my mother's counsel better ;
Best of all my own opinion.
I will set myself against him,
And defy him to a contest,
I myself my songs will sing him,
I myself will speak my mantras ;
Sing until the best of minstrels
Shall become the worst of singers.   60
Shoes of stone will I provide him,
Wooden trousers on his haunches ;
On his breast a stony burden,
And a rock upon his shoulders ;

Stony gloves his hands shall cover,
And his head a stony helmet."
    Then he went his way unheeding,
Went his way, and fetched his gelding,
From whose mouth the fire was flashing,
'Neath whose legs the sparks were flying.   70
Then the fiery steed he harnessed,
To the golden sledge he yoked him,
In the sledge himself he mounted,
And upon the seat he sat him,
O'er the horse his whip he brandished,
With the beaded whip he smote him,
From the place the horse sprang quickly,
And he darted lightly forwards.
    On he drove with thundering clatter,
As he drove a day, a second,   80
Driving also on the third day,
And at length upon the third day,
Came to Väinölä's sweet meadows,
Kalevala's extended heathlands.
    Väinämöinen, old and steadfast,
He, the oldest of magicians,
As it chanced was driving onward,
Peacefully his course pursuing
On through Väinölä's sweet meadows,
Kalevala's extended heathlands.   90
    Came the youthful Joukahainen
Driving on the road against him,
And the shafts were wedged together,
And the reins were all entangled,
And the collar jammed with collar,
And the runners dashed together.
    Thus their progress was arrested,
Thus they halted and reflected ;
Sweat dropped down upon the runners ;
From the shafts the steam was rising.   100
    Asked the aged Väinämöinen,
" Who are you, and what your lineage,
You who drive so reckless onward,
Utterly without reflection ?

Broken are the horses' collars,
And the wooden runners likewise ;
You have smashed my sledge to pieces,
Broke the sledge in which I travelled."
    Then the youthful Joukahainen
Answered in the words which follow :   110
" I am youthful Joukahainen ;
But yourself should also tell me,
What your race, and what your nation,
And from what vile stock you issue."
    Väinämöinen, old and steadfast,
Told his name without concealment,
And began to speak as follows :
"Youth, if you are Joukahainen,
You should move aside a little,
For remember, you are younger."   120
    But the youthful Joukahainen
Answered in the words which follow :
" Here of youthfulness we reck not ;
Nought doth youth or age concern us,
He who highest stands in knowledge,
He whose wisdom is the greatest,
Let him keep the path before him,
And the other yield the passage.
If you are old Väinämöinen,
And the oldest of the minstrels,   130
Let us give ourselves to singing,
Let us now repeat our sayings,
That the one may teach the other,
And the one surpass the other."
    Väinämöinen, old and steadfast,
Answered in the words which follow :
"What can I myself accomplish
As a wise man or a singer ?
I have passed my life in quiet,
Here among these very moorlands,   140
On the borders of my home-field
I have heard the cuckoo calling.
But apart from this at present,
I will ask you to inform me

What may be your greatest wisdom;
And the utmost of your knowledge?"
    Said the youthful Joukahainen,
"Many things I know in fulness,
And I know with perfect clearness,
And my insight shows me plainly,   150
In the roof we find the smoke-hole,
And the fire is near the hearthstone.
    "Joyful life the seal is leading,
In the waves there sports the sea-dog,
And he feeds upon the salmon,
And the powans round about him.
    "Smooth the water loved by powans,
Smooth the surface, too, for salmon;
And in frost the pike is spawning,
Slimy fish in wintry weather.   160
Sluggish is the perch, the humpback,
In the depths it swims in autumn,
But it spawns in drought of summer,
Swimming slowly to the margin.
    "If this does not yet suffice you,
I am wise in other matters,
And of weighty things can tell you.
In the north they plough with reindeer,
In the south the mare is useful,
And the elk in furthest Lapland.   170
    "Trees I know on Pisa mountain,
Firs upon the rocks of Horna,
Tall the trees on Pisa mountain,
And the firs on rocks of Horna.
    "Three great waterfalls I know of,
And as many lakes extensive,
And as many lofty mountains,
Underneath the vault of heaven.
Hälläpyörä is in Häme,
Karjala has Kaatrakoski,   180
But they do not match the Vuoksi,
There where Imatra is rushing."
    Said the aged Väinämöinen,
"Childish tales, and woman's wisdom,

But for bearded men unsuited,
And for married men unfitted.
Tell me words of deepest wisdom,
Tell me now of things eternal."

Then the youthful Joukahainen
Answered in the words which follow: 190
"Well I know whence comes the titmouse,
That the titmouse is a birdie,
And a snake the hissing viper,
And the ruffe a fish in water.
And I know that hard is iron,
And that mud when black is bitter.
Painful, too, is boiling water,
And the heat of fire is hurtful,
Water is the oldest medicine,
Cataract's foam a magic potion;   200
The Creator's self a sorcerer,
Jumala the Great Magician.

"From the rock springs forth the water,
And the fire from heaven descendeth,
And from ore we get the iron,
And in hills we find the copper.

"Marshy country is the oldest,
And the first of trees the willow.
Pine-roots were the oldest houses,
And the earliest pots were stone ones."   210

Väinämöinen, old and steadfast,
Answered in the words which follow:
"Is there more that you can tell me,
Or is this the end of nonsense?"

Said the youthful Joukahainen,
"Many little things I wot of,
And the time I well remember
When 'twas I who ploughed the ocean,
Hollowed out the depths of ocean,
And I dug the caves for fishes,   220
And I sunk the deep abysses,
When the lakes I first created,
And I heaped the hills together,
And the rocky mountains fashioned.

"Then I stood with six great heroes,
I myself the seventh among them.
When the earth was first created,
And the air above expanded;
For the sky I fixed the pillars,
And I reared the arch of heaven,   230
To the moon assigned his journey,
Helped the sun upon his pathway,
To the Bear his place appointed,
And the stars in heaven I scattered."

Said the aged Väinämöinen,
"Ay, indeed, a shameless liar!
You at least were never present
When the ocean first was furrowed,
And the ocean depths were hollowed,
And the caves were dug for fishes,   240
And the deep abysses sunken,
And the lakes were first created,
When the hills were heaped together,
And the rocky mountains fashioned.

"No one ever yet had seen you,
None had seen you, none had heard you,
When the earth was first created,
And the air above expanded,
When the posts of heaven were planted,
And the arch of heaven exalted,   250
When the moon was shown his pathway,
And the sun was taught to journey,
When the Bear was fixed in heaven,
And the stars in heaven were scattered."

But the youthful Joukahainen
Answered in the words which follow:
"If I fail in understanding,
I will seek it at the sword-point.
O thou aged Väinämöinen,
O thou very broad-mouthed minstrel,   260
Let us measure swords together,
Let the blade decide between us."

Said the aged Väinämöinen,
"I have little cause to fret me

Either for your sword or wisdom,
For your sword-point or your judgment.
But, apart from this at present,
I will draw no sword upon you,
So contemptible a fellow,
And so pitiful a weakling."   270
  Then the youthful Joukahainen
Shook his head, his mouth drawn crooked,
And he tossed his locks of blackness,
And he spake the words which follow :
  " He who shuns the sword's decision,
Nor betakes him to his sword-blade,
To a swine I soon will sing him,
To a snouted swine transform him.
Heroes I have thus o'erpowered,
Hither will I drive and thither.   280
And will pitch them on the dunghill,
Grunting in the cowshed corner."
  Angry then was Väinämöinen,
Filled with wrath and indignation,
And himself commenced his singing,
And to speak his words of wisdom.
But he sang no childish ditties,
Children's songs and women's jesting,
But a song for bearded heroes,
Such as all the children sing not,   290
Nor a half the boys can master,
Nor a third can lovers compass,
In the days of dark misfortune,
When our life is near its ending.
  Sang the aged Väinämöinen ;
Lakes swelled up, and earth was shaken,
And the coppery mountains trembled,
And the mighty rocks resounded.
And the mountains clove asunder ;
On the shore the stones were shivered.   300
Then he sang of Joukahainen,
Changed his runners into saplings,
And to willows changed the collar,
And the reins he turned to alder,

And he sang the sledge all gilded,
To the lake among the rushes,
And the whip, with beads embellished,
To a reed upon the water,
And the horse, with front white-spotted
To a stone beside the torrent.　　　　310

Then he sang his sword, gold-hilted,
To a lightning-flash in heaven,
And his ornamented crossbow,
To a rainbow o'er the water,
And he sang his feathered arrows,
Into hawks that soar above him ;
And his dog, with upturned muzzle,
Stands a stone in earth embedded.

From his head, his cap, by singing,
Next became a cloud above him,　　　　320
From his hands, his gloves, by singing,
Next were changed to water-lilies,
And the blue coat he was wearing,
Floats a fleecy cloud in heaven,
And the handsome belt that girt him,
In the sky as stars he scattered.

As he sang, sank Joukahainen
Waist-deep in the swamp beneath him,
Hip-deep in the marshy meadow,
To his arm-pits in a quicksand.　　　　330
Then indeed young Joukahainen
Knew at last, and comprehended ;
And he knew his course was finished,
And his journey now was ended.
For in singing he was beaten,
By the aged Väinämöinen.

He would raise his foot to struggle
But he could no longer lift it ;
Then he tried to lift the other,
But as shod with stone he felt it.　　　　340

Then the youthful Joukahainen
Felt the greatest pain and anguish,
And he fell in grievous trouble,
And he spoke the words which follow :

"O thou wisest Väinämöinen,
O thou oldest of magicians,
Speak thy words of magic backwards,
And reverse thy songs of magic.
Loose me from this place of terror,
And release me from my torment.   350
I will pay the highest ransom,
And the fixed reward will give thee."

Said the aged Väinämöinen,
"What do you propose to give me,
If I turn my words of magic,
And reverse my songs of magic,
Loose you from this place of terror,
And release you from your torment?"

Said the youthful Joukahainen,
"I've two crossbows I could give you,   360
Ay, a pair of splendid crossbows,
One shoots forth with passing quickness,
Surely hits the mark the other.
If it please you, choose between them."

Said the aged Väinämöinen,
"No, your bows I do not covet,
For the wretched bows I care not;
I myself have plenty of them.
All the walls are decked with crossbows,
All the pegs are hung with crossbows;   370
In the woods they wander hunting,
Nor a hero needs to span them."

Then the youthful Joukahainen
In the swamp he sang yet deeper.

Said the youthful Joukahainen,
"I have yet two boats to offer;
Splendid boats, as I can witness,
One is light, and fit for racing,
Heavy loads will bear the other;
If it please you, choose between them."   380

Said the aged Väinämöinen,
"No, your boats I do not covet,
And I will not choose between them,
I myself have plenty of them.

All the staves are full already,
Every creek is crowded with them,
Boats to face the gale adapted,
Boats against the wind that travel."
　　Then the youthful Joukahainen,
In the swamp he sang yet deeper.　　　　　　390
　　Said the youthful Joukahainen,
"I have still two noble stallions;
Ay, a pair of handsome horses;
One of these of matchless swiftness,
And the other best in harness.
If it please you, choose between them."
　　Said the aged Väinämöinen,
"No, I do not want your horses;
Do not need your steeds, white-footed.
I myself have plenty of them.　　　　　　400
Every stall has now its tenant,
Every stable's filled with horses,
With their backs like water shining;
Lakes of fat upon their haunches."
　　Then the youthful Jaukahainen,
In the swamp he sang yet deeper.
　　Said the youthful Joukahainen,
"O thou aged Väinämöinen,
Speak thy words of magic backwards,
And reverse thy songs of magic.　　　　　　410
I will give a golden helmet,
And a hat filled up with silver,
Which my father won in warfare,
Which he won in battle-struggle."
　　Said the aged Väinämöinen,
"No, I do not want your silver,
And for gold, I only scorn it.
I myself have both in plenty.
Every store-room crammed with treasure,
Every chest is overflowing.　　　　　　420
Gold as ancient as the moonlight,
Silver with the sun coeval."
　　Then the youthful Joukahainen
In the swamp he sang yet deeper.

Said the youthful Joukahainen,
" O thou aged Väinämöinen,
Loose me from this place of terror,
And release me from my torment.
All my stacks at home I'll give thee,
And my fields I likewise promise,   430
All to save my life I offer,
If you will accept my ransom."
Said the aged Väinämöinen,
" No, your barns I do not covet,
And your fields are 'neath my notice.
I myself have plenty of them.
Fields are mine in all directions,
Stocks are reared on every fallow,
And my own fields please me better,
And my stacks of corn are finest."   440
Then the youthful Joukahainen
In the swamp he sang yet deeper.
Then the youthful Joukahainen,
Felt at length the greatest anguish,
Chin-deep in the swamp while sinking,
In the mud his beard was draggled,
In the moss his mouth was sunken,
And his teeth among the tree-roots.
Said the youthful Joukahainen,
" O thou wisest Väinämöinen,   450
O thou oldest of magicians,
Sing once more thy songs of magic,
Grant the life of one so wretched,
And release me from my prison.
In the stream my feet are sunken,
With the sand my eyes are smarting.
" Speak thy words of magic backwards,
Break the spell that overwhelms me !
You shall have my sister Aino,
I will give my mother's daughter.   460
She shall dust your chamber for you,
Sweep the flooring with her besom,
Keep the milk-pots all in order ;
And shall wash your garments for you.

Golden fabrics she shall weave you,
And shall bake you cakes of honey."
Then the aged Väinämöinen,
Heard his words, and grew full joyful,
Since to tend his age was promised
Joukahainen's lovely sister.   470

On the stone of joy he sat him,
On the stone of song he rested,
Sang an hour, and sang a second,
And again he sang a third time:
Thus reversed his words of magic,
And dissolved the spell completely.

Then the youthful Joukahainen
From the mud his chin uplifted,
And his beard he disentangled,
From the rock his steed led forward,   480
Drew his sledge from out the bushes,
From the reeds his whip unloosing.

Then upon his sledge he mounted,
And upon the seat he sat him,
And with gloomy thoughts he hastened,
With a heart all sad and doleful,
Homeward to his dearest mother,
Unto her, the aged woman.

On he drove with noise and tumult,
Home he drove in consternation,   490
And he broke the sledge to pieces,
At the door the shafts were broken.

Then the noise alarmed his mother,
And his father came and asked him,
"Recklessly the sledge was broken;
Did you break the shafts on purpose?
Wherefore do you drive so rashly,
And arrive at home so madly?"

Then the youthful Joukahainen
Could not keep his tears from flowing;   500
Sad he bowed his head in sorrow,
And his cap awry he shifted,
And his lips were dry and stiffened,
O'er his mouth his nose was drooping.

Then his mother came and asked him
Wherefore was he sunk in sorrow.
"O my son, why weep so sadly?
O my darling, why so troubled,
With thy lips so dry and stiffened,
O'er thy mouth thy nose thus drooping?"   510
Said the youthful Joukahainen,
"O my mother, who hast borne me,
There is cause for what has happened,
For the sorcerer has o'ercome me.
Cause enough have I for weeping,
And the sorcerer's brought me sorrow.
I myself must weep for ever,
And must pass my life in mourning,
For my very sister Aino,
She, my dearest mother's daughter,   520
I have pledged to Väinämöinen,
As the consort of the minstrel,
To support his feeble footsteps,
And to wait upon him always."
Joyous clapped her hands his mother,
Both her hands she rubbed together,
And she spoke the words which follow:
"Do not weep, my son, my dearest,
For thy tears are quite uncalled for.
Little cause have we to sorrow,   530
For the hope I long have cherished,
All my lifetime I have wished it,
And have hoped this high-born hero
Might akin to us be reckoned,
And the minstrel Väinämöinen
Might become my daughter's husband."
But when Joukahainen's sister
Heard, she wept in deepest sorrow,
Wept one day, and wept a second,
At the threshold ever weeping,   540
Wept in overwhelming sorrow,
In the sadness of her spirit.
Then her mother said consoling,
"Wherefore weep, my little Aino?

You have gained a valiant bridegroom,
And the home of one most noble,
Where you'll look from out the window,
Sitting on the bench and talking."

But her daughter heard and answered,
"O my mother, who hast borne me, 550
Therefore have I cause for weeping,
Weeping for the beauteous tresses,
Now my youthful head adorning,
And my hair so soft and glossy,
Which must now be wholly hidden,
While I still am young and blooming.

"Then must I through lifetime sorrow
For the splendour of the sunlight,
And the moonbeam's charming lustre
And the glory of the heavens, 560
Which I leave, while still so youthful,
And as child must quite abandon,
I must leave my brother's work-room,
Just beyond my father's window."

Said the mother to the daughter,
To the girl the crone made answer,
"Cast away this foolish sorrow,
Cease your weeping, all uncalled for,
Little cause have you for sorrow,
Little cause for lamentation. 570
God's bright sun is ever shining
On the world in other regions,
Shines on other doors and windows
Than your father's or your brother's ;
Berries grow on every mountain,
Strawberries on the plains are growing,
You can pluck them in your sorrow
Wheresoe'er your steps may lead you ;
Not alone on father's acres,
Or upon your brother's clearings.' 580

RUNO IV.—THE FATE OF AINO

Argument

Väinämöinen meets Aino in the wood and addresses her (1–20). Aino hurries home weeping, and informs her mother (21–116). Her mother forbids her to weep, and tells her to rejoice, and to adorn herself handsomely (117–188). Aino continues to weep, and declares that she will never take a very old man as her husband (189–254). She wanders sorrowfully into the wild woods, and reaches the banks of a strange unknown lake, where she goes to bathe, and is lost in the water (255–370). The animals commission the hare to carry the tidings of Aino's death to her home (371–434). Her mother weeps for her night and day (435–518).

THEN the little maiden Aino,
Youthful Joukahainen's sister,
Went for besoms to the greenwood,
Sought for bath-whisks in the bushes;
One she gathered for her father,
And a second for her mother,
And she gathered yet another,
For her young and ruddy brother.

As she turned her footsteps homeward,
Pushing through the alder-bushes,   10
Came the aged Väinämöinen,
And he saw her in the thicket,
Finely clad among the herbage,
And he spoke the words which follow:
"Maiden, do not wear for others,
But for me alone, O maiden,
Round thy neck a beaded necklace,
And a cross upon thy bosom.
Plait for me thy beauteous tresses,
Bind thy hair with silken ribands."   20

But the young maid gave him answer,
"Not for thee, and not for others,
Rests the cross upon my bosom,
And my hair is bound with ribands.

Nought I care for sea-borne raiment ;
Wheaten bread I do not value.
I will walk in home-spun garments,
And with crusts will still my hunger,
In my dearest father's dwelling,
And beside my much-loved mother."   30
    From her breast she took the crosslet,
Drew the rings from off her fingers,
From her neck the beaded necklace,
From her head the scarlet ribands.
Down upon the ground she threw them,
Scattered them among the bushes ;
Then she hastened, ever weeping,
Loud lamenting, to the homestead.
    At the window sat her father,
While he carved a hatchet-handle.   40
" Wherefore weepest thou, my daughter,
Young, and yet so full of sadness ? "
    " Cause enough have I for weeping,
Cause for weeping and lamenting.
Therefore weep I, dearest father,
Weep, and feel so full of sorrow.
From my breast I lost the crosslet,
From my belt I dropped the buckle,
From my breast my silver crosslet,
From my waist the copper girdle."   50
    At the gate, her brother sitting,
For the sledge was shaping runners.
" Wherefore weepest thou, my sister,
Young, and yet so full of sorrow ? "
    " Cause enough have I for weeping,
Cause for weeping and lamenting.
Therefore do I weep, poor brother,
Weep, and feel so full of sorrow.
Rings I lost from off my fingers,
From my neck my beaded necklace,   60
And my finger-rings were golden,
And my necklace-beads were silver."
    At the window sat her sister,
As she wove a golden girdle

"Wherefore weepest thou, poor sister,
Young, and yet so full of sorrow?"
    "Cause enough have I for weeping,
Cause for weeping and lamenting.
Therefore do I weep, poor sister,
Weep and feel so full of sorrow.   70
From my brow the gold has fallen,
From my hair I lost the silver,
Tore the blue bands from my temples,
From my head the scarlet braiding."
    On the threshold of the storehouse,
Skimming milk, she found her mother.
"Wherefore weepest thou, my daughter,
Young, and yet so full of sorrow?"
    "O my mother, who hast borne me,
O my mother, who hast nursed me,   80
Cause enough have I for anguish,
Cause enough for bitter sorrow.
Therefore do I weep, poor mother,
Therefore grieve I, O my mother,
To the wood I went for besoms,
Gathered bath-whisks from the bushes;
One I gathered for my father,
One I gathered for my mother,
And I gathered yet another,
For my young and ruddy brother.   90
As I turned my footsteps homeward,
And across the heath was tripping,
From the dell there called Osmoinen,
From the field cried Kalevainen,
    "Do not wear, fair maid, for others,
But for me alone, poor maiden,
Round thy neck a beaded necklace,
And a cross upon thy bosom.
Plait for me thy beauteous tresses,
Braid thy hair with silken ribands."   100
    "From my breast I took the crosslet,
From my neck the beaded necklace,
Tore the blue bands from my temples,
From my head the scarlet ribands,

Then upon the ground I threw them,
Scattered them among the bushes,
And I answered him in this wise :
" Not for thee, and not for others,
Rests my cross upon my bosom,
And my hair is bound with ribands.   110
Nought I care for sea-borne raiment,
Wheaten bread I do not value.
I will walk in home-spun garments,
And with crusts will still my hunger,
In my dearest father's dwelling,
And beside my much-loved mother."

 And her mother answered thus wise,
Said the old crone to the maiden,
" Do not weep, my dearest daughter,
Do not grieve (and thou so youthful) ;   120
Eat a whole year long fresh butter,
That your form may grow more rounded,
Eat thou pork the second season,
That your form may grow more charming,
And the third year eat thou cream-cakes,
That you may become more lovely.
Seek the storehouse on the mountain,
There the finest chamber open.
There are coffers piled on coffers,
Chests in heaps on chests are loaded,   130
Open then the finest coffer,
Raise the painted lid with clangour,
There you'll find six golden girdles,
Seven blue robes of finest texture,
Woven by the Moon's own daughter,
By the Sun's own daughter fashioned.

 " In the days when I was youthful,
In my youthful days of girlhood,
In the wood I sought for berries,
Gathered raspberries on the mountain,   140
Heard the moonlight's daughter weaving,
And the sunlight's daughter spinning,
There beside the wooded island,
On the borders of the greenwood.

"Thereupon I softly neared them,
And beside them took my station,
And began to ask them gently,
In the words that I repeat you :
'Give you of your gold, O Kuutar,
And your silver give, Päivätär,   150
To the maiden poorly dowered,
To the child who now implores you !'

"Then her gold did Kuutar give me,
And her silver gave Päivätär.
With the gold I decked my temples,
And adorned my head with silver,
Homeward like a flower I hastened,
Joyful, to my father's dwelling.

"These I wore one day, a second,
Then upon the third day after   160
Took the gold from off my temples,
From my head removed the silver,
Took them to the mountain storehouse ;
In the chest with care I laid them,
There until this day I left them,
And since then I have not seen them.

"On thy brows bind silken ribands,
On thy temples gold adornments,
Round thy neck a beaded necklace,
On thy breast a golden crosslet.   170
Put thou on a shift of linen,
Of the finest flax that's woven,
Lay thou on a robe of woollen,
Bind it with a silken girdle,
Then the finest silken stockings,
And of shoes the very finest,
Then in plaits thy hair arranging,
Bind it up with silken ribands,
Slip the gold rings on thy fingers,
Deck thy wrists with golden bracelets.   180
After this return thou homewards
From thy visit to the storehouse,
As the joy of all thy kindred,
And of all thy race the fairest,

Like a floweret by the wayside,
Like a raspberry on the mountain,
Far more lovely than aforetime,
Fairer than in former seasons."

Thus the mother urged her counsel,
Thus she spoke unto her daughter,   190
But the daughter did not heed her,
Heeded not her mother's counsel.
From the house she wandered weeping,
From the homestead went in sorrow,
And she said the words which follow,
And expressed herself in this wise :

'What may be the joyous feelings,
And the thoughts of one rejoicing ?
Such may be the joyous feelings,
And the thoughts of one rejoicing ;   200
Like the dancing of the water
On the waves when gently swelling.
What do mournful thoughts resemble ?
What the long-tailed duck may ponder ?
Such may mournful thoughts resemble,
Thus the long-tailed duck may ponder,
As 'neath frozen snow embedded,
Water deep in well imprisoned.

"Often now my life is clouded,
Often is my childhood troubled,   210
And my thoughts like withered herbage,
As I wander through the bushes,
Wandering on through grassy meadows,
Pushing through the tangled thickets,
And my thoughts are pitch for blackness
And my heart than soot not brighter.

"Better fortune had befel me,
And it would have been more happy,
Had I not been born and nurtured,
And had never grown in stature,   220
Till I saw these days of sorrow,
And this joyless time o'ertook me,
Had I died in six nights only,
Or upon the eighth had perished

Much I should not then have needed,
But a shroud a span-long only,
And of earth a tiny corner.
Little then had wept my mother,
Fewer tears had shed my father,
And my brother not a tearlet."   230

Thus she wept a day, a second,
And again her mother asked her,
"Wherefore dost thou weep, poor maiden,
Wherefore thus lament and sorrow ? "

" Therefore weep I, hapless maiden,
Therefore do I weep for ever,
That yourself have pledged me, hapless,
And your daughter you have promised
Thus to be an old man's comfort,
As a solace to the old man,   240
To support his feeble footsteps,
And to wait upon him always.
Better were it had you sent me
Deeply down beneath the billows,
There to be the powan's sister,
And companion of the fishes.
In the lake 'tis surely better
There beneath the waves to sojourn,
There to be the powan's sister,
And companion of the fishes,   250
Than to be an old man's comfort,
To support his aged footsteps,
So that I can mend his stockings,
And may be a staff to prop him."

Then she sought the mountain storehouse,
And the inner room she entered ;
And the finest chest she opened,
Raised the painted lid with clangour,
And she found six golden girdles,
Seven blue robes of finest texture,   260
And she robed her in the finest,
And completed her adornment.
Set the gold upon her temples,
On her hair the shining silver,

On her brow the sky-blue ribands,
On her head the bands of scarlet.
    Then she wandered from the storehouse,
And across the fields she wandered,
Past the marshes, and the heathlands,
Through the shady, gloomy forests.   270
Thus she sang, as on she hastened,
Thus she spoke, as on she wandered:
"All my heart is filled with trouble;
On my head a stone is loaded.
But my trouble would not vex me,
And the weight would less oppress me,
If I perished, hapless maiden,
Ending thus my life of sorrow,
In the burden of my trouble,
In the sadness of my sorrow.   280
    "Now my time perchance approaches,
From this weary world to hasten,
Time to seek the world of Mana,
Time to Tuonela to hasten,
For my father will not mourn me,
Nor my mother will lament me,
Nor my sister's cheeks be moistened,
Nor my brother's eyes be tearful,
If I sank beneath the waters,
Sinking where the fish are sporting,   290
To the depths beneath the billows,
Down amid the oozy blackness."
    On she went, one day, a second,
And at length, upon the third day,
Came she to a lake's broad margin,
To the bank, o'ergrown with rushes.
And she reached it in the night-time,
And she halted in the darkness.
    In the evening wept the maiden,
Through the darksome night lamented,   300
On the rocks that fringed the margin,
Where a bay spread wide before her.
At the earliest dawn of morning,
As she gazed from off a headland,

Just beyond she saw three maidens,
Bathing there amid the waters,
Aino made the fourth among them,
And the fifth a slender sapling.

Then her shift she cast on willows,   310
And her dress upon the aspens,
On the open ground her stockings,
Threw her shoes upon the boulders,
On the sand her beads she scattered,
And her rings upon the shingle.

In the waves a rock was standing,
Brightly hued and golden shining ;
And she swam and sought to reach it,
As a refuge in her trouble.

When at length she stood upon it,
And would rest upon the summit,   320
On the stone of many colours,
On the rock so smooth and shining,
In the waves it sank beneath her,
Sinking to the very bottom.
With the rock, the maiden Aino
Sank beneath the water's surface.

There the dove for ever vanished,
Thus the luckless maiden perished,
She herself exclaimed in dying,
When she felt that she was sinking :   330
" To the lake I went to bathe me,
And to swim upon its surface,
But, like tender dove, I vanished,
Like a bird by death o'ertaken.
Never may my dearest father,
Never while his life endureth,
Cast his net amid the waters,
In these waves, so wide extending.

" To the shore I went to wash me,
To the lake I went to bathe me,   340
But, like tender dove, I vanished,
Like a bird by death o'ertaken.
Never may my dearest mother,
Never while her life endureth,

Fetch the water for her baking,
From the wide bay near her dwelling.
"To the shore I went to wash me,
To the lake I went to bathe me,
But, like tender dove, I vanished,
Like a bird by death o'ertaken.   350
Never may my dearest brother,
Never while his life endureth,
Water here his prancing courser,
Here upon the broad lake's margin.

"To the shore I went to wash me,
To the lake I went to bathe me,
But, like tender dove, I vanished,
Like a bird by death o'ertaken.
Never may my dearest sister,
Never while her life endureth,   360
Hither stay to wash her eyebrows,
On the bridge so near her dwelling.
In the lake the very water
Is as blood that leaves my veinlets;
Every fish that swims this water,
Is as flesh from off my body;
All the bushes on the margin
Are as ribs of me unhappy;
And the grass upon the margin
As my soiled and tangled tresses."   370
    Thus the youthful maiden perished,
And the dove so lovely vanished.
    Who shall now the tidings carry,
And repeat the mournful story,
At the dwelling of the maiden,
At the homestead of the fair one?
    First the bear would take the tidings,
And repeat the mournful story;
But the bear conveyed no tidings,
For he strayed among the cattle.   380
    Who shall now the tidings carry,
And repeat the mournful story,
At the dwelling of the maiden,
At the homestead of the fair one?

Then the wolf would take the message,
And repeat the mournful story;
But the wolf conveyed no tidings,
For among the sheep he wandered.
 Who shall now the tidings carry,
And repeat the mournful story,   390
At the dwelling of the maiden,
At the homestead of the fair one?
 Then the fox would take the message,
And repeat the mournful story;
But the fox conveyed no tidings,
For among the geese he wandered.
 Who shall now the tidings carry,
And repeat the mournful story,
At the dwelling of the maiden,
At the homestead of the fair one?   400
 'Twas the hare who took the tidings,
And conveyed the mournful story;
For the hare replied discreetly,
"I will not forget the message."
 Then the hare sprang quickly onward,
Sped the Long-ear with his story,
On his crooked legs he hastened,
With his cross-like mouth he hurried,
To the dwelling of the maiden,
To the homestead of the fair one.   410
 Thus he hastened to the bath-house
And he crouched upon the threshold.
Full of maidens is the bath-house,
In their hands the bath-whisks holding.
"Scamp, come here; and shall we boil you,
Or, O Broad-eye, shall we roast you,
Either for the master's supper,
Or perchance the mistress' breakfast,
For the luncheon of the daughter,
Or perchance the son to dine on?"   420
 Thereupon the hare responded,
And the Round-eye answered boldly,
"Would that Lempo might come hither
For the cooking in the kettle!

I am come to give you tidings,
And to bring a message to you.
Vanished from you is the fair one,
Perished has the tin-adorned one,
Sunken with her silver buckle,
Drowning with her belt of copper,   430
Diving in the muddy water,
To the depths below the billows,
There to be the powan's sister,
And companion of the fishes."

Then her mother fell to weeping,
And her bitter tears flowed freely,
And she loud lamented, speaking
In her grief the words which follow :
"Never, O unhappy mothers,
Never while your life endureth,   440
Never may you urge your daughters,
Or attempt to force your children
To a marriage that repels them,
Like myself, O wretched mother,
Urging vainly thus my daughter,
Thus my little dove I fostered."

Thus the mother wept, lamenting,
And her bitter tears flowed freely
From her blue eyes in her sadness,
O'er her cheeks, so pale with sorrow.   450
After one tear flowed another,
And her bitter tears flowed freely
From her cheeks, so pale with sorrow,
To her breast, so sadly heaving.
After one tear flowed another,
And her bitter tears flowed freely
From her breast, so sadly heaving,
On the borders of her garments.
After one tear flowed another,
And her bitter tears flowed freely   460
From the borders of her garments
Down upon her scarlet stockings.
After one tear flowed another,
And her bitter tears flowed freely

Down from off her scarlet stockings
To her shoes, all gold-embroidered.
    After one tear flowed another,
And her bitter tears flowed freely
From her shoes, all gold-embroidered,
On the ground where she was standing.   470
As they flowed, the ground they moistened,
And they swelled to streams of water.
    On the ground the streams were flowing,
And became the source of rivers;
Thence arose three mighty rivers
From the tears of bitter weeping,
Which were ever ceaseless flowing
From the weeping mother's eyelids.
    From each stream that thus was fashioned,
Rushed three waterfalls in fury,   480
And amid each cataract's flowing,
Three great rocks arose together,
And on every rocky summit
There arose a golden mountain,
And on every mountain summit
Up there sprang three beauteous birch-trees,
In the crown of every birch-tree,
Golden cuckoos three were perching.
    All at once they called together,
And the first cried, "Sweetheart, sweetheart!" 490
And the second, "Lover, lover!"
And the third cried, "Gladness, gladness!"
    He who cried out, "Sweetheart, sweetheart!"
Sang his song for three months running,
For the young and loveless maiden,
Resting now beneath the water.
    He who cried out, "Lover, lover!"
Sang his song for six months running,
Sang to the unhappy suitor,
Who must sorrow through his lifetime.   500
    He who cried out, "Gladness, gladness!"
Sang his song for all a lifetime;
Sang to the unhappy mother,
Who must daily weep for ever.

And the mother spoke as follows,
As she listened to the cuckoo :
" Never may a hapless mother
Listen to the cuckoo crying !
When I hear the cuckoo calling,
Heavy beats my heart within me.   510
From my eyes the tears are falling,
O'er my cheeks are waters rolling,
And the drops like peas are swelling,
Than the largest broad-beans larger.
By an ell my life is shortened,
By a span-length I am older,
And my strength has wholly failed me,
Since I heard the cuckoo calling."

Runo V.—Väinämöinen's Fishing

Argument

Väinämöinen fishes for Joukahainen's sister in the lake, and draws
her into his boat in the form of a fish (1–72). He is about to cut her
to pieces when she slips from his hand into the lake, and tells him who
she is (73–133). Väinämöinen tries to persuade her to return to him,
and then fishes for her, but in vain (134–163). He returns home
disconsolate, and his dead mother advises him to woo the Maiden of
Pohja (164–241).

Now the tidings were repeated,
And the news was widely rumoured,
How the youthful maid had perished,
And the fair one had departed.
Väinämöinen, old and steadfast,
Deeply sorrowed at the tidings ;
Wept at evening, wept at morning,
Spent the livelong night in weeping,
For the fair one who had perished,
For the maiden who had slumbered,   10
In the muddy lake downsunken
To the depths below the billows.

Then he went, in sorrow sighing,
While his heart was filled with anguish,
To the blue lake's rocky margin,
And he spoke the words which follow:
"Tell me, Untamo, thou sleeper,
Tell me all thy dreams, O idler,
Where to find the realm of Ahto,
Where dwell Vellamo's fair maidens?"   20

Sleeper Untamo made answer,
And his dreams he thus repeated:
"There has Ahto fixed his country,
There dwell Vellamo's fair maidens,
Near the cloud-encompassed headland,
Near the ever-misty island,
In the depths below the billows,
On the black ooze at the bottom.

"There has Ahto fixed his country,
There dwell Vellamo's fair maidens,   30
Living in a narrow chamber,
In a little room abiding,
With the walls of varied marble,
In the depths beside the headland."

Then the aged Väinämöinen
Hastened to his little vessel,
And he scanned his fishing-tackle,
And his hooks with care inspected;
Put the tackle in his pocket,
And the barbed hooks in his wallet.   40
Through the waves his boat he ferried,
Making for the jutting headland,
To the cape, with clouds encompassed,
And the ever-misty island.

Then he set about his fishing,
And he watched his angle closely,
And he held his hand-net ready,
Dropped his angle in the water,
And he fished, and tried his fortune,
While the rod of copper trembled,   50
And the thread of silver whistled,
And the golden line whirred loudly.

And at length one day it happened,
Very early in the morning,
On his hook a fish was hanging,
And a salmon-trout was captured.
In the boat he drew it quickly,
And upon the planks he cast it.

Then he scanned the fish, and turned it,
And he spoke the words which follow:　　60
"'Tis a fish, among the fishes,
For I never saw its equal,
Smoother is it than a powan,
Than a salmon-trout more yellow,
Greyer than a pike I deem it,
For a female fish too finless,
For a male 'tis far too scaleless;
Has no tresses, like a maiden,
Nor, like water-nymphs, 'tis belted;
Nor is earless like a pigeon;　　70
It resembles most a salmon,
Or a perch from deepest water."

In his waistband Väinämöinen
Bore a case-knife, silver-hafted,
And he drew the knife of sharpness,
Drew the case-knife, silver-hafted,
And prepared to slit the salmon,
And to cut the fish to pieces,
Thought to eat it for his breakfast,
Or a snack to make his luncheon,　　80
To provide him with a dinner,
And a plenteous supper likewise.

As he would have slit the salmon,
And would cut the fish to pieces,
Sprang the salmon in the water,
For the beauteous fish jumped sideways
From the planking of the red boat,
From the boat of Väinämöinen.

Thereupon her head she lifted,
Raised her shoulders from the water,　　90
On the fifth wave's watery hillock,
From the sixth high wave emerging,

Then her hands in air uplifted,
And displayed her left foot also,
When the seventh wave rose, upswelling,
And upon the ninth wave's summit.
　　Thereupon the fish addressed him,
And it spoke, and thus protested :
" O thou aged Väinämöinen,
Surely I have not come hither,　　　　　　　　　100
Like a salmon, to be slaughtered,
Or a fish, to cut to pieces,
Only to become your breakfast,
Or a snack to make your luncheon,
To provide you with a dinner,
And a plenteous supper likewise."
　　Said the aged Väinämöinen,
" Wherefore didst thou then come hither ? "
　　" Therefore 'tis that I have sought thee,
In thine arm like dove to nestle,　　　　　　　110
By thy side to sit for ever,
On thy knee, as consort sitting,
To prepare the couch to rest thee,
And to smooth thy pillow for thee,
Keep thy little room in order,
And to sweep the flooring for thee,
In thy room to light the fire,
And to fan the flames up brightly,
There large loaves of bread to bake thee,
Cakes of honey to prepare thee,　　　　　　　120
And thy jug of beer to fill thee,
And thy dinner set before thee.
　　" I am not a water-salmon,
Not a perch from deepest water,
But a young and lovely maiden,
Youthful Joukahainen's sister,
Whom thou all thy life hast longed for,
Whom thou hast so long desired.
　　" O thou pitiful old creature,
Väinämöinen, void of wisdom,　　　　　　　　130
Thou hadst not the wit to hold me,
Vellamo's young water-maiden,

Me, the darling child of Ahto!"
Said the aged Väinämöinen,
Head bowed down, and deeply grieving,
"Sister thou of Joukahainen,
Once again return, I pray thee."
But she never more came near him,
Ne'er again throughout his lifetime;
For she turned away, and, diving,   140
Vanished from the water's surface
Down among the rocks so varied,
In a liver-coloured crevice.
Väinämöinen, old and steadfast,
Pondered deeply, and reflected,
What to do, and what was needful.
Quick he wove a net all silken,
And he drew it straight and crossways,
Through the reach, and then across it,
Drew it through the quiet waters,   150
Through the depths beloved by salmon,
And through Väinölä's deep waters,
And by Kalevala's sharp headlands,
Through the deep, dark watery caverns,
And the wide expanse of water,
And through Joukola's great rivers,
And across the bays of Lapland.
Other fish he caught in plenty,
All the fishes of the waters,
Only not the fish he sought for,   160
Which he kept in mind for ever,
Never Vellamo's fair maiden,
Not the dearest child of Ahto.
Then the aged Väinämöinen,
Bowed his head, lamenting deeply,
With his cap adjusted sideways,
And he spoke the words which follow:
"O how grievous is my folly,
Weak am I in manly wisdom,
Once indeed was understanding,   170
Insight too conferred upon me,
And my heart was great within me;

Such in former times my portion.
But in days that now are passing,
In the evil days upon me,
Now my strength with age is failing,
All my understanding weakens
And my insight has departed,
All my judgment is perverted.

"She for whom long years I waited,   180
Whom for half my life I longed for,
Vellamo's fair water-maiden,
Youngest daughter of the surges,
Who should be my friend for ever,
And my wife throughout my lifetime,
Came and seized the bait I offered,
In my boat sprang unresisting,
But I knew not how to hold her,
To my home I could not take her,
But she plunged amid the waters,   190
Diving to the depths profoundest."

Then he wandered on a little,
And he walked, in sadness sighing,
To his home direct returning,
And he spoke the words which follow:
"Once indeed the birds were singing,
And my joyous cuckoo hailed me,
Both at morning and at evening,
Likewise, too, in midday hours.
What has stilled their lively music,   200
And has hushed their charming voices?
Care has stilled their lively music,
Sorrow checked their cheerful voices,
Therefore do they sing no longer,
Neither at the sun's declining,
To rejoice me in the evening,
Nor to cheer me in the morning.

"Now no more can I consider
How to shape my course of action,
How upon the earth to sojourn,   210
How throughout the world to travel.
Would my mother now were living,

And my aged mother waking !
She would surely tell me truly
How to best support my trouble,
That my grief may not o'erwhelm me,
And my sorrow may not crush me,
In these weary days of evil,
In this time of deep depression."

    In her grave his mother wakened,   220
Answered from beneath the billows :
" Still thy mother lives and hears thee,
And thy aged mother wakens,
That she plainly may advise thee,
How to best support thy trouble,
That thy grief may not o'erwhelm thee,
And thy sorrow may not crush thee,
In these weary days of evil,
In these days of deep depression.
Seek thou out the maids of Pohja,   230
Where the daughters are more handsome,
And the maidens twice as lovely,
And are five or six times nimbler,
Not like lazy girls of Jouko,
Lapland's fat and sluggish daughters.

    " Thence a wife, O son, provide thee,
From the fairest maids of Pohja ;
Choose a maid of fair complexion,
Lovely, too, in every feature,
One whose feet are always nimble,   240
Always active in her movements."

RUNO VI.—JOUKAHAINEN'S CROSSBOW

Argument

Joukahainen cherishes hatred against Väinämöinen and lies in wait
for him on his journey to Pohjola (1–78). He sees him riding past and
shoots at him, but only kills his horse (79–182). Väinämöinen falls into
the water and is driven out to sea by a tempest, while Joukahainen
rejoices, because he thinks he has at last overcome Väinämöinen (183–
234).

VÄINÄMÖINEN, old and steadfast,
Now resolved upon a journey
To the cold and dreary regions
Of the gloomy land of Pohja.
  Then he took his straw-hued stallion
Like a pea-stalk in his colour,
And the golden bit adjusted,
Bridle on his head of silver,
On his back himself he seated,
And he started on his journey,   10
And he trotted gently onward,
At an easy pace he journeyed,
Mounted on the straw-hued courser,
Like a pea-stalk in his colour.
  Thus through Väinölä he journeyed,
Over Kalevala's wide heathlands,
And the horse made rapid progress,
Home behind, and journey shortened,
Then across the sea he journeyed,
O'er the far-extending billows,   20
With the horse's hoofs unwetted,
And his feet unsunk in water.
  But the youthful Joukahainen,
He, the puny son of Lapland,
Long had cherished his resentment,
And had long indeed been envious
Of the aged Väinämöinen,
Of the ever-famous minstrel.

Then he wrought a mighty crossbow,
And a splendid bow he fashioned,   30
And he formed the bow of iron,
Overlaid the back with copper,
And with gold inlaid it also,
And with silver he adorned it.

Where did he obtain the bowstring?
Whence a cord to match the weapon?
Sinews from the elk of Hiisi,
And the hempen cord of Lempo.
Thus at length the bow was finished,
And the stock was quite completed,   40
And the bow was fair to gaze on,
And its value matched its beauty.
At its back a horse was standing,
On the stock a foal was running,
On the curve a sleeping woman,
At the catch a hare was couching.

Shafts of wood he likewise fashioned,
Every arrow triply feathered,
And the shafts were formed of oakwood,
And he made the heads of pinewood;   50
Thus the arrows were completed,
And he fixed the feathers on them,
From the swallows' plumage taken,
Likewise from the tails of sparrows.

After this, the points he sharpened,
And the arrow-points he poisoned,
In the black blood of the serpent,
In the blood of hissing adders.

Thus he made his arrows ready,
And his bow was fit for bending,   60
And he watched for Väinämöinen,
Waited for Suvantolainen,
Watched at morning, watched at evening,
Waited also through the noontide.

Long he watched for Väinämöinen,
Waited long, and wearied never,
Sitting gazing from the window,
Or upon the stairs he waited,

Sometimes lurking by the pathway,
Sometimes watching in the meadow, 70
On his back his well-filled quiver,
'Neath his arm his crossbow ready.
   Then he waited further onwards,
Lurking near another building,
On the cape that juts out sharply,
Where the tongue of land curves outward,
Near a waterfall, all foaming,
Past the banks of sacred rivers.
   And at length one day it happened,
Very early in the morning, 80
As he turned his eyes to westward,
And he turned his head to eastward
Something dark he spied on ocean,
Something blue upon the billows.
" Is a cloud in east arising,
Or the dawn of day appearing ? "
   In the east no cloud was rising,
Nor the dawn of day appearing.
'Twas the aged Väinämöinen,
'Twas the ever-famous minstrel, 90
Who to Pohjola was hasting,
As to Pimentola he journeyed,
Mounted on his straw-hued courser,
Like a pea-stalk in his colour.
   Then the youthful Joukahainen,
He, the meagre son of Lapland,
Spanned in haste his mighty crossbow,
And he aimed the splendid weapon
At the head of Väinämöinen,
Thus to kill Suvantolainen. 100
   Then his mother came and asked him,
And the aged one inquired,
" Wherefore do you span your weapon,
Bending thus the iron crossbow ? "
   Then the youthful Joukahainen
Answered in the words which follow:
" Therefore do I span the weapon,
Bending thus the iron crossbow,

For the head of Väinämöinen,
Thus to kill Suvantolainen, 110
I will shoot old Väinämöinen,
Strike the ever-famous minstrel,
Through the heart, and through the liver,
'Twixt the shoulders I will shoot him."
But his mother straight forbade him,
And dissuaded him from shooting.
"Do not shoot at Väinämöinen,
Do not Kalevalainen slaughter.
Of a noble race is Väinö ;
He's my sister's son, my nephew. 120
"If you shoot at Väinämöinen,
And should Kalevalainen slaughter,
Gladness from the world will vanish,
And from earth will song be banished.
In the world is gladness better,
And on earth is song more cheerful,
Than to Manala if banished,
And to Tuonela's darkest regions."
Then the youthful Joukahainen
Paused a moment and reflected, 130
And he pondered for an instant,
Though his hands to shoot were ready,
One would shoot, and one restrained him,
But his sinewy fingers forced him.
And at length these words he uttered,
And expressed his own decision :
"What if twice from earth in future
Every gladness should be banished ?
Let all songs for ever vanish ;
I will shoot my arrows, heedless ! " 140
Then he spanned the mighty crossbow,
And he drew the bow of copper,
And against his left knee bent it,
Steady with his foot he held it,
Took an arrow from his quiver,
Chose a triple-feathered arrow,
Took the strongest of his arrows,
Chose the very best among them.

Then upon the groove he laid it,
On the hempen cord he fixed it,   150
Then his mighty bow he lifted,
And he placed it to his shoulder,
Ready now to shoot the arrow,
And to shoot at Väinämöinen.
And he spoke the words which follow:
" Do thou strike, O birchwood arrow,
Strike thou in the back, O pinewood.
Twang thy best, O hempen bowstring!
If my hand is leaning downward,
Let the arrow then strike higher,   160
If my hand is bending upward,
Let the arrow then strike downward!"
    Quickly then he drew the trigger,
Shot the first among his arrows.
Far too high the shaft flew upward,
High above his head to skyward,
And it whizzed among the cloudlets,
Through the scattered clouds it wandered.
    Thus he shot, in reckless fashion,
Shot the second of his arrows.   170
Far too low the shot flew downwards,
Deep in Mother Earth 'twas sunken.
Earth was almost sunk to Mana,
And the hills of sand were cloven.
    Then he shot again, a third time,
And the third shaft, straighter flying,
In the blue elk's spleen was buried,
Under aged Väinämöinen.
Thus he shot the straw-hued courser,
Like a pea-stalk in his colour;   180
Through the flesh beneath his shoulder,
In the left side deep he pierced him.
    Then the aged Väinämöinen
Plunged his fingers in the water,
With his hands the waves he parted,
Grasping at the foaming billows,
From the blue elk's back he tumbled.
From the steed of pea-stalk colour.

Then a mighty wind arising
Raised upon the sea a billow,   190
And it bore old Väinämöinen,
Swimming from the mainland further,
O'er the wide expanse of water,
Out into the open ocean.

Then the youthful Joukahainen
Uttered words of boastful triumph:
"Now thou ancient Väinämöinen,
Never while thy life endureth,
In the course of all thy lifetime,
While the golden moon is shining,   200
Walk in Väinölä's fair meadows,
Or on Kalevala's broad heathlands!

"May you toss for six years running,
Seven long summers ever drifting,
Tossed about for over eight years,
On the wide expanse of water,
On the surface of the billows,
Drift for six years like a pine-tree,
And for seven years like a fir-tree,
And for eight years like a tree-stump!"   210

Then the house again he entered,
And at once his mother asked him,
"Have you shot at Väinämöinen?
Slaughtered Kaleva's famous offspring?"

Then the youthful Joukahainen
Answered in the words which follow:
"I have shot at Väinämöinen,
And have o'erthrown Kalevalainen,
Sent him swimming in the water,
Swept him out upon the billows,   220
On the restless waves of ocean
Where the waves are wildly tossing,
And the old man plunged his fingers
And his palms amid the waters,
Then upon his side he tumbled,
And upon his back he turned him,
Drifting o'er the waves of ocean,
Out upon the foaming billows."

But his mother made him answer,
"Very evil hast thou acted,   230
Thus to shoot at Väinämöinen
And to o'erthrow Kalevalainen.
Of Suvantola the hero,
Kalevala's most famous hero."

RUNO VII.—VÄINÄMÖINEN AND LOUHI

Argument

Väinämöinen swims for several days on the open sea (1–88). The
eagle, grateful to him for having spared the birch-tree for him to rest
on, when he was felling the trees, takes Väinämöinen on his wings, and
carries him to the borders of Pohjola, where the Mistress of Pohjola
takes him to her abode, and receives him hospitably (89–274).
Väinämöinen desires to return to his own country, and the Mistress of
Pohjola permits him to depart, and promises him her daughter in
marriage if he will forge the Sampo in Pohjola (275–322). Väinämöinen
promises that when he returns home he will send the smith Ilmarinen
to forge the Sampo, and the Mistress of Pohjola gives him a horse and
a sledge to convey him home (323–368).

VÄINÄMÖINEN, old and steadfast,
Swam upon the open ocean,
Drifting like a fallen pine-tree,
Like a rotten branch of fir-tree,
During six days of the summer,
And for six nights in succession,
While the sea spread wide before him,
And the sky was clear above him.
    Thus he swam for two nights longer,
And for two days long and dreary.   10
When the ninth night darkened round him,
And the eighth day had passed over,
Sudden anguish came upon him,
And his pain grew ever greater.
From his toes his nails were dropping,
And the joints from off his fingers.

Then the aged Väinämöinen
Spoke in words like those which follow:
"Woe to me, unhappy creature,
Overburdened with misfortune!   20
I have wandered from my country,
And my ancient home abandoned.
'Neath the open sky for ever,
Driven along in sun and moonlight,
Rocked about by winds for ever,
Tossed about by every billow,
On the wide expanse of water,
Out upon the open ocean,
Here I live a cold existence,
And 'tis painful thus to wallow,   30
Always tossing on the billows,
On the surface of the waters.

"Now, alas, I know no longer
How to lead this life of sadness
In this everlasting trouble,
In an age when all is fleeting.
Shall I rear in wind a dwelling,
Build a house upon the waters?

"If I rear in wind a dwelling,
Then the wind would not sustain it;   40
If I build a house on water,
Then the waves will drift it from me."

Came a bird from Lapland flying,
From the north-east came an eagle,
Not the largest of the eagles,
Nor was he among the smallest,
With one wing he swept the water,
To the sky was swung the other;
On the sea his tail he rested,
On the cliffs his beak he rattled.   50

Slowly back and forwards flying,
Turning all around, and gazing,
Soon he saw old Väinämöinen
On the blue waves of the ocean.
"What has brought you here, O hero,
Wandering through the waves of ocean?"

Väinämöinen, old and steadfast,
Answered in the words which follow :
"This has brought the man to ocean,
Plunged the hero in the sea-waves.   60
I would seek the maid of Pohja,
Woo the maiden of Pimentola.

"On my journey swift I hasted,
On the ocean's watery surface,
Till about the time of daybreak,
Came I, after many mornings,
Where is Luotola's deep embayment,
Hard by Joukola's rapid river,
When my horse was shot beneath me,
By an arrow launched against me.   70

"Thus I fell into the water,
In the waves I plunged my fingers,
And the wind impels me onward,
And the billows drift me forward.

"Then there came a gale from north-west,
From the east a mighty tempest,
Far away the tempest drove me,
Swimming from the land still further,
Many days have I been floating,
Many days have I been swimming,   80
On this wide expanse of water,
Out upon the open ocean.
And I cannot now conjecture,
Cannot guess, nor e'en imagine,
How I finally shall perish,
And what death shall overtake me
Whether I shall die of hunger,
Or shall sink beneath the waters."

Said the bird of air, the eagle,
"Let thy heart be free from trouble ;   90
Climb upon my back, and seat thee,
Standing up upon my wing-tips,
From the sea will I transport thee,
Wheresoever thou may'st fancy.
For the day I well remember,
And recall a happier season,

When fell Kaleva's green forest,
Cleared was Osmola's famed island,
But thou didst protect the birch-tree,
And the beauteous tree left'st standing,   100
That the birds might rest upon it,
And that I myself might sit there."
    Then the aged Väinämöinen
Raised his head from out the water,
From the sea the man sprang upward,
From the waves the hero mounted,
On the eagle's wings he sat him,
On the wing-tips of the eagle.
    Then the bird of air, the eagle,
Raised the aged Väinämöinen,   110
Through the path of wind he bore him,
And along the east-wind's pathway,
To the utmost bounds of Pohja,
Onwards to the misty Sariola,
There abandoned Väinämöinen,
Soared into the air, and left him.
    There stood Väinämöinen weeping,
There stood weeping and lamenting,
On the borders of the ocean,
On a land whose name he knew not,   120
With a hundred wounds upon him,
By a thousand winds belaboured,
And his beard was much disordered,
And his hair was all entangled.
    Thus he wept for two, and three nights,
For as many days stood weeping,
For the country round he knew not,
And no path could he discover,
Which perchance might lead him homeward,
Back to a familiar country,   130
To his own, his native country,
Where he passed his days aforetime.
    But the little maid of Pohja,
Fair-haired damsel of the household,
With the sun had made agreement,
And both sun and moon had promised,

They would always rise together,
And they would awake together.
She herself arose before them,
Ere the sun or moon had risen,   140
Long before the time of cockcrow,
Or the chirping of a chicken.

From five sheep she shore the fleeces,
Clipped the wool from off six lambkins,
In her loom she wove the fleeces,
And the whole with care she carded,
Long before the dawn of morning,
Long before the sun had risen.

After this she washed the tables,
Swept the wide-extended flooring,   150
With the broom of twigs all leafless,
Then with broom of leafy branches.
Then the sweepings she collected
In the dustpan made of copper ;
Out of doors she took the rubbish,
To the field beyond the farmyard,
To the field's extremest limit,
Where the lowest fence has opening.
There she stood upon the sweepings,
And she turned around, and listened.   160
From the lake she heard a weeping,
Sounds of woe across the river.

Quickly then she hastened homeward,
And she hurried to the parlour.
As she came, she told her tidings,
In such words as those which follow :
"From the lake I hear a weeping,
Sounds of woe across the river."

Louhi, Pohjola's old Mistress,
Old and gap-toothed dame of Pohja,   170
Hastened forth into the farmyard,
Hurried to the fence's opening,
Where she bent her ear to listen,
And she spoke the words which follow :
"This is not like childhood's weeping
Nor like women's lamentation,

But a bearded hero weeping;
Thus weep men whose chins are bearded."

Three planks high the boat was builded, 180
Which she pushed into the water,
And herself began to row it,
And she rowed, and hastened onward
To the spot where Väinämöinen,
Where the hero was lamenting.

There was Väinämöinen weeping,
There Uvanto's swain lamented,
By the dreary clumps of willow,
By the tangled hedge of cherry.
Moved his mouth, his beard was shaking,
But his lips he did not open. 190

Then did Pohjola's old Mistress,
Speak unto, and thus addressed him:
"O thou aged man unhappy,
Thou art in a foreign country!"

Väinämöinen, old and steadfast,
Lifted up his head and answered
In the very words that follow:
"True it is, and well I know it,
I am in a foreign country,
Absolutely unfamiliar. 200
I was better in my country,
Greater in the home I came from."

Louhi, Pohjola's old Mistress,
Answered in the words which follow:
"In the first place you must tell me,
If I may make bold to ask you,
From what race you take your lineage,
And from what heroic nation?"

Väinämöinen, old and steadfast,
Answered in the words which follow: 210
"Well my name was known aforetime,
And in former days was famous,
Ever cheerful in the evening,
Ever singing in the valleys,
There in Väinölä's sweet meadows,
And on Kalevala's broad heathlands;

But my grief is now so heavy
That I know myself no longer."
  Louhi, Pohjola's old Mistress,
Answered in the words which follow: 220
"Rise, O man, from out the marshes,
Hero, seek another pathway.
Tell me now of thy misfortunes,
And relate me thy adventure."
  Thus she made him cease his weeping,
Made the hero cease lamenting,
And into her boat she took him,
Bade him at the stern be seated,
And herself resumed the oars,
And she then began to row him   230
Unto Pohjola, o'er water,
And she brought him to her dwelling.
Then she fed the famished stranger,
And she dried his dripping garments,
Then she rubbed his limbs all stiffened,
And she warmed him and shampooed him,
Till she had restored his vigour,
And the hero had recovered.
After this, she spoke and asked him,
In the very words which follow: 240
"Why did'st weep, O Väinämöinen,
Why lament, Uvantolainen,
In that miserable region,
On the borders of the lakelet?"
  Väinämöinen, old and steadfast,
Answered in the words which follow:
"Cause enough have I for weeping,
Reason, too, for lamentation,
In the sea I long was swimming,
Tossed about upon the billows,   250
On the wide expanse of water,
Out upon the open ocean.
  "I must weep throughout my lifespan,
And lament throughout my lifetime,
That I swam beyond my country,
Left the country so familiar,

And have come to doors I know not,
And to hedge-gates that I know not,
All the trees around me pain me,
All the pine-twigs seem to pierce me,   260
Every birch-tree seems to flog me,
Every alder seems to wound me,
But the wind is friendly to me,
And the sun still shines upon me,
In this unaccustomed country,
And within the doors I know not."
    Louhi, Pohjola's old Mistress,
Answered in the words which follow :
" Do not weep, O Väinämöinen,
Nor lament, Uvantolainen.   270
Here 'tis good for thee to sojourn,
And to pass thy days in comfort.
Salmon you can eat at table,
And beside it pork is standing."
    But the aged Väinämöinen
Answered in the words which follow .
" Foreign food I do not relish,
In the best of strangers' houses.
In his land a man is better,
In his home a man is greater.   280
Grant me, Jumala most gracious,
O compassionate Creator,
Once again to reach my country,
And the land I used to dwell in !
Better is a man's own country,
Water from beneath the sabot,
Than in unfamiliar countries,
Mead to drink from golden goblets."
    Louhi, Pohjola's old Mistress,
Answered in the words which follow :   290
" What are you prepared to give me,
If I send you to your country,
To the borders of your cornfields,
Or the bath-house of your dwelling ? "
    Said the aged Väinämöinen,
" Tell me then what I shall give you,

If you send me to my country,
To the borders of my cornfields,
There to hear my cuckoo calling,
And my birds so sweetly singing.   300
Will you choose a gold-filled helmet,
Or a hat filled up with silver?"
    Louhi, Pohjola's old Mistress,
Answered in the words which follow:
"O thou wisest Väinämöinen,
Thou the oldest of the sages,
Golden gifts I do not ask for,
And I wish not for thy silver.
Gold is but a toy for children,
Silver bells adorn the horses,   310
But if you can forge a Sampo,
Weld its many-coloured cover,
From the tips of swan's white wing-plumes,
From the milk of barren heifer,
From a single grain of barley,
From a single fleece of ewe's wool,
Then will I my daughter give you,
Give the maiden as your guerdon,
And will bring you to your country,
There to hear the birds all singing,   320
There to hear your cuckoo calling,
On the borders of your cornfields."
    Väinämöinen, old and steadfast,
Answered in the words which follow:
"No, I cannot forge a Sampo,
Nor can weld its pictured cover.
Only bring me to my country,
And I'll send you Ilmarinen,
Who shall forge a Sampo for you,
Weld its many-coloured cover.   330
He perchance may please the maiden,
Win your daughter's young affections.
    "He's a smith without an equal,
None can wield the hammer like him,
For 'twas he who forged the heaven,
And who wrought the air's foundations,

Yet we find no trace of hammer,
Nor the trace of tongs discover."
    Louhi, Pohjola's old Mistress,
Answered in the words which follow: 340
" I will only yield my daughter,
And my child I promise only
To the man who welds a Sampo
With its many-coloured cover,
From the tips of swan's white wing-plumes,
From the milk of barren heifer,
From a single grain of barley,
From a single fleece of ewe's wool."
    Thereupon the colt she harnessed,
In the front she yoked the bay one,   350
And she placed old Väinämöinen
In the sledge behind the stallion.
And she spoke and thus addressed him,
In the very words which follow :
" Do not raise your head up higher,
Turn it not to gaze about you,
That the steed may not be wearied,
Till the evening shall have gathered.
If you dare to raise your head up,
Or to turn to gaze around you,   360
Then misfortune will o'ertake you,
And an evil day betide you."
    Then the aged Väinämöinen
Whipped the horse, and urged him onward,
And the white-maned courser hastened
Noisily upon the journey,
Forth from Pohjola's dark regions,
Sariola for ever misty.

RUNO VIII.—VÄINÄMÖINEN'S WOUND

Argument

On his journey Väinämöinen encounters the magnificently-clad Maiden of Pohja, and makes advances to her (1–50). The maiden at length consents to his wishes if he will make a boat from the splinters of her spindle, and move it into the water without touching it (51–132). Väinämöinen sets to work, but wounds his knee severely with his axe, and cannot stanch the flow of blood (133–204). He goes in search of some magic remedy and finds an old man who promises to stop the bleeding (205–282).

LOVELY was the maid of Pohja,
Famed on land, on water peerless,
On the arch of air high-seated,
Brightly shining on the rainbow,
Clad in robes of dazzling lustre,
Clad in raiment white and shining.
There she wove a golden fabric,
Interwoven all with silver,
And her shuttle was all golden,
And her comb was all of silver.   10

From her hand flew swift the shuttle,
In her hands the reel was turning,
And the copper shafts they clattered,
And the silver comb resounded,
As the maiden wove the fabric,
And with silver interwove it.

Väinämöinen, old and steadfast,
Thundered on upon his journey,
From the gloomy land of Pohja,
Sariola for ever misty.   20
Short the distance he had travelled,
Short the way that he had journeyed,
When he heard the shuttle whizzing,
High above his head he heard it.

Thereupon his head he lifted,
And he gazed aloft to heaven,

And beheld a glorious rainbow ;
On the arch the maiden seated,
As she wove a golden fabric,
As the silver comb resounded.   30
Väinämöinen, old and steadfast,
Stayed his horse upon the instant,
And he raised his voice, and speaking,
In such words as these addressed her :
" Come into my sledge, O maiden,
In the sledge beside me seat thee."
Then the maiden made him answer,
And in words like these responded :
" Wherefore should the maiden join you,
In the sledge beside you seated ? "   40
Väinämöinen, old and steadfast,
Heard her words, and then responded :
" Therefore should the maiden join me,
In the sledge beside me seat her ;
Bread of honey to prepare me,
And the best of beer to brew me,
Singing blithely on the benches,
Gaily talking at the window,
When in Väinölä I sojourn,
At my home in Kalevala."   50
Then the maiden gave him answer,
And in words like these addressed him :
" As I wandered through the bedstraw,
Tripping o'er the yellow meadows,
Yesterday, in time of evening,
As the sun was slowly sinking,
In the bush a bird was singing,
And I heard the fieldfare trilling,
Singing of the whims of maidens,
And the whims of new-wed damsels.   60
" Thus the bird was speaking to me,
And I questioned it in this wise :
' Tell me O thou little fieldfare,
Sing thou, that my ears may hear it,
Whether it indeed is better,
Whether thou hast heard 'tis better,

For a girl in father's dwelling,
Or in household of a husband?'
  "Thereupon the bird made answer,
And the fieldfare answered chirping :   70
  'Brilliant is the day in summer,
But a maiden's lot is brighter.
And the frost makes cold the iron,
Yet the new bride's lot is colder.
In her father's house a maiden
Lives like strawberry in the garden,
But a bride in house of husband,
Lives like house-dog tightly fettered.
To a slave comes rarely pleasure ;
To a wedded damsel never.'"   80
  Väinämöinen, old and steadfast,
Answered in the words which follow :
"Song of birds is idle chatter,
And the throstle's, merely chirping ;
As a child a daughter's treated,
But a maid must needs be married.
Come into my sledge, O maiden,
In the sledge beside me seat thee.
I am not a man unworthy,
Lazier not than other heroes."   90
  But the maid gave crafty answer,
And in words like these responded :
"As a man I will esteem you,
And as hero will regard you,
If you can split up a horsehair
With a blunt and pointless knife-blade,
And an egg in knots you tie me,
Yet no knot is seen upon it."
  Väinämöinen, old and steadfast,
Then the hair in twain divided,   100
With a blunt and pointless knife-blade,
With a knife completely pointless,
And an egg in knots he twisted,
Yet no knot was seen upon it.
Then again he asked the maiden
In the sledge to sit beside him.

But the maid gave crafty answer,
" I perchance at length may join you,
If you'll peel the stone I give you,
And a pile of ice will hew me,   110
But no splinter scatter from it,
Nor the smallest fragment loosen."
Väinämöinen, old and steadfast,
Did not find the task a hard one.
From the stone the rind he severed,
And a pile of ice he hewed her,
But no splinters scattered from it,
Nor the smallest fragment loosened.
Then again he asked the maiden
In the sledge to sit beside him.   120
But the maid gave crafty answer,
And she spoke the words which follow :
" No, I will not yet go with you,
If a boat you cannot carve me,
From the splinters of my spindle,
From the fragments of my shuttle,
And shall launch the boat in water,
Push it out upon the billows,
But no knee shall press against it,
And no hand must even touch it ;   130
And no arm shall urge it onward,
Neither shall a shoulder guide it."
Väinämöinen, old and steadfast,
Answered in the words which follow :
" None in any land or country,
Under all the vault of heaven,
Like myself can build a vessel,
Or so deftly can construct it."
Then he took the spindle-splinters,
Of the reel he took the fragments,   140
And began the boat to fashion,
Fixed a hundred planks together,
On a mount of steel he built it,
Built it on the rocks of iron.
At the boat with zeal he laboured,
Toiling at the work unresting,

Working thus one day, a second,
On the third day likewise working,
But the rocks his axe-blade touched not,
And upon the hill it rang not.   150
    But at length, upon the third day,
Hiisi turned aside the axe-shaft,
Lempo turned the edge against him,
And an evil stroke delivered.
On the rocks the axe-blade glinted,
On the hill the blade rang loudly,
From the rock the axe rebounded,
In the flesh the steel was buried,
In the victim's knee 'twas buried,
In the toes of Väinämöinen,   160
In the flesh did Lempo drive it,
To the veins did Hiisi guide it,
From the wound the blood flowed freely,
Bursting forth in streaming torrents.
    Väinämöinen, old and steadfast,
He, the oldest of magicians,
Uttered words like those which follow,
And expressed himself in this wise :
" O thou evil axe ferocious,
With thy edge of gleaming sharpness,   170
Thou hast thought to hew a tree-trunk,
And to strike upon a pine-tree,
Match thyself against a fir-tree,
Or to fall upon a birch-tree.
'Tis my flesh that thou hast wounded,
And my veins thou hast divided."
    Then his magic spells he uttered,
And himself began to speak them,
Spells of origin, for healing,
And to close the wound completely.   180
But he could not think of any
Words of origin of iron,
Which might serve to bind the evil,
And to close the gaping edges
Of the great wound from the iron,
By the blue edge deeply bitten.

But the blood gushed forth in torrents,
Rushing like a foaming river,
O'er the berry-bearing bushes,
And the heath the ground that covered.   190
There remained no single hillock,
Which was not completely flooded
By the overflowing blood-stream,
Which came rushing forth in torrents
From the knee of one most worthy,
From the toes of Väinämöinen.

Väinämöinen, old and steadfast,
Gathered from the rocks the lichen,
From the swamps the moss collected,
Earth he gathered from the hillocks,   200
Hoping thus to stop the outlet
Of the wound that bled so freely,
But he could not check the bleeding,
Nor restrain it in the slightest.
And the pain he felt oppressed him,
And the greatest trouble seized him.

Väinämöinen, old and steadfast,
Then began to weep full sorely.
Thereupon his horse he harnessed,
In the sledge he yoked the chestnut,   210
On the sledge himself he mounted,
And upon the seat he sat him.
O'er the horse his whip he brandished,
With the bead-decked whip he lashed him,
And the horse sped quickly onward.
Rocked the sledge, the way grew shorter,
And they quickly reached a village,
Where the path in three divided.

Väinämöinen, old and steadfast,
Drove along the lowest pathway,   220
To the lowest of the homesteads,
And he asked upon the threshold,
"Is there no one in this household,
Who can cure the wounds of iron,
Who can soothe the hero's anguish,
And can heal the wound that pains him?"

On the floor a child was playing,
By the stove a boy was sitting,
And he answered him in this wise :
" There is no one in this household   230
Who can heal the wounds of iron,
Who can soothe the hero's anguish,
To the rock can fix it firmly,
And can heal the wound that pains him.
Such may dwell in other houses :
Drive away to other houses."

Väinämöinen, old and steadfast,
O'er the horse his whip then brandished,
And the sledge went rattling onward.
Thus a little way he travelled,   240
On the midmost of the pathways,
To the midmost of the houses,
And he asked upon the threshold,
And beseeching at the window,
" Is there no one in this household,
Who can heal the wounds of iron,
Who can stanch the blood when flowing,
And can check the rushing bloodstream ? "

'Neath the quilt a crone was resting,
By the stove there sat a gossip,   250
And she spoke and answered plainly,
As her three teeth gnashed together,
" There is no one in this household,
Who can heal the wounds of iron,
None who knows efficient blood-spells,
And can close the wound that pains you.
Such may dwell in other houses :
Drive away to other houses."

Väinämöinen, old and steadfast,
O'er the horse his whip then brandished,   260
And the sledge went rattling onward.
Thus a little way he travelled,
On the highest of the pathways,
To the highest of the houses,
And he asked upon the threshold,
Calling from beside the doorpost,

" Is there any in this household,
Who can heal the wounds of iron,
Who can check this rushing bloodstream,
And can stay the dark red torrent ? "   270
    By the stove an old man rested,
On the stove-bed lay a greybeard,
From the stove the old man mumbled,
And the greybeard cried in answer,
" Stemmed before were greater torrents,
Greater floods than this were hindered,
By three words of the Creator,
By the mighty words primeval.
Brooks and streams were checked from flowing,
Mighty streams in cataracts falling,   280
Bays were formed in rocky headlands,
Tongues of land were linked together."

Runo IX.—The Origin of Iron

Argument

Väinämöinen repeats to the old man the legend of the origin of iron
(1–266). The old man reviles the iron and repeats spells for the stop-
ping of blood, and the flow of blood is stayed (267–416). The old man
directs his son to prepare a salve, and dresses and binds up the wound.
Väinämöinen is cured, and thanks Jumala for his merciful assistance
(417–586).

Then the aged Väinämöinen
In the sledge at once stood upright,
From the sledge he sprang unaided,
And courageously stood upright.
To the room he hastened quickly,
And beneath the roof he hurried.
    There they brought a silver beaker,
And a golden goblet likewise,
But they proved by far too little,
Holding but the smallest measure   10
Of the blood of aged Väinö,
From the hero's foot that spouted.

From the stove the old man mumbled,
Cried the greybeard when he saw him,
"Who among mankind may'st thou be,
Who among the roll of heroes?
Seven large boats with blood are brimming,
Eight large tubs are overflowing
From your knee, O most unhappy,
On the floor in torrents gushing.   20
Other words I well remember,
But the oldest I recall not,
How the iron was first created,
And the unworked ore was fashioned."
    Then the aged Väinämöinen
Answered in the words that follow:
"Well I know the birth of Iron,
And how steel was first created.
Air is the primeval mother,
Water is the eldest brother,   30
Iron is the youngest brother,
And the Fire in midst between them.
    "Ukko, mightiest of Creators,
He, the God above in heaven,
From the Air the Water parted,
And the continents from water,
When unborn was evil Iron,
Uncreated, undeveloped.
    "Ukko, God of realms supernal,
Rubbed his mighty hands together.   40
Both his hands he rubbed together,
On his left knee then he pressed them,
And three maidens were created,
Three fair Daughters of Creation,
Mothers of the rust of Iron,
And of blue-mouthed steel the fosterers.
    "Strolled the maids with faltering footsteps
On the borders of the cloudlets,
And their full breasts were o'erflowing,
And their nipples pained them sorely.   50
Down on earth their milk ran over,
From their breasts' o'erflowing fulness,

Milk on land, and milk on marshes,
Milk upon the peaceful waters.
  "Black milk from the first was flowing,
From the eldest of the maidens,
White milk issued from another,
From the second of the maidens,
Red milk by the third was yielded,
By the youngest of the maidens.   60
  "Where the black milk had been dropping,
There was found the softest Iron,
Where the white milk had been flowing,
There the hardest steel was fashioned,
Where the red milk had been trickling,
There was undeveloped Iron.
  "But a short time had passed over,
When the Iron desired to visit
Him, its dearest elder brother,
And to make the Fire's acquaintance.   70
  "But the Fire arose in fury,
Blazing up in greatest anger,
Seeking to consume its victim,
E'en the wretched Iron, its brother.
  "Then the Iron sought out a refuge,
Sought for refuge and protection
From the hands of furious Fire,
From his mouth, all bright with anger.
  "Then the Iron took refuge from him,
Sought both refuge and protection   80
Down amid the quaking marshes,
Where the springs have many sources,
On the level mighty marshes,
On the void and barren mountains,
Where the swans their eggs deposit,
And the goose her brood is rearing.
  "In the swamps lay hid the Iron,
Stretched beneath the marshy surface,
Hid for one year and a second,
For a third year likewise hidden,   90
Hidden there between two tree-stumps,
'Neath three roots of birch-trees hidden

But it had not yet found safety
From the fierce hands of the Fire,
And a second time it wandered
To the dwelling of the Fire,
That it should be forged to weapons,
And to sword-blades should be fashioned.
    " On the marshes wolves were running,
On the heath the bears came trooping,   100
'Neath the wolves' feet quaked the marshes,
'Neath the bears the heath was shaken,
Thus was ore of iron uncovered,
And the bars of steel were noticed,
Where the claws of wolves had trodden,
And the paws of bears had trampled.
    " Then was born smith Ilmarinen,
Thus was born, and thus was nurtured,
Born upon a hill of charcoal,
Reared upon a plain of charcoal,   110
In his hands a copper hammer,
And his little pincers likewise.
    " Ilmari was born at night-time,
And at day he built his smithy,
Sought a place to build his smithy,
Where he could construct his bellows.
In the swamp he found a land-ridge,
And a small place in the marshes,
So he went to gaze upon it,
And examined the surroundings,   120
And erected there his bellows,
And his anvil there constructed.
    " Then he hastened to the wolf-tracks,
And the bear-tracks also followed,
And the ore of iron he saw there,
And the lumps of steel he found there,
In the wolves' enormous footprints ;
Where the bears' paws left their imprints.
Then he spoke the words which follow :
" ' O thou most unlucky Iron,   130
In an ill abode thou dwellest,
In a very lowly station,

'Neath the wolf-prints in the marshes,
And the imprints of the bear-paws.'

"Then he pondered and reflected,
'What would be the upshot of it,
If I cast it in the fire,
And I laid it on the anvil?'

"Sore alarmed was hapless Iron,
Sore alarmed, and greatly startled,   140
When of Fire it heard him speaking,
Speaking of the furious Fire.

"Said the smith, said Ilmarinen,
'But indeed it cannot happen;
Fire his friends will never injure,
Nor will harm his dear relations.
If you seek the Fire's red chamber,
All illumined with its brightness,
You will greatly gain in beauty,
And your splendour greatly increase.   150
Fitted thus for men's keen sword-blades
Or as clasps for women's girdles.'

"Therefore when the day was ended,
Was the Iron from out the marshes,
Delved from all the swampy places,
Carried homeward to the smithy.

"Then he cast it in the furnace,
And he laid it on the anvil,
Blew a blast, and then a second,
And he blew again a third time,   160
Till the Iron was fully softened,
And the ore completely melted,
Like to wheaten dough in softness,
Soft as dough for rye-bread kneaded,
In the furnace of the smithy,
By the bright flame's softening power.

"Then exclaimed the Iron unhappy,
'O thou smith, O Ilmarinen,
Take me quickly from this furnace,
From the red flames that torment me.'   170

"Said the smith, said Ilmarinen,
'If I take you from the furnace,

Perhaps you might become outrageous,
And commit some furious action.
Perhaps you might attack your brother,
And your mother's child might injure.'

"Therefore swore the Iron unhappy,
By the oaths of all most solemn,
By the forge and by the anvil,
By the hammer and the mallet,   180
And it said the words which follow,
And expressed itself in this wise:
'Give me trees that I can bite them,
Give me stones that I may break them,
I will not assault my brother,
Nor my mother's child will injure.
Better will be my existence,
And my life will be more happy,
If I dwell among companions,
As the tools of handicraftsmen,   190
Than to wound my own relations,
And disgrace my own connections.'

"Then the smith, e'en Ilmarinen,
He, the great primeval craftsman,
From the fire removed the Iron;
Laid it down upon the anvil,
Welded it till it was wearied,
Shaped it into pointed weapons,
Into spears, and into axes,
Into tools of all descriptions.   200
Still there was a trifle wanting,
And the soft Iron still defective,
For the tongue of Iron had hissed not,
And its mouth of steel was formed not,
For the Iron was not yet hardened,
Nor with water had been tempered.

"Then the smith, e'en Ilmarinen,
Pondered over what was needed,
Mixed a small supply of ashes,
And some lye he added to it,   210
To the blue steel's smelting mixture,
For the tempering of the Iron.

"With his tongue he tried the liquid,
Tasted it if it would please him,
And he spoke the words which follow :
'Even yet it does not please me
For the blue steel's smelting mixture,
And perfecting of the Iron.'
From without a bee came flying,
Blue-winged from the grassy hillocks,   220
Hovering forwards, hovering backwards,
Hovering all around the smithy.

"Then the smith spoke up as follows :
'O thou bee, my nimble comrade,
Honey on thy wings convey me,
On thy tongue from out the forest,
From the summits of six flowerets,
And from seven tall grass-stems bring it,
For the blue steel's smelting mixture,
And the tempering of the Iron.'   230

" But the hornet, Bird of Hiisi,
Looked around him, and he listened,
Gazing from beside the roof-tree,
Looking from below the birch-bark,
At the tempering of the Iron,
And the blue steel's smelting mixture.

" Thence he flew on whirring pinions,
Scattering all of Hiisi's terrors,
Brought the hissing of the serpents,
And of snakes the dusky venom,   240
And of ants he brought the acid,
And of toads the hidden poison,
That the steel might thus be poisoned,
In the tempering of the Iron.

"Then the smith, e'en Ilmarinen,
He, the greatest of the craftsmen,
Was deluded, and imagined
That the bee returned already,
And had brought the honey needed,
Brought the honey that he wanted,   250
And he spoke the words which follow :
'Here at last is what will please me,

For the blue steel's smelting mixture,
And the tempering of the Iron.'
    "Thereupon the steel he lifted,
In he plunged the luckless Iron,
As from out the fire he took it,
And he took it from the anvil.
    "Then indeed the steel was angry,
And the Iron was seized with fury.   260
And its oath the wretch has broken,
Like a dog has soiled its honour,
Brutally its brother bitten,
Striking at its own relations,
Let the blood rush forth in torrents,
From the wound in torrents gushing."
    From the stove the old man mumbled,
(Shook his beard, his head he nodded)
"Now I know whence comes the Iron,
And of steel the evil customs.   270
    "O thou most unhappy Iron,
Wretched Iron, slag most worthless,
Steel thou art of evil witchcraft,
Thou hast been for nought developed,
But to turn to evil courses,
In the greatness of thy power.
    "Once thou wast devoid of greatness;
Neither wast thou great nor little,
Neither noted for thy beauty,
Nor remarkable for evil,   280
When as milk thou wast created,
When the sweet milk trickled over
From the breasts of youthful maidens,
From the maidens' swelling bosoms,
On the borders of the cloudland,
'Neath the broad expanse of heaven.
    "Thou wast then devoid of greatness,
Thou wast neither great nor little,
When thou in the mud wast resting,
Sunk below the sparkling water,   290
Overspreading all the marshland,
At the base of rocky mountains.

And in loose earth thou wast altered,
And to iron-ore converted.

"Thou wast still devoid of greatness,
Thou wast neither great nor little,
When the elks were trampling o'er thee,
And the reindeer, in the marshes,
When the wolves' claws trod upon thee,
And the bears' paws passed above thee.　　300

"Thou wast still devoid of greatness,
Thou wast neither great nor little,
When thou from the marsh wast gathered,
From the ground with care uplifted,
Carried thence into the smithy,
To the forge of Ilmarinen.

"Thou wast still devoid of greatness,
Thou wast neither great nor little,
When as ore thou there wast hissing,
Plunged amid the boiling water,　　310
Or amid the fiery furnace,
When the mighty oath thou sworest,
By the forge and by the anvil,
By the hammer and the mallet,
Where the smith himself was standing,
On the flooring of the smithy.

"Now that thou hast grown to greatness,
Thou hast wrought thyself to frenzy,
And thy mighty oath hast broken,
Like a dog hast soiled thy honour,　　320
For thy kinsman thou hast wounded,
Raised thy mouth against thy kinsman.

"Who hast led thee to this outrage,
To this wickedness incited?
Perhaps thy father or thy mother,
Or the eldest of thy brothers,
Or the youngest of thy sisters,
Or some other near relation?

"Not thy father, not thy mother,
Nor the eldest of thy brothers,　　330
Nor the youngest of thy sisters
Nor some other near relation.

Thou thyself hast wrought the evil,
And hast done a deadly outrage.
Come thyself to see the mischief,
And to remedy the evil.
Come, before I tell thy mother,
And complain unto thy parents,
More will be thy mother's trouble,
Great the anguish of thy parents,   340
That their son had wrought this evil,
And their son had wrought this folly.

"Hear me, Blood, and cease thy flowing,
O thou Bloodstream, rush no longer,
Nor upon my head spirt further,
Nor upon my breast down-trickle.
Like a wall, O Blood, arrest thee,
Like a fence, O Bloodstream, stand thou,
As a flag in lakelet standing,
Like a reed in moss-grown country,   350
Like the bank that bounds the cornfield,
Like a rock in raging torrent.

"But thy own sense ought to teach thee
How that thou should'st run more smoothly.
In the flesh should'st thou be moving,
With thy current smoothly flowing.
In the body is it better,
Underneath the skin more lovely
Through the veins to trace thy pathway,
With thy current smoothly flowing,   360
Than upon the earth rush downward,
And among the dust to trickle.

"Flow not, milk, upon the flooring,
Soil thou not, O Blood, the meadows,
Nor the grass, O crown of manhood,
Nor the hillocks, gold of heroes.
In the heart should be thy dwelling,
And among the lungs' dark cellars.
Thither then withdraw thou quickly,
There withdraw upon the instant.   370
Do not issue like a river,
Nor as pond extend thy billows,

Trickling forth from out the marshes,
Nor to leak like boats when damaged.
"Therefore, dear one, cease thy flowing,
Crimson Blood, drip down no longer,
Not impeded, but contented.
Dry were once the Falls of Tyrja,
Likewise Tuonela's dread river,
Dry the lake and dry the heaven,   380
In the mighty droughts of summer,
In the evil times of bush-fires.

"If thou wilt not yet obey me,
Still I know another method,
And resort to fresh enchantments:
And I call for Hiisi's caldron,
And will boil the blood within it
All the blood that forth has issued,
So that not a drop escapes me,
That the red blood flows no longer,   390
Nor the blood to earth drops downward,
And the blood no more may issue.

"But if manly strength has failed me,
Nor is Ukko's son a hero,
Who can stop this inundation,
Stem the swift arterial torrent,
Thou our Father in the heavens,
Jumala, the clouds who rulest,
Thou hast manly strength sufficient,
Thou thyself the mighty hero,   400
Who shall close the blood's wide gateway,
And shall stem the blood escaping.

"Ukko, O thou great Creator,
Jumala, aloft in heaven,
Hither come where thou art needed,
Hither come where we implore thee,
Press thy mighty hands upon it,
Press thy mighty thumbs upon it,
And the painful wound close firmly,
And the door whence comes the evil,   410
Spread the tender leaves upon it,
Leaves of golden water-lily,

Thus to close the path of bleeding,
And to stem the rushing torrent,
That upon my beard it spirts not,
Nor upon my rags may trickle."
　Thus he closed the bleeding opening,
Stemming thus the bloody torrent,
Sent his son into the smithy,
To prepare a healing ointment　　　　　**420**
From the blades of magic grasses,
From the thousand-headed yarrow,
And from dripping mountain-honey,
Falling down in drops of sweetness.
Then the boy went to the smithy,
To prepare the healing ointment,
On the way he passed an oak-tree,
And he stopped and asked the oak-tree,
" Have you honey on your branches ?
And beneath your bark sweet honey ? "　　**430**
　And the oak-tree gave him answer,
" Yesterday, throughout the evening,
Dripped the honey on my branches,
On my summit splashed the honey,
From the clouds dropped down the honey,
From the scattered clouds distilling."
　Then he took the slender oak-twigs,
From the tree the broken fragments,
Took the best among the grasses,
Gathered many kinds of herbage,　　　　**440**
Herbs one sees not in this country ;
Such were mostly what he gathered.
　Then he placed them o'er the furnace,
And the mixture brought to boiling ;
Both the bark from off the oak-tree,
And the finest of the grasses.
Thus the pot was boiling fiercely,
Three long nights he kept it boiling,
And for three days of the springtime,
While he watched the ointment closely,　　**450**
If the salve was fit for using,
And the magic ointment ready.

I—D 259

But the salve was still unfinished,
Nor the magic ointment ready;
Grasses to the mass he added,
Added herbs of many species,
Which were brought from other places,
Gathered on a hundred pathways,
These were culled by nine magicians,
And by eight wise seers discovered.   460

Then for three nights more he boiled it,
And for nine nights in succession;
Took the pot from off the furnace,
And the salve with care examined,
If the salve was fit for using,
And the magic ointment ready.

Here there grew a branching aspen,
On the borders of the cornfield,
And in twain he broke the aspen,
And the tree completely severed,   470
With the magic salve he smeared it,
Carefully the ointment tested,
And he spoke the words which follow:
"As I with this magic ointment
Smear the injured crown all over,
Let no harm be left upon it,
Let the aspen stand uninjured,
Even as it stood aforetime."

Then at once was healed the aspen,
Even as it stood aforetime,   480
And its crown was far more lovely,
And the trunk below was healthy.

Then again he took the ointment,
And the salve again he tested,
And on broken stones he tried it,
And on shattered rocks he rubbed it,
And the stone with stone knit firmly,
And the cracks were fixed together.

From the forge the boy came homeward,
When the salve was fit for using,   490
With the ointment quite perfected,
In the old man's hands he placed it.

"Here I bring a perfect ointment,
And the magic salve is ready.
It could fuse the hills together,
In a single rock unite them."
    With his tongue the old man tried it,
With his mouth the liquid tasted,
And the ointment tasted perfect,
And the salve was most efficient.   500
    This he smeared on Väinämöinen,
And with this he healed the sufferer;
Stroked him downward, stroked him upward,
Rubbed him also on the middle,
And he spoke the words which follow,
And expressed himself in this wise:
"'Tis not I who use my muscles,
But 'tis the Creator moves them;
With my own strength do not labour,
But with strength from the Almighty.   510
With my mouth I speak not to you;
Jumala's own mouth speaks with you,
If my speech is sweet unto you,
Jumala's own speech is sweeter.
Even if my hands are lovely,
The Creator's hands are fairer."
    When the salve was rubbed upon him,
And the healing ointment touched him,
Almost fainting with the anguish,
Väinämöinen writhed and struggled.   520
Turning this way, turning that way,
Seeking ease, but never finding.
    Then the old man banned the suffering,
Far away he drove the anguish,
To the central Hill of Tortures,
To the topmost Mount of Suffering,
There to fill the stones with anguish,
And the slabs of rock to torture.
    Then he took a silken fabric,
And in strips he quickly cut it;   530
From the edge he tore the fragments,
And at once he formed a bandage;

Then he took the silken bandage,
And with utmost care he wound it,
Round the knees he wound it deftly,
Round the toes of Väinämöinen.
  Then he spoke the words which follow,
And expressed himself in this wise:
"Thus I use God's silken bandage,
The Creator's mantle wind I   540
Round the great knees of the patient,
Round the toes of one most noble.
Watch thou, Jumala most gracious,
Give thy aid, O great Creator,
That we fall not in misfortune,
That no evil may o'ertake us."
  Then the aged Väinämöinen
Felt he had regained his vigour,
And that he was healed completely,
And his flesh again was solid,   550
And beneath it all was healthy.
In his body he was painless,
And his sides were quite uninjured,
From above the wounds had vanished,
Stronger felt he than aforetime,
Better than in former seasons.
On his feet he now was walking
And could bend his knees in stamping;
Not the least of pain he suffered,
Not a trace remained of aching.   560
  Then the aged Väinämöinen,
Lifted up his eyes to heaven,
Gazing up to God most gracious,
Lifting up his head to heaven,
And he spoke the words which follow,
And expressed himself in this wise:
"Thence all mercy flows for ever,
Thence comes aid the most effective,
From the heaven that arches o'er us,
From the omnipotent Creator.   570
  "Praise to Jumala most gracious,
Praise to thee, O great Creator,

That thy aid thou hast vouchsafed me,
Granted me thy strong protection,
When my suffering was the greatest,
From the edge of sharpest Iron."
    Then the aged Väinämöinen
Further spoke these words of warning :
" People, henceforth in the future
On your present welfare build not,   580
Make no boat in mood of boasting,
Nor confide too much in boat-ribs.
God foresees the course of by-ways,
The Creator orders all things ;
Not the foresight of the heroes,
Nor the might of all the great ones."

Runo X.—The Forging of the Sampo

Argument

Väinämöinen reaches home and urges Ilmarinen to depart to woo the Maiden of Pohja, because he would be able to forge a Sampo (1–100). Ilmarinen refuses to go to Pohjola, but Väinämöinen conveys him thither without his consent by a stratagem (101–200). Ilmarinen arrives in Pohjola, where he is very well received, and promises to forge a Sampo (201–280). He forges the Sampo, and the Mistress of Pohjola conceals it in the Rocky Mountain of Pohjola (281–432). Ilmarinen asks for the maiden as his reward, but she makes excuses, saying that she is not yet ready to leave home (433–462). Ilmarinen receives a boat, returns home, and informs Väinämöinen that he has forged the Sampo in Pohjola (463–510).

Väinämöinen, old and steadfast,
Took his horse of chestnut colour,
And between the shafts he yoked him,
Yoked before the sledge the chestnut,
On the sledge himself he mounted,
And upon the seat he sat him.
    Quickly then his whip he flourished,
Cracked his whip, all bead-embroidered,
Quick he sped upon his journey,
Lurched the sledge, the way was shortened,   10

Loudly rang the birchwood runners,
And the rowan cumber rattled.
    On he rushed with speed tremendous,
Through the swamps and open country,
O'er the heaths, so wide extending.
Thus he drove a day, a second,
And at length, upon the third day,
Reached the long bridge-end before him
Kalevala's extended heathlands,
Bordering on the field of Osmo.   20
    Then he spoke the words which follow,
And expressed himself in this wise :
"Wolf, do thou devour the dreamer,
Seize the Laplander, O sickness,
He who said that I should never
In my lifetime reach my homestead,
Nor again throughout my lifetime,
Nor as long as shines the moonlight,
Neither tread Väinölä's meadows,
Kalevala's extended heathlands."   30
    Then the aged Väinämöinen,
Spoke aloud his songs of magic,
And a flower-crowned birch grew upward,
Crowned with flowers, and leaves all golden,
And its summit reached to heaven,
To the very clouds uprising.
In the air the boughs extended,
And they spread themselves to heaven.
    Then he sang his songs of magic,
And he sang a moon all shining,   40
On the pine-tree's golden summit ;
And the Great Bear in the branches.
    On he drove with speed tremendous,
Straight to his beloved homestead,
Head bowed down, and thoughts all gloomy,
And his cap was tilted sideways,
For the great smith Ilmarinen,
He the great primeval craftsman,
He had promised as his surety,
That his own head he might rescue   50

Out of Pohjola's dark regions,
Sariola for ever misty.
  Presently his horse he halted
At the new-cleared field of Osmo,
And the aged Väinämöinen,
In the sledge his head uplifted,
Heard the noise within the smithy,
And the clatter in the coal-shed.
  Väinämöinen, old and steadfast,
Then himself the smithy entered,   60
And he found smith Ilmarinen,
Wielding mightily his hammer.
  Said the smith, said Ilmarinen,
"O thou aged Väinämöinen,
Where have you so long been staying,
Where have you so long been living?"
  Väinämöinen, old and steadfast,
Answered in the words which follow:
"There have I so long been staying,
There have I so long been living,   70
In the gloomy land of Pohja,
Sariola for ever misty.
Long I coursed on Lapland snowshoes,
With the world-renowned magicians."
  Then the smith, e'en Ilmarinen,
Answered in the words which follow:
"O thou aged Väinämöinen,
Thou the great primeval sorcerer,
Tell me of your journey thither;
Tell me of your homeward journey."   80
  Said the aged Väinämöinen,
"Much indeed have I to tell you:
Lives in Pohjola a maiden,
In that village cold a virgin,
Who will not accept a suitor,
Mocks the very best among them.
Half of all the land of Pohja
Praises her surpassing beauty.
From her temples shines the moonlight,
From her breasts the sun is shining,   90

And the Great Bear from her shoulders,
From her back the starry Seven.
   "Thou thyself, smith Ilmarinen,
Thou, the great primeval craftsman,
Go thyself to woo the maiden,
And behold her shining tresses.
If you can but forge a Sampo,
With its many-coloured cover,
You will then receive the maiden,
And the fair maid be your guerdon."   100
   Said the smith, e'en Ilmarinen,
"O thou aged Väinämöinen,
You have perhaps already pledged me
To the gloomy land of Pohja,
That your own head you might rescue,
And might thus secure your freedom.
Not in course of all my lifetime,
While the golden moon is shining,
Hence to Pohjola I'll journey,
Huts of Sariola so dreary,   110
Where the people eat each other,
And they even drown the heroes."
   Then the aged Väinämöinen
Answered in the words which follow :
"There is wonder after wonder ;
There's a pine with flowery summit,
Flowery summit, leaves all golden,
Near where Osmo's field is bordered.
On the crown the moon is shining,
In the boughs the Bear is resting."   120
   Said the smith, e'en Ilmarinen,
"This I never can believe in,
If I do not go to see it,
And my own eyes have not seen it."
   Said the aged Väinämöinen,
"If you cannot then believe it,
We will go ourselves, and witness
Whether true or false the story."
   Then they both went forth to see it,
View the pine with flowery summit,   130

First walked aged Väinämöinen,
And smith Ilmarinen second.
When they reached the spot they sought for,
On the edge of Osmo's cornfield,
Then the smith his steps arrested,
In amazement at the pine-tree,
With the Great Bear in the branches,
And the moon upon its summit.
  Then the aged Väinämöinen,
Spoke the very words which follow: 140
"Now thou smith, my dearest brother,
Climb and fetch the moon above us,
Bring thou, too, the Great Bear shining
On the pine-tree's golden summit."
  Then the smith, e'en Ilmarinen,
Climbed aloft into the pine-tree,
Up he climbed into the daylight,
Climbed to fetch the moon above him,
And the Great Bear, shining brightly,
On the pine-tree's golden summit.   150
  Said the pine-tree's golden summit,
Said the widely-branching pine-tree,
"Mighty man, of all most foolish,
O most thoughtless of the heroes!
In my branches, fool, thou climbest,
To my summit, as a boy might,
And would'st grasp the moon's reflection,
And the false stars thou beholdest!"
  Then the aged Väinämöinen,
Lifted up his voice in singing.   160
As he sang uprose a tempest,
And the wind rose wildly furious,
And he spoke the words which follow,
And expressed himself in thiswise:
"In thy boat, O wind, convey him,
In thy skiff, O breeze, convey him,
Bear him to the distant regions
Of the gloomy land of Pohja."
  Then there rose a mighty tempest,
And the wind so wildly furious   170

Carried off smith Ilmarinen,
Hurried him to distant regions,
To the gloomy land of Pohja,
Sariola for ever misty.
　Then the smith, e'en Ilmarinen,
Journeyed forth, and hurried onwards,
On the tempest forth he floated,
On the pathway of the breezes,
Over moon, and under sunray,
On the shoulders of the Great Bear,　　　　　180
Till he reached the halls of Pohja,
Baths of Sariola the gloomy,
Yet the tailed-dogs were not barking,
And the watch-dogs were not yelping.
　Louhi, Pohjola's old Mistress,
Old and gap-toothed dame of Pohja,
In the house she stood and listened,
And at length she spoke as follows:
"Who then are you among mortals,
Who among the roll of heroes,　　　　　190
On the tempest-path who comest,
On the sledgeway of the breezes,
Yet the dogs ran forth not, barking,
And the shaggy-tailed ones barked not."
　Said the smith, e'en Ilmarinen,
"Surely I have not come hither
That the village dogs should shame me,
Or the shaggy-tailed ones hurt me,
Here behind these foreign portals,
And behind these unknown fences."　　　　　200
　Then did Pohjola's old Mistress
Question thus the new-come stranger:
"Have you ever on your travels,
Heard reports of, or encountered
Him, the great smith Ilmarinen,
Most accomplished of the craftsmen?
Long have we been waiting for him,
Long been anxious for his coming
Here to Pohjola's dark regions,
That a Sampo he might forge us."　　　　　210

Then the smith, e'en Ilmarinen,
Answered in the words which follow:
"I have met upon my journey
With the smith named Ilmarinen;
I myself am Ilmarinen,
And a most accomplished craftsman."

Louhi, Pohjola's old Mistress,
Old and gap-toothed dame of Pohja,
Hurried back into her dwelling,
And she spoke the words which follow: 220
"Come my daughter, thou the youngest,
Thou the fairest of my children,
Robe thyself in choicest raiment,
Clothe thee in the brightest-coloured,
In the finest of your dresses,
Brightest beads upon thy bosom,
Round thy neck the very finest,
And upon thy temples shining.
See thou that thy cheeks are rosy,
And thy countenance is cheerful.   230
Here's the smith named Ilmarinen,
He the great primeval craftsman,
Who will forge the Sampo for us,
With its brightly-pictured cover."

Then the lovely maid of Pohja,
Famed on land, on water peerless,
Took the choicest of her dresses,
And the brightest of her garments,
And the fifth at last selected.
Then her headdress she adjusted,   240
And her copper belt girt round her,
And her wondrous golden girdle.

Back she came from out the storeroom,
Dancing back into the courtyard,
And her eyes were brightly shining.
As she moved, her earrings jingled,
And her countenance was charming,
And her lovely cheeks were rosy.
Gold was shining on her bosom,
On her head was silver gleaming.   250

Then did Pohjola's old Mistress,
Lead the smith named Ilmarinen,
Into Pohjola's great castle,
Rooms of Sariola the gloomy.
There she set a meal before him,
Gave the hero drink in plenty,
And she feasted him profusely,
And at length she spoke as follows :
" O thou smith, O Ilmarinen,
Thou the great primeval craftsman,   260
If you can but forge a Sampo,
With its many-coloured cover,
From the tips of swans' white wing-plumes,
From the milk of barren heifer,
From a little grain of barley,
From the wool of sheep of summer,
Will you then accept this maiden,
As reward, my charming daughter ? "
    Then the smith named Ilmarinen
Answered in the words which follow :   270
" I will go to forge the Sampo,
Weld its many-coloured cover,
From the tips of swans' white wing-plumes,
From the milk of barren heifer,
From a little grain of barley,
From the wool of sheep of summer,
For 'twas I who forged the heavens,
And the vault of air I hammered,
Ere the air had yet beginning,
Or a trace of aught was present."   280
    Then he went to forge the Sampo,
With its many-coloured cover,
Sought a station for a smithy,
And he needed tools for labour ;
But no place he found for smithy,
Nor for smithy, nor for bellows,
Nor for furnace, nor for anvil,
Not a hammer, nor a mallet.
    Then the smith, e'en Ilmarinen,
Spoke aloud the words which follow :   290

"None despair, except old women,
Scamps may leave their task unfinished ;
Not a man, how weak soever,
Not a hero of the laziest !"
   For his forge he sought a station,
And a wide place for the bellows,
In the country round about him,
In the outer fields of Pohja.
So he sought one day, a second,
And at length upon the third day   300
Found a stone all streaked with colours,
And a mighty rock beside it.
Here the smith his search abandoned,
And the smith prepared his furnace,
On the first day fixed the bellows,
And the forge upon the second.
   Thereupon smith Ilmarinen,
He the great primeval craftsman,
Heaped the fuel upon the fire,
And beneath the forge he thrust it,   310
Made his servants work the bellows,
To the half of all their power.
   So the servants worked the bellows,
To the half of all their power,
During three days of the summer,
During three nights of the summer.
Stones beneath their heels were resting,
And upon their toes were boulders.
   On the first day of their labour
He himself, smith Ilmarinen,   320
Stooped him down, intently gazing,
To the bottom of the furnace,
If perchance amid the fire
Something brilliant had developed.
   From the flames there rose a crossbow,
Golden bow from out the furnace ;
'Twas a gold bow tipped with silver,
And the shaft shone bright with copper.
   And the bow was fair to gaze on,
But of evil disposition,   330

And a head each day demanded,
And on feast-days two demanded.
He himself, smith Ilmarinen,
Was not much delighted with it,
So he broke the bow to pieces,
Cast it back into the furnace,
Made his servants work the bellows,
To the half of all their power.
So again upon the next day,
He himself, smith Ilmarinen,   340
Stooped him down, intently gazing
To the bottom of the furnace,
And a boat rose from the furnace,
From the heat rose up a red boat,
And the prow was golden-coloured,
And the rowlocks were of copper.
    And the boat was fair to gaze on,
But of evil disposition ;
It would go to needless combat,
And would fight when cause was lacking.   350
    Therefore did smith Ilmarinen
Take no slightest pleasure in it,
And he smashed the boat to splinters,
Cast it back into the furnace ;
Made his servants work the bellows,
To the half of all their power.
Then upon the third day likewise,
He himself, smith Ilmarinen,
Stooped him down, intently gazing
To the bottom of the furnace,   360
And a heifer then rose upward,
With her horns all golden-shining,
With the Bear-stars on her forehead ;
On her head appeared the Sun-disc.
    And the cow was fair to gaze on,
But of evil disposition ;
Always sleeping in the forest,
On the ground her milk she wasted.
    Therefore did smith Ilmarinen
Take no slightest pleasure in her,   370

And he cut the cow to fragments,
Cast her back into the furnace,
Made his servants work the bellows,
To the half of all their power.
    So again upon the fourth day,
He himself, smith Ilmarinen
Stooped him down, and gazed intently
To the bottom of the furnace,
And a plough rose from the furnace,
With the ploughshare golden-shining,   380
Golden share, and frame of copper,
And the handles tipped with silver.
    And the plough was fair to gaze on,
But of evil disposition,
Ploughing up the village cornfields,
Ploughing up the open meadows.
    Therefore did smith Ilmarinen
Take no slightest pleasure in it.
And he broke the plough to pieces,
Cast it back into the furnace,   390
Called the winds to work the bellows
To the utmost of their power.
    Then the winds arose in fury,
Blew the east wind, blew the west wind,
And the south wind yet more strongly,
And the north wind howled and blustered.
Thus they blew one day, a second,
And upon the third day likewise.
Fire was flashing from the windows,
From the door the sparks were flying   400
And the dust arose to heaven;
With the clouds the smoke was mingled.
Then again smith Ilmarinen,
On the evening of the third day,
Stooped him down, and gazed intently
To the bottom of the furnace,
And he saw the Sampo forming,
With its many-coloured cover.
    Thereupon smith Ilmarinen,
He the great primeval craftsman,   410

Welded it and hammered at it,
Heaped his rapid blows upon it,
Forged with cunning art the Sampo,
And on one side was a corn-mill,
On another side a salt-mill,
And upon the third a coin-mill.

Now was grinding the new Sampo,
And revolved the pictured cover,
Chestfuls did it grind till evening,
First for food it ground a chestful,   420
And another ground for barter,
And a third it ground for storage.

Now rejoiced the Crone of Pohja,
And conveyed the bulky Sampo,
To the rocky hills of Pohja,
And within the Mount of Copper,
And behind nine locks secured it.
There it struck its roots around it,
Fathoms nine in depth that measured,
One in Mother Earth deep-rooted,   430
In the strand the next was planted,
In the nearest mount the third one.

Afterwards smith Ilmarinen,
Asked the maiden as his guerdon,
And he spoke the words which follow:
"Will you give me now the maiden,
For the Sampo is completed,
With its beauteous pictured cover?"

Then the lovely maid of Pohja
Answered in the words which follow: 440
"Who in years that this shall follow,
For three summers in succession,
Who shall hear the cuckoo calling,
And the birds all sweetly singing,
If I seek a foreign country,
As in foreign lands a berry?

"If the dove had thus departed,
And the maiden thus should wander,
Strayed away the mother's darling,
Likewise would the cranberries vanish,   450

All the cuckoos vanish with them,
And the nightingales would migrate,
From the summit of this mountain,
From the summits of these uplands.
    "Not as yet can I abandon
My delightful life as maiden,
And my innocent employments
In the glowing heat of summer.
All unplucked the mountain-berries,
And the lakeshore will be songless,   460
And unvisited the meadows,
And in woods I sport no longer."
    Thereupon smith Ilmarinen,
He the great primeval craftsman,
Sad, and with his head down-hanging,
And his cap in grief thrust sideways,
Presently began to ponder,
In his head long time debating
How he now should journey homeward,
To his own familiar country,   470
From the gloomy land of Pohja,
Sariola for ever misty.
    Then said Pohjola's old Mistress,
"O thou smith, O Ilmarinen
Wherefore is thy mind so saddened,
And thy cap in grief pushed sideways?
Are you thinking how to journey,
Homeward to your native country?"
    Said the smith, e'en Ilmarinen,
"Yes, my thoughts are there directed   480
To my home that I may die there,
And may rest in scenes familiar."
    Then did Pohjola's old Mistress
Set both meat and drink before him,
At the boat-stern then she placed him,
There to work the copper paddle,
And she bade the wind blow strongly,
And the north wind fiercely bluster.
    Thus it was smith Ilmarinen
He the great primeval craftsman,   490

Travelled homeward to his country,
O'er the blue sea's watery surface.
Thus he voyaged one day, a second,
And at length upon the third day,
Reached the smith his home in safety,
In the land where he was nurtured.

Asked the aged Väinämöinen,
When he saw smith Ilmarinen,
" Ilmarinen, smith and brother,
Thou the great primeval craftsman, 500
Hast thou forged a new-made Sampo,
With its many-coloured cover? "

Then replied smith Ilmarinen,
Ready with a fitting answer,
" Grinds forth meal, the new-made Sampo,
And revolves the pictured cover,
Chestfuls does it grind till evening,
First for food it grinds a chestful,
And another grinds for barter,
And a third it grinds for storage." 510

Runo XI.—Lemminkainen and Kyllikki

Argument

Lemminkainen goes to seek a wife among the noble maidens of Saari
(1–110). At first they laugh at him, but afterwards become very
friendly (111–156). But Kyllikki, on whose account he has come,
will not listen to him, and at length he carries her off by force, drags her
into his sledge, and drives away with her (157–222). Kyllikki weeps,
and especially reproaches Lemminkainen with his fondness for
war, and Lemminkainen promises not to go to war if Kyllikki promises
never to go to the village dances, and both swear to observe these
conditions (223–314). Lemminkainen drives home, and his mother
rejoices in her young daughter-in-law (315–402).

Now 'tis time to speak of Ahti,
Of that lively youth to gossip.
Ahti, dweller in the island,
He the scapegrace son of Lempi,

In a noble house was nurtured,
By his dear and much-loved mother,
Where the bay spread out most widely,
Where the cape extended furthest.

Kauko fed himself on fishes,
Ahti was reared up on perches,   10
And he grew a man most handsome,
Very bold and very ruddy,
And his head was very handsome,
And his form was very shapely,
Yet he was not wholly faultless,
But was careless in his morals,
Passing all his time with women,
Wandering all around at night-time,
When the maidens took their pleasure
In the dance, with locks unbraided.   20

Kylli, beauteous maid of Saari,
Saari's maiden, Saari's flower,
In a noble house was nurtured,
And her stature grew most graceful,
Sitting in her father's dwelling,
Resting there in seat of honour.

Long she grew, and wide was famous:
Suitors came from distant regions,
To the far-famed maiden's homestead,
To the dwelling of the fair one.   30

For his son, the Sun had wooed her,
But she would not go to Sunland,
Where the Sun is ever shining
In the burning heats of summer.

For his son, the Moon had wooed her,
But she would not go to Moonland,
Where the Moon is ever shining,
In the realms of air to wander.

For his son, a Star had wooed her,
But she would not go to Starland,   40
Through the live-long night to glimmer,
In the open skies of winter.
Many suitors came from Viro,
And from Ingerland came others;

None among them pleased the maiden,
And she answered all as follows:
" 'Tis for nought your gold you squander,
And your silver waste for nothing.
Never will I go to Viro,
Neither go, nor in the future   50
Row a boat through Viro's waters,
Nor will move a punt from Saari,
Nor will eat the fish of Viro,
Nor the fish-soup eat of Viro.

"Nor to Ingerland I'll travel,
Nor its slopes and shores will visit.
There is hunger, nought but hunger,
Want of trees, and want of timber,
Want of water, want of wheatfields,
There is even want of ryebread."   60
Then the lively Lemminkainen,
He the handsome Kaukomieli,
Now resolved to make a journey
And to woo the Flower of Saari,
Seek at home the peerless fair one,
With her beauteous locks unbraided.

But his mother would dissuade him,
And the aged woman warned him:
"Do not seek, my son, my darling,
Thus to wed above your station.   70
There are none would think you noble
Of the mighty race of Saari."
Said the lively Lemminkainen,
Said the handsome Kaukomieli,
"If my house is not as noble,
Nor my race esteemed so mighty,
For my handsome shape they'll choose me,
For my noble form will take me."

But his mother still opposed her
Unto Lemminkainen's journey,   80
To the mighty race of Saari,
To the clan of vast possessions.
"There the maidens all will scorn you,
And the women ridicule you."

Little heeded Lemminkainen,
And in words like these he answered :
" I will check the women's laughter,
And the giggling of their daughters.
Sons I'll give unto their bosoms,
Children in their arms to carry ;   90
Then they will no longer scorn me,
Thus I'll stop their foolish jesting."
    Then his mother made him answer :
"Woe to me, my life is wretched.
If you mock the Saari women,
Bring to shame the modest maidens,
You will bring yourself in conflict,
And a dreadful fight will follow.
All the noble youths of Saari,
Full a hundred skilful swordsmen,   100
All shall rush on thee unhappy,
Standing all alone amidst them."
    Little heeded Lemminkainen
All the warnings of his mother ;
Chose the best among his stallions,
And the steed he quickly harnessed,
And he drove away with clatter,
To the village famed of Saari,
There to woo the Flower of Saari,
She, the peerless maid of Saari.   110
    But the women ridiculed him,
And the maidens laughed and jeered him.
In the lane he drove most strangely,
Strangely to the farm came driving,
Turned the sledge all topsy-turvy,
At the gate he overturned it.
    Then the lively Lemminkainen
Mouth awry, and head downsunken,
While his black beard he was twisting,
Spoke aloud the words which follow :   120
"Never aught like this I witnessed,
Never saw I, never heard I,
That the women laughed about me,
And the maidens ridiculed me."

Little troubled Lemminkainen,
And he spoke the words which follow:
"Is there not a place in Saari,
On the firm ground of the island,
For the sport that I will show you,
And for dancing on the greensward,　　　　130
With the joyous girls of Saari,
With their fair unbraided tresses?"
　　Then the Saari maidens answered,
Spoke the maidens of the headland:
"There is room enough in Saari,
On the firm ground of the island,
For the sport that you shall show us,
And for dancing on the greensward,
For the milkmaids in the meadows,
And the herd-boys in their dances;　　　　140
Very lean are Saari's children,
But the foals are sleek and fattened."
　　Little troubled Lemminkainen,
But engaged himself as herd-boy,
Passed his days among the meadows,
And his nights 'mid lively maidens,
Sporting with the charming maidens,
Toying with their unbound tresses.
　　Thus the lively Lemminkainen,
He the handsome Kaukomieli,　　　　150
Ended soon the women's laughter,
And the joking of the maidens.
There was not a single daughter,
Not a maid, however modest,
But he did not soon embrace her,
And remain awhile beside her.
　　One alone of all the maidens,
Of the mighty race of Saari,
Would not list to any lover,
Not the greatest man among them;　　　　160
Kyllikki, the fairest maiden,
Loveliest flower of all in Saari.
　　Then the lively Lemminkainen,
He the handsome Kaukomieli,

Wore a hundred boats to tatters,
Rowed in twain a hundred oars,
As he strove to win the maiden,
Kyllikki herself to conquer.
Kyllikki the lovely maiden
Answered him in words that follow :   170
"Wherefore wander here, O weakling,
Racing round me like a plover,
Always seeking for a maiden,
With her tin-adorned girdle?
I myself will never heed you
Till the stone is ground to powder,
Till the pestle's stamped to pieces,
And the mortar smashed to atoms.

"Nought I care for such a milksop,
Such a milksop, such a humbug ;   180
I must have a graceful husband,
I myself am also graceful ;
I must have a shapely husband,
I myself am also shapely ;
And a well-proportioned husband,
I myself am also handsome."
But a little time thereafter,
Scarce had half a month passed over,
On a certain day it happened,
As was usual in the evenings,   190
All the girls had met for pleasure,
And the beauteous maids were dancing,
In a grove near open country,
On a lovely space of heathland.
Kyllikki was first among them,
She the far-famed Flower of Saari.
Thither came the ruddy scoundrel,
There drove lively Lemminkainen,
With the best among his horses,
With the horse that he had chosen,   200
Right into the green arena
Where the beauteous maids were dancing.
Kyllikki he seized and lifted,
Then into the sledge he pushed her,

And upon the bearskin sat her,
That upon the sledge was lying.
  With his whip he lashed the stallion,
And he cracked the lash above him,
And he started on his journey,
And he cried while driving onward: 210
"O ye maidens, may ye never
In your lives betray the secret,
Speak of how I drove among you,
And have carried off the maiden.
  "But if you will not obey me,
You will fall into misfortune;
To the war I'll sing your lovers,
And the youths beneath the sword-blades,
That you hear no more about them,
See them not in all your lifetime,   220
Either in the streets when walking,
Or across the fields when driving."
  Kyllikki lamented sorely,
Sobbed the beauteous Flower of Saari:
"Let me but depart in safety,
Let the child depart in safety,
Set me free to journey homeward
To console my weeping mother.
  "If you will not now release me,
Set me free to journey homeward,   230
O then I have five strong brothers,
And my uncle's sons are seven,
Who can run with hare-like swiftness,
And will haste the maid to rescue."
  When she could not gain her freedom,
She began to weep profusely,
And she spoke the words which follow:
"I, poor maid, was born for nothing,
And for nought was born and fostered,
And my life was lived for nothing,   240
Since I fall to one unworthy,
In a worthless fellow's clutches,
One for battle always ready,
And a rude ferocious warrior."

Answered lively Lemminkainen,
Said the handsome Kaukomieli :
" Kyllikki, my dearest heart-core,
Thou my sweetest little berry,
Do not vex yourself so sorely,
Do not thus give way to sadness.   250
I will cherish you when eating,
And caress you on my journeys,
Whether sitting, whether standing,
Always near when I am resting.

" Wherefore then should you be troubled,
Wherefore should you sigh for sorrow ?
Are you therefore grieved so sorely,
Therefore do you sigh for trouble,
Lest the cows or bread might fail you,
Or provisions be deficient ?   260
" Do not vex yourself so sorely,
I have cows enough and plenty,
Plenty are there, milk to yield me,
Some, Muurikkis, in the marshes,
Some, Mansikkis, on the hillsides,
Some, Puolukkas, on the clearing.
Sleek they are, although unfoddered.
Fine they are, although untended.
In the evening none need bind them,
In the evening none need loose them,   270
No one need provide them fodder,
Nor give salt in morning hours.

" Or perchance are you lamenting,
Sighing thus so full of trouble,
That I am not high descended,
Nor was born of noble lineage ?

" If I am not high descended,
Nor was born of noble lineage,
Yet have I a sword of keenness,
Gleaming brightly in the battle.   280
This is surely high descended,
And has come of noble lineage,
For the blade was forged by Hiisi,
And by Jumala 'twas polished,

Thus am I so high descended,
And I come of noblest lineage,
With my sword so keenly sharpened
Gleaming brightly in the battle."

But the maiden sighed with anguish,
And in words like these made answer: 290
"O thou Ahti, son of Lempi,
If you would caress the maiden,
Keep her at your side for ever,
Dove-like in thy arms for ever,
Pledge thyself by oaths eternal,
Not again to join in battle,
Whether love of gold may lure you,
Or your wish is fixed on silver."

Then the lively Lemminkainen
Answered in the words which follow: 300
"Here I swear, by oaths eternal,
Not again to join in battle,
Whether love of gold may lure me,
Or my wish is fixed on silver.
But thyself on oath must pledge thee,
Not to wander to the village,
Whether for the love of dancing,
Or to loiter in the pathways."

Then they took the oaths between them,
And with oaths eternal bound them,   310
There in Jumala's high presence,
In the sight of the Almighty,
Ahti should not go to battle,
Nor should Kylli seek the village.

Then the lively Lemminkainen
Whipped his steed to faster running,
Shook the reins to urge him onward,
And he spoke the words which follow:
"Now farewell to Saari's meadows,
Roots of pine, and trunks of fir-trees,   320
Where I wandered for a summer,
Where I tramped throughout the winter,
And on cloudy nights took shelter,
Hiding from the stormy weather,

While I waited for my dear one,
And to bear away my darling."
    On he urged his prancing courser,
Till he saw his home before him,
And the maiden spoke as follows,
And in words like these addressed him :   330
" Lo, I see a hut before us,
Looking like a place of famine.
Tell me whose may be the cottage,
Whose may be this wretched dwelling ? "
    Then the lively Lemminkainen
Answered in the words which follow :
" Do not grieve about the hovel,
Sigh not for the hut before you.
We will build us other houses,
And establish better dwellings,   340
Built of all the best of timber,
With the very best of planking."
    Thus the lively Lemminkainen
Reached again his home in safety,
Finding there his dearest mother,
She, his old and much-loved mother.
    And his mother spoke as follows,
And expressed herself in thiswise :
" Long, my son, have you been absent,
Long in foreign lands been roaming."   350
    Said the lively Lemminkainen,
And he spoke the words which follow :
" I have brought to shame the women,
With the modest girls have sported,
And have well repaid the laughter,
And the jests they heaped upon me.
To my sledge the best I carried,
And upon the rug I sat her,
And between the runners laid her,
And beneath the rug I hid her ;   360
Thus repaid the laughing women,
And the joking of the maidens.
    "O my mother, who hast borne me,
O my mother, who hast reared me,

I have gained what I have sought for,
And have won what most I longed for.
Now prepare the best of bolsters,
And the softest of the cushions,
In my native land to rest me,
With the young and lovely maiden."   370
    Then his mother spoke as follows,
And in words like these expressed her:
" Now to Jumala be praises,
Praise to thee, O great Creator,
For the daughter thou hast sent me,
Who can fan the flames up brightly,
Who can work at weaving deftly,
And is skilful, too, in spinning,
And accomplished, too, in washing,
And can bleach the clothes to whiteness.   380
    " For thy own weal thank him also ;
Good is won, and good brought homeward :
Good decreed by the Creator,
Good that's granted by his mercy.
On the snow is fair the bunting,
Fairer yet is she beside thee ;
White the foam upon the water,
Whiter yet this noble lady :
On the lake the duck is lovely,
Lovelier yet thy cherished darling ;   390
Brilliant is a star in heaven,
Brighter yet thy promised fair one.
    " Let the floors be wide expanded,
And the windows widened greatly,
Let new walls be now erected,
All the house be greatly bettered,
And the threshold new-constructed,
Place new doors upon the threshold,
For the youthful bride beside you,
She, of all the very fairest,   400
She, the best of all the maidens,
And the noblest in her lineage."

RUNO XII.—LEMMINKAINEN'S FIRST EXPEDITION
TO POHJOLA

Argument

Kyllikki forgets her oath and goes to the village, whereupon Lemminkainen is enraged and resolves to divorce her immediately, and to set forth to woo the Maiden of Pohja (1-128). His mother does her utmost to dissuade him, telling him that he will very probably be killed. Lemminkainen, who is brushing his hair, throws the brush angrily out of his hand and declares that blood shall flow from the brush if he should come to harm (129-212). He makes ready, starts on his journey, comes to Pohjola, and sings all the men out of the homestead of Pohjola ; and only neglects to enchant one wicked cowherd (213-504).

THEN did Ahti Lemminkainen,
He the handsome Kaukolainen
Live awhile a life of quiet
With the young bride he had chosen,
And he went not forth to battle,
Nor went Kylli to the village.

But at length one day it happened
In the early morning hours,
Forth went Ahti Lemminkainen
To the place where spawn the fishes,   **10**
And he came not home at evening,
And at nightfall he returned not.
Kyllikki then sought the village,
There to dance with sportive maidens.

Who shall now the tidings carry,
Who will now convey a message?
Ainikki 'twas, Ahti's sister,
She it was who brought the tidings,
She it was conveyed the message.
" Ahti, O my dearest brother,   **20**
Kyllikki has sought the village,
Entered there the doors of strangers,
Where the village girls are sporting,
Dancing with unbraided tresses."

Ahti then, for ever boyish,
He the lively Lemminkainen,

Grew both sorrowful and angry,
And for long was wild with fury,
And he spoke the words which follow:
"O my mother, aged woman,   30
Wash my shirt, and wash it quickly
In the black snake's deadly venom,
Dry it then, and dry it quickly
That I may go forth to battle,
And contend with youths of Pohja,
And o'erthrow the youths of Lapland.
Kyllikki has sought the village,
Entered there the doors of strangers,
There to dance with sportive maidens,
With their tresses all unbraided."   40
    Kyllikki made answer promptly,
She his favoured bride responded:
"Ahti, O my dearest husband,
Do not now depart to battle!
I beheld while I was sleeping,
While my slumber was the deepest,
From the hearth the flames were flashing,
Flashing forth with dazzling brightness,
Leaping up below the windows,
To the furthest walls extending,   50
Then throughout the house blazed fiercely,
Like a cataract in its fury,
O'er the surface of the flooring,
And from window unto window."
    But the lively Lemminkainen
Answered in the words which follow:
"Nought I trust in dreams of women,
Nor rely on woman's insight.
O my mother who hast borne me,
Bring me here my war-shirt quickly,   60
Bring me, too, my mail for battle,
For my inclination leads me
Hence to drink the beer of battle,
And to taste the mead of combat."
    Then his mother spoke in answer:
"O my son, my dearest Ahti,

Do thou not go forth to battle !
In the house is beer in plenty,
In the barrels made of alder,
And behind the taps of oakwood.   70
It is seasoned now for drinking,
And all day canst thou be singing."
    Said the lively Lemminkainen,
" But for home-brewed ale I care not,
Rather would I drink stream-water,
From the end of tarry rudder,
And this drink were sweeter to me
Than the beer in all our cellars.
Bring me here my war-shirt quickly,
Bring me, too, my mail for battle.   80
I will seek the homes of Pohja,
And o'erthrow the youths of Lapland,
And for gold will ask the people,
And I will demand their silver."
    Then said Lemminkainen's mother,
" O my son, my dearest Ahti,
We ourselves have gold in plenty,
Silver plenty in the storeroom.
Only yesterday it happened,
In the early hours of morning,   90
Ploughed the slave a field of vipers,
Full of twining, twisting serpents,
And a chest-lid raised the ploughshare,
And the chest was full of money.
Coins by hundreds there were hidden,
Thousands there were squeezed together,
To our stores the chest was carried,
In the loft we stored it safely."
    Said the lively Lemminkainen,
" Nought I care for home-stored treasures.   100
I will win me marks in battle,
Treasures won by far are better,
Than the gold in all our storerooms,
Or the silver found in ploughing.
Bring me here my war-shirt quickly,
Bring me, too, my mail for battle,

I will go to war in Pohja,
To destroy the sons of Lapland.

"There my inclination leads me
And my understanding drives me,   110
And my own ears shall inform me,
And my own eyes show me truly,
If in Pohjola a maiden,
In Pimentola a maiden,
Is not longing for a lover,
For the best of men desirous."

Then said Lemminkainen's mother,
"O my son, my dearest Ahti,
Kyllikki at home is with thee,
Fairest she of all the housewives.   120
Strange it were to see two women
In a bed beside one husband."

Said the lively Lemminkainen,
"Kyllikki has sought the village.
Let her go to all the dances,
Let her sleep in all the houses,
Where the village girls are sporting,
Dancing with unbraided tresses."

Still his mother would dissuade him,
And the aged woman warned him :   130
"Yet beware, my son, and go not
Unto Pohjola's dread homestead,
Destitute of magic knowledge,
Destitute of all experience,
There to meet the youths of Pohja,
And to conquer Lapland's children !
There the Laplanders will sing you,
And the Turja men will thrust you,
Head in clay, and mouth in charcoal,
With your arms where sparks are flying,   140
And your hands in glowing embers,
There upon the burning hearthstones."

Lemminkainen heard and answered :
"Once some sorcerers would enchant me,
Wizards charm, and snakes would blast me,
As three Laplanders attempted

Through the night in time of summer,
On a rock all naked standing,
Wearing neither clothes nor waistband ;
Not a rag was twisted round them,   150
But they got what I could give them,
Like the miserable codfish,
Like the axe on stone that's battered,
Or against the rock the auger,
Or on slippery ice a sabot,
Or like Death in empty houses.

    " Otherwise indeed they threatened,
Otherwise events had happened,
For they wanted to o'erthrow me,
Threatened they would sink me deeply   160
In the swamp when I was walking,
That in mire I might be sunken,
In the mud my chin pushed downward,
And my beard in filthy places.
But indeed a man they found me,
And they did not greatly fright me.
I myself put forth my magic,
And began my spells to mutter,
Sang the wizards with their arrows,
And the archers with their weapons,   170
Sorcerers with their knives of iron,
Soothsayers with their pointed weapons,
Under Tuoni's mighty Cataract,
Where the surge is most terrific,
Underneath the highest cataract,
'Neath the worst of all the whirlpools.
There the sorcerers now may slumber,
There repose beneath their blankets,
Till the grass may spring above them,
Through their heads and caps sprout upward, 180
Through the arm-pits of the sorcerers,
Piercing through their shoulder-muscles,
While the wizards sleep in soundness,
Sleeping there without protection."
    Still his mother would restrain him,
Hinder Lemminkainen's journey,

Once again her son dissuaded,
And the dame held back the hero.
" Do not go, O do not venture
To that cold and dreary village,　　　　190
To the gloomy land of Pohja.
There destruction sure awaits you,
Evil waits for thee, unhappy,
Ruin, lively Lemminkainen !
Hadst thou hundred mouths to speak with,
Even so, one could not think it,
Nor that by thy songs of magic
Lapland's sons would be confounded,
For you know not Turja's language,
Not the tongue they speak in Lapland."　　200
　　Then the lively Lemminkainen,
He the handsome Kaukomieli,
As it chanced, his hair was brushing,
And with greatest neatness brushed it.
To the wall his brush then cast he,
To the stove the comb flung after,
And again he spoke and answered,
In the very words which follow :
" Ruin falls on Lemminkainen,
Evil waits for him unhappy,　　　　210
When the brush with blood is running,
And the comb with blood is streaming."
　　Then went lively Lemminkainen,
To the gloomy land of Pohja,
'Spite the warnings of his mother,
'Gainst the aged woman's counsel.
　　First he armed him, and he girt him,
In his coat of mail he clad him,
With a belt of steel encompassed,
And he spoke the words which follow :　　220
"Stronger feels a man in armour,
In the best of iron mail-coats,
And of steel a magic girdle,
As a wizard 'gainst magicians.
Then no trouble need alarm him,
Nor the greatest evil fright him."

Then he grasped his sword so trusty,
Took his blade, like flame that glittered,
Which by Hiisi's self was whetted,
And by Jumala was polished.   230
By his side the hero girt it,
Thrust in sheath with leather lining.

How shall now the man conceal him,
And the mighty hero hide him?
There a little time he hid him,
And the mighty one concealed him,
'Neath the beam above the doorway,
By the doorpost of the chamber,
In the courtyard by the hayloft,
By the gate of all the furthest.   240

Thus it was the hero hid him
From the sight of all the women,
But such art is not sufficient,
And such caution would not serve him,
For he likewise must protect him
From the heroes of the people,
There where two roads have their parting,
On a blue rock's lofty summit,
And upon the quaking marshes,
Where the waves are swiftly coursing,   250
Where the waterfall is rushing,
In the winding of the rapids.

Then the lively Lemminkainen
Spoke the very words which follow:
"Rise ye up from earth, O swordsmen,
You, the earth's primeval heroes,
From the wells arise, ye warriors,
From the rivers rise, ye bowmen!
With thy dwarfs arise, O woodland,
Forest, come with all thy people,   260
Mountain-Ancient, with thy forces,
Water-Hiisi, with thy terrors,
Water-Mistress, with thy people,
With thy scouts, O Water-Father,
All ye maidens from the valleys,
Richly robed, among the marshes,

Come ye to protect a hero,
Comrades of a youth most famous,
That the sorcerers' arrows strike not,
Nor the swords of the magicians,   270
Nor the knife-blades of enchanters,
Nor the weapons of the archers.

" If this be not yet sufficient,
Still I know of other measures,
And implore the very Highest,
Even Ukko in the heavens,
He of all the clouds the ruler,
Of the scattered clouds conductor.

" Ukko, thou of Gods the highest,
Aged Father in the heavens,   280
Thou amidst the clouds who breathest,
Thou amid the air who speakest,
Give me here a sword of fire,
By a sheath of fire protected,
That I may resist misfortune,
And I may avoid destruction,
Overthrow the powers infernal,
Overcome the water-sorcerers,
That all foes that stand before me,
And the foes who stand behind me,   290
And above me and beside me,
May be forced to own my power.
Crush the sorcerers, with their arrows,
The magicians, with their knife-blades,
And the wizards with their sword-blades,
All the scoundrels with their weapons."

Then the lively Lemminkainen,
He the handsome Kaukomieli,
From the bush his courser whistled,
From the grass, the gold-maned courser.   300
Thereupon the horse he harnessed,
In the shafts the fiery courser,
In the sledge himself he seated,
And the sledge began to rattle.
O'er the horse his whip he flourished,
Cracked the whip, and urged him onward,

Started quickly on his journey.
Rocked the sledge, the way grew shorter,
And the silver sand was scattered,
And the golden heather crackled.   310
    Thus he drove one day, a second,
Drove upon the third day likewise,
And at length upon the third day
Came the hero to a village.
Then the lively Lemminkainen
Drove the rattling sledge straight onward
Forth along the furthest pathway,
To the furthest of the houses,
And he asked upon the threshold,
Speaking from behind the window: 320
"Is there some one in this household
Who can loose my horse's harness,
And can sink the shaft-poles for me,
And can loose the horse's collar?"
    From the floor a child made answer,
And a boy from out the doorway:
"There is no one in this threshold,
Who can loose your horse's harness,
Or can sink the shaft-poles for you,
Or can loose the horse's collar."   330
    Little troubled Lemminkainen,
O'er the horse his whip he brandished,
With the beaded whip he smote him,
Drove the rattling sledge straight onward,
On the midmost of the pathways
To the midmost of the houses,
And he asked upon the threshold,
And beneath the eaves he shouted:
"Is there no one in this household
Who will hold the horse-reins for me,   340
And the chest-bands will unloosen,
That the foaming steed may rest him?"
    From the stove a crone responded
From the stove-bench cried a gossip:
"There are plenty in this household
Who can hold the horse-reins for you,

And the chest-bands can unloosen,
And can sink the shaft-poles for you.
Perhaps ten men may be sufficient,
Or a hundred if you need them,   350
Who would raise their sticks against you,
Give you, too, a beast of burden,
And would drive you homeward, rascal,
To your country, wretched creature,
To the household of your father,
To the dwelling of your mother,
To the gateway of your brother,
To the threshold of your sister,
Ere this very day is ended,
Ere the sun has reached its setting."   360
Little heeded Lemminkainen,
And he spoke the words which follow :
" May they shoot the crone, and club her,
On her pointed chin, and kill her."
Then again he hurried onward,
Thundering on upon his journey,
On the highest of the pathways,
To the highest of the houses.
Then the lively Lemminkainen
Reached the house to which he journeyed,   370
And he spoke the words which follow,
And expressed himself in thiswise :
" Stop the barker's mouth, O Hiisi,
And the dog's jaws close, O Lempo,
And his mouth securely muzzle,
That his gagged teeth may be harmless,
That he may not bark a warning
When a man is passing by him."
As he came into the courtyard,
On the ground he slashed his whiplash,   380
From the spot a cloud rose upward,
In the cloud a dwarf was standing,
And he quickly loosed the chest-bands,
And the shafts he then let downward.
Then the lively Lemminkainen
Listened with his ears attentive,

But no person there observed him,
So that no one present knew it.
Out of doors he heard a singing,
Through the moss he heard them speaking,   390
Through the walls heard music playing,
Through the shutters heard a singing.

In the house he cast his glances,
Gazed into the room in secret,
And the house was full of wizards,
And the benches full of singers,
By the walls there sat musicians.
Seers were sitting in the doorway,
On the upper benches sorcerers,
By the hearth were soothsayers seated,   400
There a Lapland bard was singing,
Hoarsely singing songs of Hiisi.

Then the lively Lemminkainen
Thought it wise to change his figure,
To another shape transformed him,
Left his hiding place, and entered,
Thrust himself into the chamber,
And he spoke the words which follow :
" Fine a song may be when ended,
Grandest are the shortest verses,   410
Wisdom better when unspoken,
Than in midmost interrupted."

Then came Pohjola's old Mistress,
On the floor advancing swiftly,
Till she reached the chamber's middle,
And she spoke these words in answer :
" Once there was a dog among us,
And a shaggy iron-haired puppy,
Eating flesh, of bones a biter,
One who licked the blood when freshest.   420
Who among mankind may you be,
Who among the list of heroes,
Boldly thus the house to enter,
Pushing right into the chamber,
Yet the dogs have never heard you,
Nor have warned us with their barking?"

Said the lively Lemminkainen,
"Surely I have not come hither,
Void of art and void of knowledge,
Void of strength and void of cunning,   430
Taught not magic by my father,
And without my parents' counsel,
That the dogs should now devour me,
And the barkers should attack me.

" But it was my mother washed me,
When a boy both small and slender,
Three times in the nights of summer,
Nine times in the nights of autumn,
And she taught me all the pathways,
And the knowledge of all countries,   440
And at home sang songs of magic,
Likewise too in foreign countries."

Then the lively Lemminkainen,
He the handsome Kaukomieli,
Soon began his songs of magic,
All at once began his singing,
Fire flashed from his fur-cloak's borders,
And his eyes with flame were shining
With the songs of Lemminkainen,
As he sang his spells of magic.   450

Sang the very best of singers
To the worst of all the singers,
And he fed their mouths with pebbles,
And he piled up rocks above them,
On the best of all the singers,
And most skilful of magicians.

Then he sang the men thereafter
Both to one side and the other,
To the plains, all bare and treeless,
To the lands, unploughed for ever,   460
To the ponds, devoid of fishes,
Where no perch has ever wandered,
To the dreadful falls of Rutja,
And amid the roaring whirlpools,
Underneath the foaming river,
To the rocks beneath the cataract.

There to burn as if 'mid fire,
And to scatter sparks around them.
Then the lively Lemminkainen
Sang his songs against the swordsmen.   470
Sang the heroes with their weapons,
Sang the young men, sang the old men,
And the men of age between them,
And his songs spared one man only,
And he was a wicked cowherd,
Old, with eyes both closed and sightless.
    Märkähattu then, the cowherd,
Spoke the very words which follow :
" O thou lively son of Lempi,
Thou hast banned the young and old men,   480
Banned the men of age between them,
Wherefore hast not banned me likewise ? "
    Said the lively Lemminkainen,
" Therefore 'tis that I have spared thee,
That thou dost appear so wretched,
Pitiful without my magic.
In the days when thou wast younger,
Thou wast worst of all the cowherds,
Hast destroyed thy mother's children,
And disgraced thy very sister,   490
All the horses hast thou crippled,
All the foals hast thou outwearied,
In the swamps or stony places,
Plashing through the muddy waters."
    Märkähattu then, the cowherd,
Greatly vexed, and greatly angry,
Through the open door went quickly,
Through the yard to open country,
Ran to Tuonela's deep river,
To the dreadful river's whirlpool,   500
Waited there for Kaukomieli,
Waited there for Lemminkainen,
Till on his return from Pohja,
He should make his journey homeward.

Runo XIII.—Hiisi's Elk

Argument

Lemminkainen asks the old woman of Pohja for her daughter, but
she demands that he should first capture the Elk of Hiisi on snowshoes
(1–30). Lemminkainen starts off in high spirits to hunt the elk, but it
escapes, and he breaks his snowshoes and spear (31–270).

THEN the lively Lemminkainen
Said to Pohjola's old Mistress,
" Give me, old one, now your maiden,
Bring me here your lovely daughter,
She the best of all among them,
She the tallest of the maidens."
　　Then did Pohjola's old Mistress
Answer in the words which follow :
" Nay, I will not give my maiden,
And you shall not have my daughter, 　　　10
Not the best or worst among them,
Not the tallest, not the shortest,
For you have a wife already,
Long the mistress of your household."
　　Said the lively Lemminkainen,
" Kylli in the town lies fettered,
At the steps before the village,
By the gate where strangers enter,
So a better wife I wish for,
Therefore give me now your daughter, 　　　20
She the fairest of your daughters,
Lovely with unbraided tresses."
　　Then said Pohjola's old Mistress,
" Never will I give my daughter
To a vain and worthless fellow,
To a hero good for nothing.
Therefore you may woo my daughter,
Win the far-famed flower-crowned maiden,
If you hunt the elk on snowshoes,
In the distant field of Hiisi." 　　　30

Then the lively Lemminkainen
Fixed the point upon his javelin,
And his bowstring made of sinew,
And with bone he tipped his arrows,
And he said the words which follow :
" Now my javelin I have pointed,
All my shafts with bone have pointed,
And have strung my bow with sinew,
Not the snowshoe left put forward,
Nor the right one stamped behind it."   40

Then the lively Lemminkainen
Pondered deeply and reflected
How he should procure his snowshoes,
How they best should be constructed.
Then to Kauppi's house he hastened,
And to Lyylikki's forge hurried.
" O thou wisest Vuojalainen,
Thou the handsome Lapland Kauppi,
Make me snowshoes that will suit me,
Fitted with the finest leather ;   50
I must chase the elk of Hiisi,
In the distant field of Hiisi."

Lyylikki then spoke as follows,
Kauppi gave him ready answer :
"Vainly goest thou, Lemminkainen,
Forth to hunt the elk of Hiisi ;
For a piece of rotten timber,
Only will reward your labour."

Little troubled Lemminkainen,
And he spoke the words which follow :   60
" Make a snowshoe left to run with,
And a right one to put forward !
I must chase the elk on snowshoes,
In the distant field of Hiisi."

Lyylikki, the smith of snowshoes,
Kauppi, maker of the snowshoes,
In the autumn shaped the left one,
In the winter carved the right one,
And he fixed the frames on one day,
Fixed the rings upon another.   70

Now the left was fit to run with,
And the right for wearing ready,
And the frames were now completed,
And the rings were also fitted.
Frames he lined with skins of otter,
And the rings with ruddy foxskin.
Then he smeared with grease the snowshoes,
Smeared them with the fat of reindeer,
And himself reflected deeply,
And he spoke the words which follow :   80
"Can you, in this youthful frolic,
You, a young and untried hero,
Forward glide upon the left shoe,
And push forward with the right one ?"
Said the lively Lemminkainen,
Answered him the ruddy rascal :
"Yes, upon this youthful frolic
Of a young and untried hero,
I can glide upon the left shoe,
And push forward with the right one."   90
On his back he bound his quiver,
And his new bow on his shoulder,
In his hands his pole grasped firmly,
On the left shoe glided forward,
And pushed onward with the right one,
And he spoke the words which follow :
"In God's world may there be nothing,
Underneath the arch of heaven,
In the forest to be hunted,
Not a single four-foot runner,   100
Which may not be overtaken,
And can easily be captured
Thus by Kaleva's son with snowshoes,
And with Lemminkainen's snowshoes."
But the boast was heard by Hiisi,
And by Juutas comprehended ;
And an elk was formed by Hiisi,
And a reindeer formed by Juutas,
With a head of rotten timber,
Horns composed of willow-branches,   110

Feet of ropes the swamps which border,
Shins of sticks from out the marshes;
And his back was formed of fence-stakes,
Sinews formed of dryest grass-stalks,
Eyes of water-lily flowers,
Ears of leaves of water-lily,
And his hide was formed of pine-bark,
And his flesh of rotten timber.

Hiisi now the elk instructed,
Thus he spoke unto the reindeer: 120
"Now rush forth thou elk of Hiisi,
On thy legs, O noble creature,
To the breeding-place of reindeer,
Grassy plains of Lapland's children,
Till the snowshoe-men are sweating;
Most of all, this Lemminkainen!"

Then rushed forth the elk of Hiisi,
Sped away the fleeing reindeer,
Rushing past the barns of Pohja,
To the plains of Lapland's children,   130
In the house the tubs kicked over,
On the fire upset the kettles,
Threw the meat among the ashes,
Spilt the soup among the cinders.

Then arose a great commotion,
On the plains of Lapland's children,
For the Lapland dogs were barking,
And the Lapland children crying,
And the Lapland women laughing,
And the other people grumbling.   140

He, the lively Lemminkainen,
Chased the elk upon his snowshoes,
Glided o'er the land and marshes,
O'er the open wastes he glided.
Fire was crackling from his snowshoes,
From his staff's end smoke ascending,
But as yet the elk he saw not;
Could not see it; could not hear it.

O'er the hills and dales he glided,
Through the lands beyond the ocean,   150

Over all the wastes of Hiisi,
Over all the heaths of Kalma,
And before the mouth of Surma,
And behind the house of Kalma.
Surma's mouth was quickly opened,
Down was bowed the head of Kalma,
That he thus might seize the hero,
And might swallow Lemminkainen;
But he tried, and failed to reach him,
Failed completely in his effort.   160

O'er all lands he had not skated,
Nor had reached the desert's borders,
In the furthest bounds of Pohja,
In the distant realms of Lapland,
So he skated further onward,
Till he reached the desert's borders.

When he reached this distant region,
Then he heard a great commotion,
In the furthest bounds of Pohja,
On the plains of Lapland's children.   170
And he heard the dogs were barking,
And the Lapland children crying,
And the Lapland women laughing,
And the other Lapps were grumbling.

Then the lively Lemminkainen
Skated on in that direction,
Where he heard the dogs were barking
On the plains of Lapland's children ;
And he said on his arrival,
And he asked them on his coming :   180
"Wherefore are the women laughing,
Women laughing, children crying,
And the older folks lamenting,
And the grey dogs all are barking?"

"Therefore are the women laughing,
Women laughing, children crying,
And the older folks lamenting,
And the grey dogs all are barking.
Here has charged the elk of Hiisi,
With its hoofs all cleft and polished,   190

In the house the tubs kicked over,
On the fire upset the kettles,
Shaken out the soup within them,
Spilt it all among the ashes."
　　Thereupon the ruddy rascal,
He the lively Lemminkainen,
Struck his left shoe in the snowdrift,
Like an adder in the meadow,
Pushed his staff of pinewood forward,
As it were a living serpent,   200
And he said as he was gliding,
Grasping firm the pole he carried :
"Let the men who live in Lapland,
Help me all to bring the elk home;
And let all the Lapland women
Set to work to wash the kettles ;
And let all the Lapland children
Hasten forth to gather splinters ;
And let all the Lapland kettles
Help to cook the elk when captured."   210
　　Then he poised himself and balanced,
Forward pushed, his strength exerting,
And the first time he shot forward,
From before their eyes he vanished.
Once again he speeded onward,
And they could no longer hear him,
But the third time he rushed onward,
Then he reached the elk of Hiisi.
Then he took a pole of maple,
And he made a birchen collar ;   220
Hiisi's elk he tethered with it,
In a pen of oak he placed it.
"Stand thou there, O elk of Hiisi,
Here remain, O nimble reindeer ! "
　　Then upon the back he stroked it,
Patted it upon the belly.
"Would that I awhile might tarry,
And might sleep awhile and rest me,
Here beside a youthful maiden,
With a dove of blooming beauty."   230

Then did Hiisi's elk grow furious,
And the reindeer kicked out wildly,
And it spoke the words which follow:
"Lempo's self shall reckon with you,
If you sleep beside a maiden,
And beside a girl should tarry."

Then it gave a mighty struggle,
And it snapped the birchen collar,
And it broke the pole of maple,
And the pen of oak burst open,   240
And the elk rushed wildly onwards,
And began to hurry forwards,
Over land and over marshes,
Over slopes o'ergrown with bushes,
Till the eyes no more could see it,
And the ears no longer hear it.

Thereupon the ruddy rascal
Grew both sorrowful and angry,
Very vexed and very angry,
And would chase the elk of Hiisi,   250
But as he was rushing forward,
In a hole he broke his left shoe,
And his snowshoe fell to pieces,
On the ground he broke the right one,
Broke the tips from off his snowshoes,
And the frames across the joinings.
While rushed on the elk of Hiisi,
Till its head he saw no longer.

Then the lively Lemminkainen,
Bowed his head in deep depression,   260
Gazed upon the broken snowshoes,
And he spoke the words which follow:
"Nevermore in all his lifetime
May another hunter venture
Confidently to the forest,
Chasing Hiisi's elk on snowshoes!
Since I went, O me unhappy,
And have spoilt the best of snowshoes,
And the splendid frames have shattered,
And my spearpoint likewise broken."   270

Runo XIV.—Lemminkainen's Death

Argument

Lemminkainen invokes the forest deities, and at length succeeds in capturing the elk, and brings it to Pohjola (1-270). Another task is given him, to bridle the fire-breathing steed of Hiisi. He bridles it and brings it to Pohjola (271-372). A third task is assigned him, to shoot a swan on the river of Tuonela. Lemminkainen comes to the river, but the despised cowherd, who is lying in wait for him, kills him, and casts his body into the cataract of Tuoni. The son of Tuoni then cuts his body to pieces (373-460).

THEN the lively Lemminkainen
Deeply pondered and reflected,
On the path that he should follow,
Whither he should turn his footsteps,
Should he leave the elk of Hiisi,
And direct his journey homewards,
Should he make another effort,
And pursue the chase on snowshoes,
With the Forest-Queen's permission,
And the favour of the wood-nymphs?   10
    Then he spoke the words which follow,
And in words like these expressed him:
"Ukko, thou of Gods the highest,
Gracious Father in the heavens,
Make me now two better snowshoes,
Leather snowshoes fit for sliding,
That I glide upon them swiftly
Over land and over marshes,
Glide throughout the land of Hiisi,
And across the heaths of Pohja,   20
There to chase the elk of Hiisi,
And to catch the nimble reindeer.
    "In the wood alone I wander,
Toil without another hero,
Through the pathways of Tapiola,
And beside the home of Tapio.

Welcome, wooded slopes and mountains,
Welcome to the rustling pinewoods,
Welcome to the grey head aspens,
And to all who greet me, welcome !   30
    " Be propitious wood and thicket,
Gracious Tapio, do thou aid me,
Bring the hero to the islands,
To the hills in safety lead him,
Where he can attain the quarry,
Whence he may bring back the booty.
    "Nyyrikki, O son of Tapio,
Thou the mighty red-capped hero,
Blaze the path across the country,
And erect me wooden guide-posts,   40
That I trace this evil pathway,
And pursue the rightful roadway,
While I seek my destined quarry,
And the booty I am seeking.
    " Mielikki, the forest's mistress,
Thou the mighty, fair-faced mother !
Let thy gold now wander onward,
And thy silver set in motion,
Right before the man who seeks it,
On the pathway of the seeker.   50
    " Take the keys of gold, suspended
By the ring that hangs beside thee,
Open thou the stores of Tapio,
And his castle in the forest,
During this my hunting-season,
While I hunt in distant regions.
    " If thyself thou wilt not trouble,
Strictly charge thy little maidens,
Send thy serving maidens to me,
Give thy orders to thy servants !   60
If thou canst not be my hostess,
Do thou not forbid thy maidens,
For thou hast a hundred maidens,
And a thousand at thy orders,
Those on all thy herds attending,
Likewise all thy game protecting.

"Little maiden of the forest,
Tapio's girl, with mouth of honey,
Play upon thy flute of honey,
Whistle through thy pipe of honey,   70
In thy noble mistress' hearing,
Gracious queen of all the forest,
That she soon may hear the music,
And from her repose may rouse her,
For she does not hear at present,
And she but awakens rarely,
Though I supplicate for ever,
With my golden tongue imploring ! "
    Then the lively Lemminkainen
Wandered on, but found no booty,   80
Glided through the plains and marshes,
Glided through the trackless forests,
Where has Jumala his soot-hills,
To the charcoal heaths of Hiisi.
Thus he skated one day, two days,
And at length upon the third day,
Came he to a lofty mountain,
Where he climbed a rock stupendous,
And he turned his eyes to north-west,
To the north across the marshes,   90
And he saw the farms of Tapio,
With the doors all golden shining,
To the north, across the marshes,
On the slope among the thickets.
    Then the lively Lemminkainen
Quickly to the spot approaching,
Pushed his way through all obstructions,
Under Tapio's very windows.
And he looked while stooping forward,
In the sixth among the windows.   100
There were resting game-dispensers,
Matrons of the woods reposing,
All were in their work-day garments,
And with filthy rags were covered.
    Said the lively Lemminkainen,
"Wherefore, Mistress of the Forest,

Dost thou wear thy work-day garments,
Dirty ragged thresher's garments?
You are very black to gaze on,
And your whole appearance dreadful,   110
For your breast is most disgusting,
And your form is very bloated.

  " When before I tracked the forests,
I beheld three castles standing.
One was wooden, one a bone one,
And the third of stone was builded.
There were six bright golden windows
On the sides of every castle,
And if then I gazed within them,
'Neath the wall as I was standing,   120
Saw the lord of Tapio's household,
And the mistress of his household ;
Tellervo, the maid of Tapio,
And the rest of Tapio's household,
All in rustling golden garments,
And parading there in silver,
She herself, the Forest-Mistress,
Gracious Mistress of the Forest,
On her wrists were golden bracelets,
Golden rings upon her fingers,   130
On her head a golden head-dress,
And her hair adorned with ducats ;
In her ears were golden earrings,
Finest beads her neck encircling.

  "Gracious Mistress of the Forest,
Of sweet Metsola the matron !
Cast away thy hay-shoes from thee,
And discard thy shoes of birch-bark,
Cast thou off thy threshing garments,
And thy wretched work-day garments,   140
Don thy garments of good fortune,
And thy blouse for game-dispensing,
In the days I track the forest,
Seeking for a hunter's booty.
Long and wearily I wander,
Wearily I track my pathway,

Yet I wander here for nothing,
All the time without a quarry.
If you do not grant me booty,
Nor reward me for my labour,   150
Long and sad will be the evening,
Long the day when game is wanting.
  "Aged greybeard of the forest,
With thy pine-leaf hat and moss cloak,
Dress thou now the woods in linen,
And the wilds a cloth throw over.
All the aspens robe in greyness,
And the alders robe in beauty,
Clothe the pine-trees all in silver,
And with gold adorn the fir-trees.   160
Aged pine-trees belt with copper,
Belt the fir-trees all with silver,
Birch-trees with their golden blossoms,
And their trunks with gold adornments.
Make it as in former seasons
Even when thy days were better,
When the fir-shoots shone in moonlight,
And the pine-boughs in the sunlight,
When the wood was sweet with honey,
And the blue wastes flowed with honey,   170
Smelt like malt the heathlands' borders,
From the very swamps ran butter.
  "Forest-maiden, gracious virgin,
Tuulikki, O Tapio's daughter!
Drive the game in this direction,
Out into the open heathland.
If it runs with heavy footsteps,
Or is lazy in its running,
Take a switch from out the bushes,
Or a birch-twig from the valley,   180
Switch the game upon the haunches,
And upon the flanks, O whip it,
Drive it swiftly on before you,
Make it hasten quickly onward,
To the man who here awaits it,
In the pathway of the hunter.

"If the game comes on the footpath,
Drive it forward to the hero,
Do thou put thy hands together,
And on both sides do thou guide it,   190
That the game may not escape me,
Rushing back in wrong direction.
If the game should seek to fly me,
Rushing in the wrong direction,
Seize its ear, and drag it forward
By the horns upon the pathway.

"If there's brushwood on the pathway,
Drive it to the pathway's edges;
If a tree should block the pathway,
Then the tree-trunk break asunder.   200

"If a fence obstructs the pathway,
Thrust the fence aside before you,
Take five withes to hold it backward,
And seven posts whereon to bind them.

"If a river runs before thee,
Or a brook should cross the pathway,
Build thou then a bridge all silken,
With a red cloth for a gateway;
Drive the game by narrow pathways,
And across the quaking marshes,   210
Over Pohjola's wide rivers,
O'er the waterfalls all foaming.

"Master of the house of Tapio,
Mistress of the house of Tapio;
Aged greybeard of the forest,
King of all the golden forest;
Mimerkki, the forest's mistress,
Fair dispenser of its treasures,
Blue-robed woman of the bushes,
Mistress of the swamps, red-stockinged,   220
Come, with me thy gold to barter,
Come, with me to change thy silver.
I have gold as old as moonlight,
Silver old as is the sunlight,
Which I won in battle-tumult,
In the contest of the heroes,

Useful in my purse I found it,
Where it jingled in the darkness;
If thy gold thou wilt not barter,
Perhaps thou wilt exchange thy silver."   230
    Thus the lively Lemminkainen
For a week on snowshoes glided,
Sang a song throughout the forest,
There among the depths of jungle,
And appeased the forest's mistress,
And the forest's master likewise,
And delighted all the maidens,
Pleasing thus the girls of Tapio.
Then they hunted and drove onward
From its lair the elk of Hiisi,   240
Past the wooded hills of Tapio,
Past the bounds of Hiisi's mountain,
To the man who waited for it,
To the sorcerer in his ambush.
    Then the lively Lemminkainen
Lifted his lasso, and threw it
O'er the elk of Hiisi's shoulders,
Round the camel's neck he threw it,
That it should not kick in fury,
When upon its back he stroked it.   250
    Then the lively Lemminkainen
Spoke aloud the words which follow:
"Lord of woods, of earth the master,
Fairest creature of the heathlands;
Mielikki, the forest's mistress,
Loveliest of the game-dispensers!
Come to take the gold I promised,
Come ye now to choose the silver,
On the ground lay down your linen,
Spreading out of flax the finest,   260
Underneath the gold that glitters,
Underneath the shining silver,
That upon the ground it fall not,
Nor among the dirt is scattered."
    Then to Pohjola he journeyed,
And he said on his arrival:

"I have chased the elk of Hiisi
On the distant plains of Hiisi.
Give me now, old dame, your daughter,
Give the youthful bride I seek for."   270
    Louhi, Pohjola's old Mistress
Heard his words, and then made answer :
"I will only give my daughter,
Give the youthful bride you seek for,
If you rein the mighty gelding,
He the chestnut steed of Hiisi,
He the foaming foal of Hiisi,
On the bounds of Hiisi's meadow."
    Then the lively Lemminkainen
Took at once a golden bridle,   280
Took a halter all of silver,
And he went to seek the courser,
Went to seek the yellow-maned one,
On the bounds of Hiisi's meadow.
    Then he hastened on his journey,
On his way went swiftly forward,
Through the green and open meadows,
To the sacred field beyond them,
And he sought there for the courser,
Seeking for the yellow-maned one.   290
At his belt the bit he carried,
And the harness on his shoulder.
    Thus he sought one day, a second,
And at length upon the third day
Came he to a lofty mountain,
And upon a rock he clambered.
And he turned his eyes to eastward,
And he turned his head to sunwards.
On the sand he saw the courser,
'Mid the firs the yellow-maned one.   300
From his hair the flame was flashing,
From his mane the smoke was rising.
    Thereupon prayed Lemminkainen :
"Ukko, thou of Gods the highest,
Ukko, thou of clouds the leader,
Of the scattered clouds conductor,

Open now thy clefts in heaven,
And in all the sky thy windows,
Let the iron hail fall downwards,
Send thou down the frozen masses,   310
On the mane of that good courser,
On the back of Hiisi's courser."

Ukko then, the great Creator,
Jumala 'mid clouds exalted,
Heard and rent the air asunder,
Clove in twain the vault of heaven,
Scattered ice, and scattered iceblocks,
Scattered down the iron hailstones,
Smaller than a horse's head is,
Larger than a head of man is,   320
On the mane of that good courser,
On the back of Hiisi's courser.

Then the lively Lemminkainen,
Forward stepped to gaze about him,
And advanced for observation,
And he spoke the words which follow:
" Hiitola's most mighty courser,
Mountain foal, with mane all foam-flecked,
Give me now thy golden muzzle,
Stretch thou forth thy head of silver,   330
Push it in the golden bridle,
With the bit of shining silver.
I will never treat you badly,
And I will not drive you harshly,
And our way is but a short one,
And 'tis but a little journey,
Unto Pohjola's bleak homestead,
To my cruel foster-mother.
With a rope I will not flog you,
With a switch I will not drive you,   340
But with silken cords will lead you,
With a strip of cloth will drive you."

Then the chestnut horse of Hiisi,
Hiisi's horse, with mane all foam-flecked
Forward stretched his golden muzzle,
Forward reached his head of silver,

To receive the golden bridle,
With the bit of shining silver.
 Thus did lively Lemminkainen
Bridle Hiisi's mighty courser,   350
In his mouth the bit adjusted,
On his silver head the bridle,
On his broad back then he mounted,
On the back of that good courser.
 O'er the horse his whip he brandished,
With a willow switch he struck him,
And a little way he journeyed
Hasting onward through the mountains,
Through the mountains to the northward,
Over all the snow-clad mountains,   360
Unto Pohjola's bleak homestead.
From the yard the hall he entered,
And he said on his arrival,
Soon as Pohjola he entered:
"I have reined the mighty courser,
Brought the foal of Hiisi bridled,
From the green and open meadows,
And the sacred field beyond them,
And I tracked the elk on snowshoes,
On the distant plains of Hiisi.   370
Give me now, old dame, your daughter,
Give the youthful bride I seek for."
 Louhi, Pohjola's old Mistress,
Answered in the words which follow:
"I will only give my daughter,
Give the youthful bride you seek for,
If the river-swan you shoot me,
Shoot the great bird on the river.
There on Tuoni's murky river,
In the sacred river's whirlpool,   380
Only at a single trial,
Using but a single arrow."
 Then the lively Lemminkainen
He the handsome Kaukomieli,
Went and took his twanging crossbow,
Went away to seek the Long-neck,

Forth to Tuoni's murky river,
Down in Manala's abysses.
  On with rapid steps he hastened,
And he went with trampling footsteps,   390
Unto Tuonela's broad river,
To the sacred river's whirlpool,
'Neath his arm a handsome crossbow,
On his back his well-stored quiver.
  Märkähattu then, the cowherd,
Pohjola's old sightless greybeard,
There by Tuonela's broad river,
By the sacred river's whirlpool,
Long had lurked, and long had waited,
There for Lemminkainen's coming.   400
  And at length one day it happened,
Came the lively Lemminkainen
Hasting on, and swift approaching
Unto Tuonela's deep river,
To the cataract most terrific,
To the sacred river's whirlpool.
  From the waves he sent a serpent,
Like a reed from out the billows ;
Through the hero's heart he hurled it,
And through Lemminkainen's liver.   410
Through the arm-pit left it smote him,
Through the shoulder right it struck him.
  Then the lively Lemminkainen
Felt himself severely wounded,
And he spoke the words which follow :
" I have acted most unwisely,
That I asked not information
From my mother, she who bore me.
Two words only were sufficient,
Three at most might perhaps be needed,   420
How to act, and live still longer,
After this day's great misfortune.
Charm I cannot water-serpents,
Nor of reeds I know the magic.
  " O my mother who hast borne me,
And hast nurtured me in sorrow,

Would that thou might'st know, and hasten
To thy son, who lies in anguish.
Surely thou would'st hasten hither,
To my aid thou then would'st hasten,   430
To thy hapless son's assistance,
At the point of death now lying,
For indeed too young I slumber,
And I die while still so cheerful."

Then did Pohjola's blind greybeard,
Märkähattu, he the cowherd,
Fling the lively Lemminkainen,
Casting Kaleva's own offspring
Into Tuoni's murky river,
In the worst of all the whirlpools.   440

Floated lively Lemminkainen,
Down the thundering cataract floated,
Down the rushing stream he floated,
Unto Tuonela's dread dwelling.

Then the bloodstained son of Tuoni
Drew his sword, and smote the hero,
With his gleaming blade he hewed him,
While it shed a stream of flashes,
And he hewed him in five fragments,
And in pieces eight he hewed him,   450
Then in Tuonela's stream cast them,
Where are Manala's abysses.
"Thou may'st toss about for ever,
With thy crossbow and thy arrows,
Shooting swans upon the river,
Water-birds upon its borders!"

Thus did Lemminkainen perish,
Perished thus the dauntless suitor,
Down in Tuoni's murky river,
Down in Manala's abysses.   460

RUNO XV.—LEMMINKAINEN'S RECOVERY AND RETURN HOME

Argument

One day blood begins to trickle from the hair-brush at Lemminkainen's home, and his mother at once perceives that death has overtaken her son. She hastens to Pohjola and inquires of Louhi what has become of him (1-100). The Mistress of Pohjola at length tells her on what errand she has sent him, and the sun gives her full information of the manner of Lemminkainen's death (101-194). Lemminkainen's mother goes with a long rake in her hand under the cataract of Tuoni, and rakes the water till she has found all the fragments of her son's body, which she joins together, and succeeds in restoring Lemminkainen to life by charms and magic salves (195-554). Lemminkainen then relates how he perished in the river of Tuonela, and returns home with his mother (555-650).

LEMMINKAINEN'S tender mother
In her home was always thinking,
"Where has Lemminkainen wandered,
Whereabouts is Kauko roaming,
For I do not hear him coming
From his world-extended journey?"
    Ah, the hapless mother knew not,
Nor the hapless one imagined,
Where her own flesh now was floating,
Where her own blood now was flowing;   10
If he tracked the fir-clad mountains,
Or among the heaths was roaming,
Or upon a lake was floating,
Out upon the foaming billows,
Or in some terrific combat,
In the most tremendous tumult,
With his legs with blood bespattered,
To the knees with blood all crimsoned.
    Kyllikki, the lovely housewife,
Wandered round and gazed about her,   20
Through the home of Lemminkainen,
And through Kaukomieli's homestead;

On the comb she looked at evening,
On the brush she looked at morning,
And at length one day it happened,
In the early morning hours,
Blood from out the comb was oozing,
From the brush was gore distilling.

Kyllikki, the lovely housewife,
Uttered then the words which follow: 30
"Lo, my husband has departed,
And my handsome Kauko wandered
In a country void of houses,
And throughout some trackless desert.
Blood from out the comb is oozing,
Gore is from the brush distilling."

Then did Lemminkainen's mother
See herself the comb was bleeding,
And began to weep with sorrow.
"O alas, my day is wretched,   40
And my life is most unhappy,
For my son has met misfortune,
And my child all unprotected,
On an evil day was nurtured.
On the poor lad came destruction,
Lost is darling Lemminkainen,
From the comb the blood is trickling,
And the brush with blood is dripping."

In her hands her skirt she gathered,
With her arms her dress she lifted,   50
And at once commenced her journey,
Hurried on upon her journey.
Mountains thundered 'neath her footsteps,
Valleys rose and hills were levelled,
And the high ground sank before her,
And the low ground rose before her.

Thus to Pohjola she journeyed,
Asking where her son had wandered,
And she asked in words which follow:
"Tell me, Pohjola's old Mistress,   60
Whither sent you Lemminkainen,
Whither has my son departed?"

Louhi, Pohjola's old Mistress,
Then replied in words which follow:
" Of your son I know no tidings,
Where he went, or where he vanished.
In his sledge I yoked a stallion,
Chose him out a fiery courser.
Perhaps he sank in ice when rotten,
O'er the frozen lake when driving,   70
Or among the wolves has fallen,
Or some dreadful bear devoured him."
    Then said Lemminkainen's mother,
" This indeed is shameless lying,
For no wolf would touch my offspring,
Not a bear touch Lemminkainen!
Wolves he'd crush between his fingers,
Bears with naked hands would master.
If you will not truly tell me,
How you treated Lemminkainen,   80
I the malthouse doors will shatter,
Break the hinges of the Sampo."
    Then said Pohjola's old Mistress,
" I have fed the man profusely,
And I gave him drink in plenty,
Till he was most fully sated.
In a boat's prow then I placed him,
That he thus should shoot the rapids,
But I really cannot tell you
What befel the wretched creature ;   90
In the wildly foaming torrent,
In the tumult of the whirlpool."
    Then said Lemminkainen's mother,
" This indeed is shameless lying.
Tell me now the truth exactly,
Make an end of all your lying,
Whither sent you Lemminkainen,
Where has Kaleva's son perished ?
Or most certain death awaits you,
And you die upon the instant."   100
    Then said Pohjola's old Mistress,
" Now at length I'll tell you truly.

Forth to chase the elks I sent him,
And to struggle with the monsters,
And the mighty beasts to bridle,
And to put the foals in harness.
Then I sent him forth swan-hunting,
Seeking for the bird so sacred,
But I really cannot tell you
If misfortune came upon him,   110
Or what hindrance he encountered.
Nought I heard of his returning,
For the bride that he demanded,
When he came to woo my daughter."

   Then the mother sought the strayed one,
Dreading what mischance had happened,
Like a wolf she tracked the marshes,
Like a bear the wastes she traversed,
Like an otter swam the waters,
Badger-like the plains she traversed,   120
Passed the headlands like a hedgehog,
Like a hare along the lakeshores,
Pushed the rocks from out her pathway,
From the slopes bent down the tree-trunks,
Thrust the shrubs beside her pathway,
From her track she cast the branches.

   Long she vainly sought the strayed one,
Long she sought, but found him never.
Of her son the trees she questioned,
For the lost one ever seeking.   130
Said a tree, then sighed a pine-tree,
And an oak made answer wisely:
"I myself have also sorrows,
For your son I cannot trouble,
For my lot's indeed a hard one,
And an evil day awaits me,
For they split me into splinters,
And they chop me into faggots,
In the kiln that I may perish,
Or they fell me in the clearing."   140

   Long she vainly sought the strayed one,
Long she sought, but found him never,

And whene'er she crossed a pathway,
Then she bowed herself before it.
"O thou path whom God created,
Hast thou seen my son pass over;
Hast thou seen my golden apple,
Hast thou seen my staff of silver?"
But the path made answer wisely,
And it spoke and gave her answer :   150
"I myself have also sorrows,
For your son I cannot trouble,
For my lot's indeed a hard one,
And an evil day awaits me.
All the dogs go leaping o'er me,
And the horsemen gallop o'er me,
And the shoes walk heavy on me,
And the heels press hardly on me."
Long she vainly sought the strayed one,
Long she sought, but found him never.   160
Met the moon upon her pathway,
And before the moon she bowed her.
"Golden moon, whom God created,
Hast thou seen my son pass by you;
Hast thou seen my golden apple,
Hast thou seen my staff of silver?"
Then the moon whom God created,
Made a full and prudent answer :
"I myself have many sorrows,
For your son I cannot trouble,   170
For my lot's indeed a hard one,
And an evil day awaits me,
Wandering lonely in the night-time,
In the frost for ever shining,
In the winter keeping vigil,
But in time of summer waning."
Long she vainly sought the strayed one,
Long she sought, but found him never,
Met the sun upon her pathway,
And before the sun she bowed her.   180
"O thou sun, whom God created,
Hast thou seen my son pass by you,

Hast thou seen my golden apple,
Hast thou seen my staff of silver?"
And the sun knew all about it,
And the sun made answer plainly:
"There has gone your son unhappy,
He has fallen and has perished,
Down in Tuoni's murky river,
Manala's primeval river, 190
There in the tremendous cataract,
Where the torrent rushes downward,
There on Tuonela's dark frontier,
There in Manala's deep valleys."

Then did Lemminkainen's mother,
Break out suddenly in weeping.
To the craftsman's forge she wended:
"O thou smith, O Ilmarinen,
Thou hast worked before, and yestreen,
On this very day O forge me, 200
Forge a rake with copper handle,
Let the teeth of steel be fashioned,
Teeth in length a hundred fathoms,
And of fathoms five the handle."

Then the smith, e'en Ilmarinen,
He the great primeval craftsman,
Forged a rake with copper handle,
And the teeth of steel he fashioned,
Teeth in length a hundred fathoms,
And of fathoms five the handle. 210

Then did Lemminkainen's mother
Take the mighty rake of iron,
And she rushed to Tuoni's river,
To the sun her prayer addressing:
"O thou sun whom God created,
Brilliant work of the Creator!
Shine an hour with heat excessive,
Shine again with sultry shimmering,
And again with utmost vigour.
Lull to sleep the race of evil, 220
And in Manala the strong ones,
Weary out the power of Tuoni!"

Then the sun whom God created,
Shining work of the Creator,
Stooped upon a crooked birch-tree,
Sank upon a crooked alder,
Shone an hour with heat excessive,
Shone again with sultry shimmering,
And again with utmost vigour,
Lulled to sleep the race of evil,   230
And in Manala the strong ones.
Slept the young on sword-hilt resting,
And the old folks staff-supported,
And the spear-men middle-agèd.
Then again he hastened upward,
Sought again the heights of heaven,
Sought again his former station,
To his first abode soared upward.

Then did Lemminkainen's mother
Take the mighty rake of iron,   240
And to seek her son was raking
All amid the raging cataract,
Through the fiercely rushing torrent,
And she raked, yet found she nothing.

Then she went and sought him deeper,
Ever deeper in the water,
Stocking-deep into the water,
Standing waist-deep in the water.

Thus she sought her son by raking
All the length of Tuoni's river,   250
And she raked against the current,
Once and twice she raked the river,
And his shirt at length discovered,
Found the shirt of him unhappy,
And she raked again a third time,
And she found his hat and stockings,
Found his stockings, greatly sorrowing,
Found his hat, with heart-wrung anguish.

Then she waded ever deeper,
Down in Manala's abysses,   260
Raked once more along the river,
Raked again across the river,

And obliquely through the water,
And at length upon the third time,
Up she drew a lifeless carcass,
With the mighty rake of iron.
　Yet it was no lifeless carcass,
But the lively Lemminkainen,
He the handsome Kaukomieli,
Sticking fast upon the rake-prongs,　　　　　270
Sticking by his nameless finger,
And the toes upon his left foot.
　Thus she fished up Lemminkainen,
Kaleva's great offspring lifted,
On the rake all shod with copper,
To the light above the water.
Yet were many fragments wanting,
Half his head, a hand was wanting,
Many other little fragments,
And his very life was wanting.　　　　　　280
　As his mother pondered o'er it,
Thus she spoke while sorely weeping:
"Can a man from this be fashioned,
And a hero new created?"
　But by chance a raven heard her,
And he answered her in thiswise:
"No man can from this be fashioned,
Not from what you have discovered,
For his eyes the powan's eaten,
And the pike has cleft his shoulders.　　　290
Cast the man into the water,
Back in Tuonela's deep river,
Perhaps a cod may thence be fashioned,
Or a whale from thence developed."
　Lemminkainen's mother would not
Cast her son into the water,
But again began her raking,
With the mighty rake of copper,
All through Tuonela's deep river,
First along it, then across it,　　　　　　300
And his head and hand discovered,
And the fragments of his backbone.

Then she found his ribs in pieces,
Likewise many other fragments,
And her son she pieced together,
Shaped the lively Lemminkainen.
　　Then the flesh to flesh she fitted,
And the bones together fitted,
And the joints together jointed,
And the veins she pressed together.　　　　310
　　Then she bound the veins together,
All their ends she knit together,
And with care their threads she counted,
And she spoke the words which follow :
" Fairest goddess of the bloodveins,
Suonetar, O fairest woman,
Lovely weaver of the veinlets,
Working with thy loom so slender,
With the spindle all of copper,
And the wheel composed of iron,　　　　320
Come thou here, where thou art needed,
Hasten hither, where I call thee,
With a lapful of thy veinlets,
And beneath thy arm a bundle,
Thus to bind the veins together,
And to knit their ends together,
Where the wounds are gaping widely,
And where gashes still are open.
　　" If this is not yet sufficient,
In the air there sits a maiden,　　　　330
In a boat adorned with copper,
In a boat with stern of scarlet.
From the air descend, O maiden,
Virgin from the midst of heaven,
Row thy boat throughout the veinlets,
Through the joints, both forth and backwards,
Through the broken bones, O steer thou,
And throughout the joints when broken.
　　" Bind the veins together firmly,
Lay them in the right position,　　　　340
End to end the larger bloodveins,
And the arteries fit together,

Duplicate the smaller bloodveins,
Join the ends of smallest veinlets.
　"Take thou then thy finest needle,
Thread it next with silken fibre,
Sew thou with the finest needle,
Stitch thou with thy tin-made needle,
Sew the ends of veins together,
Bind them with thy silken fibre.　　　　　350
　"If this is not yet sufficient,
Help me, Jumala, Eternal,
Harness thou thy foal of swiftness,
And equip thy mighty courser,
In thy little sledge then drive thou
Through the bones and joints, O drive thou,
Through the flesh that all is mangled,
Back and forth, throughout the veinlets,
In the flesh the bone then fasten,
Ends of veins knit firm together,　　　　　360
'Twixt the bones, O fix thou silver,
Fix the veins with gold together.
　"Where the skin is rent asunder,
Let the skin be brought together;
Where the veins have snapped asunder,
Let the veins be knit together;
Where through wounds the blood has issued,
Let the blood again be flowing;
Where the bones have broke to splinters,
Let the bones be fixed together;　　　　　370
Where the flesh is torn asunder,
Let the flesh be knit together,
Fix it in the right position,
In its right position fix it,
Bone to bone and flesh to flesh fix,
Joint to joint unite thou firmly."
　　Thus did Lemminkainen's mother
Form the man, and shape the hero
To his former life restore him,
To the form he wore aforetime.　　　　　380
　　All the veins had now been counted,
And their ends were knit together,

But as yet the man was speechless,
Nor the child to speak was able.
    Then she spoke the words which follow,
And expressed herself in thiswise :
" Whence shall we obtain an ointment,
Whence obtain the drops of honey
That I may anoint the patient
And that I may cure his weakness,   390
That the man his speech recovers,
And again his songs is singing ?
    " O thou bee, thou bird of honey,
King of all the woodland flowerets,
Go thou forth to fetch me honey,
Go thou forth to seek for honey,
Back from Metsola's fair meadows,
Tapiola, for ever cheerful,
From the cup of many a flower,
And the plumes of grasses many,   400
As an ointment for the patient,
And to quite restore the sick one."
    Then the bee, the bird so active,
Flew away upon his journey,
Forth to Metsola's fair meadows,
Tapiola, for ever cheerful,
Probed the flowers upon the meadows,
With his tongue he sucked the honey
From the tips of six bright flowers,
From the plumes of hundred grasses,   410
Then came buzzing loud and louder,
Rushing on his homeward journey,
With his wings all steeped in honey,
And his plumage soaked with nectar.
    Then did Lemminkainen's mother,
Take from him the magic ointment,
That she might anoint the patient,
And she thus might cure his weakness,
But from this there came no healing,
And as yet the man was speechless.   420
Then she spoke the words which follow :
" O thou bee, my own dear birdling,

Fly thou in a new direction,
Over nine lakes fly thou quickly
Till thou reach a lovely island,
Where the land abounds with honey,
Where is Tuuri's new-built dwelling,
Palvonen's own roofless dwelling,
There is honey in profusion,
There is ointment in perfection,   430
Fit to bind the veins together,
And to heal the joints completely.
From the meadow bring this ointment,
And the salve from out the meadow,
For upon the wounds I'll spread it,
And anoint the bruises with it."

Then the bee, that active hero,
Flew again on whirring pinions,
And across nine lakes he travelled,
Half across the tenth he travelled,   440
On he flew one day, a second,
And at length upon the third day,
Never on the reeds reposing,
Nor upon a leaf reposing,
Came he to the lovely island,
Where the land abounds with honey,
Till he reached a furious torrent,
And a holy river's whirlpool.

In this spot was cooked the honey,
And the ointment was made ready   450
In the little earthen vessels,
In the pretty little kettles,
Kettles of a thumb-size only,
And a finger-tip would fill them.

Then the bee, that active hero,
Gathered honey in the meadow,
And a little time passed over,
Very little time passed over,
When he came on whirring pinions,
Coming with his mission finished,   460
In his lap six cups he carried,
Seven upon his back he carried,

Brimming o'er with precious ointment,
With the best of ointment brimming.
   Then did Lemminkainen's mother
Salve him with this precious ointment,
With nine kinds of ointment salved him,
And ten kinds of magic ointment;
Even yet there came no healing,
Still her toil was unavailing.   470
   Then she spoke the words which follow,
And expressed herself in thiswise:
"O thou bee, thou bird aërial,
Fly thou forth again the third time,
Fly thou up aloft to heaven,
And through nine heavens fly thou swiftly.
There is honey in abundance,
In the wood as much as needed,
Which was charmed by the Creator,
By pure Jumala was breathed on,   480
When his children he anointed,
Wounded by the powers of evil.
In the honey dip thy pinions,
Soak thy plumage in the nectar,
Bring me honey on thy pinions,
In thy mantle from the forest,
As an ointment for the patient,
And anoint the bruises with it."
   But the bee, the bird of wisdom,
Answered her in words that follow: 490
"How can I perform thy bidding,
I a man so small and helpless?"
   "Thou canst rise on high with swiftness,
Fly aloft with easy effort,
O'er the moon, below the daylight,
And amid the stars of heaven,
Flying windlike on the first day
Past the borders of Orion,
On the second day thou soarest
Even to the Great Bear's shoulders,   500
On the third day soaring higher,
O'er the Seven Stars thou risest,

Thence the journey is a short one,
And the distance very trifling,
Unto Jumala's bright dwelling,
And the regions of the blessed."

From the earth the bee rose swiftly,
On his honeyed wings rose whirring,
And he soared on rapid pinions,
On his little wings flew upward.   510
Swiftly past the moon he hurried,
Past the borders of the sunlight,
Rose upon the Great Bear's shoulders,
O'er the Seven Stars' backs rose upward,
Flew to the Creator's cellars,
To the halls of the Almighty.
There the drugs were well concocted,
And the ointment duly tempered
In the pots composed of silver,
Or within the golden kettles.   520
In the midst they boiled the honey,
On the sides was sweetest ointment,
To the southward there was nectar,
To the northward there was ointment.

Then the bee, that bird aërial,
Gathered honey in abundance,
Honey to his heart's contentment,
And but little time passed over,
Ere the bee again came buzzing,
Humming loudly on his journey,   530
In his lap of horns a hundred,
And a thousand other vessels,
Some of honey, some of liquid,
And the best of all the ointment.

Then did Lemminkainen's mother
Raise it to her mouth and taste it,
With her tongue the ointment tasted,
With the greatest care she proved it.
"'Tis the ointment that I needed,
And the salve of the Almighty,   540
Used when Jumala the Highest,
The Creator heals all suffering."

Then did she anoint the patient,
That she thus might cure his weakness,
Salved the bones along the fractures,
And between the joints she salved him,
Salved his head and lower portions,
Rubbed him also in the middle,
Then she spoke the words which follow,
And expressed herself in thiswise: 550
"Rise, my son, from out thy slumber,
From thy dreams do thou awaken,
From this place so full of evil,
And a resting-place unholy."

From his sleep arose the hero,
And from out his dreams awakened,
And at once his speech recovered.
With his tongue these words he uttered:
"Woe's me, long have I been sleeping,
Long have I in pain been lying,   560
And in peaceful sleep reposing,
In the deepest slumber sunken."

Then said Lemminkainen's mother,
And expressed herself in thiswise:
"Longer yet hadst thou been sleeping,
Longer yet hadst thou been resting,
But for thy unhappy mother,
But for her in pain who bore thee.

"Tell me now, my son unhappy,
Tell me that my ears may hear it,   570
Who to Manala has sent thee,
There to drift in Tuoni's river?"

Said the lively Lemminkainen,
And he answered thus his mother:
"Märkähattu, he the cowherd,
Untamola's blind old rascal,
Down to Manala has sent me,
There to drift in Tuoni's river;
And he raised a water-serpent,
From the waves a serpent lifted,   580
Sent it forth to me unhappy,
But I could not guard against it,

Knowing nought of water-evil,
Nor the evils of the reed-beds."
　　Then said Lemminkainen's mother,
"Mighty man of little foresight,
Boasting to enchant the sorcerers,
And to ban the sons of Lapland,
Knowing nought of water-evil,
Nor the evils of the reed-beds!　　　　590
　　"Water-snakes are born in water,
On the waves among the reed-beds,
From the duck's brain springs the serpent,
In the head of the sea-swallow.
Syöjätär spat in the water,
Cast upon the waves the spittle,
And the water stretched it lengthwise,
And the sunlight warmed and softened,
And the wind arose and tossed it,
And the water-breezes rocked it,　　　　600
On the shore the waves they drove it,
And amid the breakers urged it."
　　Thus did Lemminkainen's mother
Cause her son with all her efforts,
To resume his old appearance,
And ensured that in the future
He should even be superior,
Yet more handsome than aforetime,
And she asked her son thereafter
Was there anything he needed?　　　　610
　　Said the lively Lemminkainen,
"There is something greatly needed,
For my heart is fixed for ever,
And my inclination leads me
To the charming maids of Pohja,
With their lovely locks unbraided,
But the dirty-eared old woman
Has refused to give her daughter,
Till I shoot the duck she asks for,
And the swan shall capture for her,　　　　620
Here in Tuonela's dark river,
In the holy river's whirlpool."

Then spoke Lemminkainen's mother,
And she answered him in thiswise:
" Leave the poor swans unmolested,
Leave the ducks a peaceful dwelling,
Here on Tuoni's murky river,
Here amid the raging whirlpool!
Best it is to journey homeward
With your most unhappy mother.   630
Praise thou now thy happy future,
And to Jumala be praises,
That he granted his assistance,
And has thus to life awaked thee,
And from Tuoni's paths hath led thee,
And from Mana's realms hath brought thee!
I myself had never conquered,
And alone had nought accomplished,
But for Jumala's compassion,
And the help of the Creator."   640
Then the lively Lemminkainen,
Went at once his journey homeward,
With his mother, she who loved him,
Homeward with the aged woman.
Here I part awhile with Kauko,
Leave the lively Lemminkainen,
Long from out my song I leave him,
While I quickly change my subject,
Turn my song in new directions,
And in other furrows labour.   650

Runo XVI.—Väinämöinen in Tuonela

Argument

Väinämöinen orders Sampsa Pellervoinen to seek for wood for boat-building. He makes a boat, but finds himself at a loss for want of three magic words (1–118). As he cannot otherwise obtain them, he goes to Tuonela hoping to procure them there (119–362). Väinämöinen finally escapes from Tuonela, and after his return warns others not to venture there, and describes what a terrible place it is and the horrible abodes in which men dwell there (363–412).

Väinämöinen, old and steadfast,
He the great primeval sorcerer,
Set to work a boat to build him,
And upon a boat to labour,
There upon the cloudy headland,
On the shady island's summit.
But the workman found no timber,
Boards to build the boat he found not.

Who shall seek for timber for him,
And shall seek an oak-tree for him,   10
For the boat of Väinämöinen,
And a keel to suit the minstrel ?

Pellervoinen, earth-begotten,
Sampsa, youth of smallest stature,
He shall seek for timber for him,
And shall seek an oak-tree for him,
For the boat of Väinämöinen,
And a keel to suit the minstrel.

So upon his path he wandered
Through the regions to the north-east,   20
Through one district, then another,
Journeyed after through a third one,
With his gold axe on his shoulder,
With his axe, with copper handle,
Till he found an aspen standing,
Which in height three fathoms measured.

So he went to fell the aspen,
With his axe the tree to sever,
And the aspen spoke and asked him,
With its tongue it spoke in thiswise :   30
"What, O man, desire you from me?
Tell your need, as far as may be."

Youthful Sampsa Pellervoinen,
Answered in the words which follow :
"This is what I wish for from thee,
This I need, and this require I,
'Tis a boat for Väinämöinen ;
For the minstrel's boat the timber."

And the aspen said astounded,
Answered with its hundred branches :   40
"As a boat I should be leaking,
And would only sink beneath you,
For my branches they are hollow.
Thrice already in this summer,
Has a grub my heart devoured,
In my roots a worm has nestled."

Youthful Sampsa Pellervoinen
Wandered further on his journey,
And he wandered, deeply pondering,
In the region to the northward.   50

There he found a pine-tree standing,
And its height was full six fathoms,
And he struck it with his hatchet,
On the trunk with axe-blade smote it,
And he spoke the words which follow :
"O thou pine-tree, shall I take thee,
For the boat of Väinämöinen,
And as boatwood for the minstrel?"

But the pine-tree answered quickly,
And it cried in answer loudly,   60
"For a boat you cannot use me,
Nor a six-ribbed boat can fashion,
Full of knots you'll find the pine-tree.
Thrice already in this summer,
In my summit croaked a raven,
Croaked a crow among my branches."

Youthful Sampsa Pellervoinen
Further yet pursued his journey,
And he wandered, deeply pondering,
In the region to the southward, 70
Till he found an oak-tree standing,
Fathoms nine its boughs extended.

And he thus addressed and asked it:
"O thou oak-tree, shall I take thee,
For the keel to make a vessel,
The foundation of a warship?"

And the oak-tree answered wisely,
Answered thus the acorn-bearer:
"Yes, indeed, my wood is suited
For the keel to make a vessel, 80
Neither slender 'tis, nor knotted,
Nor within its substance hollow.
Thrice already in this summer,
In the brightest days of summer,
Through my midst the sunbeams wandered.
On my crown the moon was shining,
In my branches cried the cuckoos,
In my boughs the birds were resting."

Youthful Sampsa Pellervoinen
Took the axe from off his shoulder, 90
With his axe he smote the tree-trunk,
With the blade he smote the oak-tree,
Speedily he felled the oak-tree,
And the beauteous tree had fallen.

First he hewed it through the summit,
All the trunk he cleft in pieces,
After this the keel he fashioned,
Planks so many none could count them,
For the vessel of the minstrel,
For the boat of Väinämöinen. 100

Then the aged Väinämöinen,
He the great primeval sorcerer,
Fashioned then the boat with wisdom,
Built with magic songs the vessel,
From the fragments of an oak-tree,
Fragments of the shattered oak-tree.

With a song the keel he fashioned,
With another, sides he fashioned,
And he sang again a third time,
And the rudder he constructed,   110
Bound the rib-ends firm together,
And the joints he fixed together.

When the boat's ribs were constructed,
And the sides were fixed together,
Still he found three words were wanting,
Which the sides should fix securely,
Fix the prow in right position,
And the stern should likewise finish.

Väinämöinen, old and steadfast,
He the great primeval minstrel,   120
Uttered then the words which follow:
" Woe to me, my life is wretched,
For my boat unlaunched remaineth,
On the waves the new boat floats not ! "

So he pondered and reflected
How to find the words he needed,
And obtain the spells of magic,
From among the brains of swallows,
From the heads of flocks of wild swans,
From the shoulders of the goose-flocks.   130

Then he went the words to gather,
And a flock of swans he slaughtered.
And a flock of geese he slaughtered,
And beheaded many swallows,
But the spells he needed found not,
Not a word, not e'en a half one.

So he pondered and reflected,
" I shall find such words by hundreds,
'Neath the tongue of summer reindeer,
In the mouth of whitest squirrel."   140

So he went the words to gather,
That the spells he might discover,
And a field he spread with reindeer,
Loaded benches high with squirrels,
Many words he thus discovered,
But they all were useless to him.

So he pondered and reflected,
" I should find such words by hundreds
In the dark abodes of Tuoni,
In the eternal home of Mana."   150
Then to Tuonela he journeyed,
Sought the words in Mana's kingdom,
And with rapid steps he hastened,
Wandered for a week through bushes,
Through bird-cherry for a second,
And through juniper the third week,
Straight to Manala's dread island,
And the gleaming hills of Tuoni.
Väinämöinen, old and steadfast,
Raised his voice, and shouted loudly   160
There by Tuonela's deep river,
There in Manala's abysses :
" Bring a boat, O Tuoni's daughter,
Row across, O child of Mana,
That the stream I may pass over,
And that I may cross the river."
Tuoni's short and stunted daughter,
She the dwarfish maid of Mana,
At the time her clothes was washing,
And her clothes she there was beating,   170
At the river dark of Tuoni,
And in Manala's deep waters.
And she answered him in thiswise,
And she spoke the words which follow :
" Hence a boat shall come to fetch you,
When you shall explain the reason
Why to Manala you travel,
Though disease has not subdued you,
Nor has death thus overcome you,
Nor some other fate o'erwhelmed you."   180
Väinämöinen, old and steadfast,
Answered in the words which follow :
" It was Tuoni brought me hither,
Mana dragged me from my country."
Tuoni's short and stunted daughter,
She the dwarfish maid of Mana,

Answered in the words which follow :
" Ay, indeed, I know the liar !
If 'twas Tuoni brought you hither,
Mana dragged you from your country,   190
Then would Tuoni's self be with you,
Manalainen's self conduct you,
Tuoni's hat upon your shoulders,
On your hands the gloves of Mana.
Speak the truth, O Väinämöinen ;
What to Manala has brought you ? "

    Väinämöinen, old and steadfast,
Answered in the words which follow :
" Iron to Manala has brought me,
Steel to Tuonela has dragged me."   200

    Tuoni's short and stunted daughter,
She the dwarfish maid of Mana,
Answered in the words which follow :
" Now, indeed, I know the liar !
For if iron to Mana brought you,
Steel to Tuonela had dragged you,
From your clothes the blood would trickle,
And the blood would forth be flowing.
Speak the truth, O Väinämöinen,
For the second time speak truly."   210

    Väinämöinen, old and steadfast,
Answered in the words which follow :
" Water has to Mana brought me,
Waves to Tuonela have brought me."

    Tuoni's short and stunted daughter,
She the dwarfish maid of Mana,
Answered in the words which follow :
" Ay, indeed, I know the liar !
If to Mana water brought you,
Waves to Manala had floated,   220
From your clothes would water trickle,
From the borders streaming downward.
Tell me true, without evasion,
What to Manala has brought you ? "

    Then the aged Väinämöinen,
Gave again a lying answer.

"Fire to Tuonela has brought me,
Flame to Manala conveyed me."

Tuoni's short and stunted daughter,
She the dwarfish maid of Mana,   230
Once again replied in answer:
"Well indeed I know the liar!
Had the fire to Tuoni brought you,
Flame to Manala conveyed you,
Would your hair be singed and frizzled,
And your beard be scorched severely.

"O thou aged Väinämöinen,
If you wish the boat to fetch you,
Tell me true, without evasion,
Make an end at last of lying,   240
Why to Manala you travel,
Though disease has not subdued you,
Nor has death thus overcome you,
Nor some other fate o'erwhelmed you."

Said the aged Väinämöinen,
"True it is I lied a little,
And again I spoke a falsehood,
But at length I answer truly.
By my art a boat I fashioned,
By my songs a boat I builded,   250
And I sang one day, a second,
And at length upon the third day,
Broke my sledge as I was singing,
Broke the shaft as I was singing,
So I came for Tuoni's gimlet,
Sought in Manala a borer,
That my sledge I thus might finish,
And with this might form my song-sledge.
Therefore bring your boat to this side,
Ferry me across the water,   260
And across the straight convey me,
Let me come across the river."

Tuonetar abused him roundly,
Mana's maiden scolded loudly:
"O thou fool, of all most foolish,
Man devoid of understanding.

Tuonela thou seekest causeless,
Com'st to Mana free from sickness!
Better surely would you find it
Quickly to regain your country,   270
Many truly wander hither,
Few return to where they came from!"
    Said the aged Väinämöinen,
"This might perhaps deter old women,
Not a man, how weak soever,
Not the laziest of heroes!
Bring the boat, O Tuoni's daughter,
Row across, O child of Mana!"
    Brought the boat then, Tuoni's daughter,
And the aged Väinämöinen   280
Quickly o'er the straight she ferried,
And across the river rowed him,
And she spoke the words which follow:
"Woe to thee, O Väinämöinen,
For thou com'st to Mana living,
Com'st to Tuonela undying!"
    Tuonetar the noble matron,
Manalatar, aged woman,
Fetched some beer within a tankard,
And in both her hands she held it,   290
And she spoke the words which follow:
"Drink, O aged Väinämöinen!"
    Väinämöinen, old and steadfast,
Looked for long within the tankard,
And within it frogs were spawning,
At the sides the worms were wriggling,
And he spoke the words which follow:
"Surely I have not come hither,
Thus to drink from Mana's goblets,
Or to drink from Tuoni's tankards.   300
Those who drink this beer are drunken,
Drinking from such cans they perish."
    Then said Tuonela's great mistress,
"O thou aged Väinämöinen,
Why to Manala dost travel,
Why to Tuonela hast ventured,

Though by Tuoni never summoned,
To the land of Mana called not?"
    Said the aged Väinämöinen,
"At my boat as I was working, 310
While my new boat I was shaping,
Then I found three words were wanting,
Ere the stern could be completed,
And the prow could be constructed,
But as I could find them nowhere,
In the world where'er I sought them,
Then to Tuonela I travelled,
Journeyed to the land of Mana,
There to find the words I needed,
There the magic words to study." 320
    Then said Tuonela's great mistress,
And she spoke the words which follow:
"Ne'er the words will Tuoni give you,
Nor his spells will Mana teach you.
Never shall you leave these regions,
Never while your life remaineth,
Shall you ever journey homeward,
To your country home returning."
    Sank the weary man in slumber,
And the traveller lay and slumbered, 330
On the bed prepared by Tuoni,
There outstretched himself in slumber,
And the hero thus was captured,
Lay outstretched, but quickly wakened.
    There's in Tuonela a witch-wife,
Aged crone with chin projecting,
And she spins her thread of iron,
And she draws out wire of copper,
And she spun of nets a hundred,
And she wove herself a thousand, 340
In a single night of summer,
On the rock amid the waters.
    There's in Tuonela a wizard,
And three fingers has the old man,
And he weaves his nets of iron,
And he makes his nets of copper,

And a hundred nets he wove him,
And a thousand nets he plaited,
In the selfsame night of summer,
On the same stone in the water.   350
    Tuoni's son with crooked fingers,
Crooked fingers hard as iron,
Took the hundred nets, and spread them
Right across the stream of Tuoni,
Both across and also lengthwise,
And in an oblique direction,
So that Väinö should not 'scape him,
Nor should flee Uvantolainen,
In the course of all his lifetime,
While the golden moon is shining,   360
From the dread abode of Tuoni,
From the eternal home of Mana.
    Väinämöinen, old and steadfast,
Uttered then the words which follow:
"May not ruin overtake me,
And an evil fate await me,
Here in Tuonela's dark dwellings,
In the foul abode of Mana?"
    Quickly then his shape transforming,
And another shape assuming,   370
To the gloomy lake he hastened,
Like an otter in the reed-beds,
Like an iron snake he wriggled,
Like a little adder hastened
Straight across the stream of Tuoni,
Safely through the nets of Tuoni.
    Tuoni's son with crooked fingers,
Crooked fingers, hard as iron,
Wandered early in the morning
To survey the nets extended,   380
Found of salmon-trout a hundred,
Smaller fry he found by thousands,
But he found not Väinämöinen,
Not the old Uvantolainen.
    Thus the aged Väinämöinen
Made his way from Tuoni's kingdom,

And he said the words which follow,
And in words like these expressed him:
" Never, Jumala the mighty,
Never let another mortal,   390
Make his way to Mana's country,
Penetrate to Tuoni's kingdom!
Many there indeed have ventured,
Few indeed have wandered homeward,
From the dread abode of Tuoni,
From the eternal home of Mana."

   Afterwards these words he added,
And expressed himself in thiswise,
To the rising generation,
And to the courageous people: 400
"Sons of men, O never venture
In the course of all your lifetime,
Wrong to work against the guiltless,
Guilt to work against the sinless,
Lest your just reward is paid you
In the dismal realms of Tuoni!
There's the dwelling of the guilty,
And the resting-place of sinners,
Under stones to redness heated,
Under slabs of stone all glowing,   410
'Neath a coverlet of vipers,
Of the loathsome snakes of Tuoni."

RUNO XVII.—VÄINÄMÖINEN AND ANTERO VIPUNEN

Argument

Väinämöinen goes to obtain magic words from Antero Vipunen, and wakes him from his long sleep under the earth (1–98). Vipunen swallows Väinämöinen, and the latter begins to torture him violently in his stomach (99–146). Vipunen tries every means that he can think of to get rid of him by promises, spells, conjurations and exorcisms, but Väinämöinen declares that he will never depart till he has obtained from Vipunen the words which he requires to finish his boat (147–526). Vipunen sings all his wisdom to Väinämöinen, who then leaves his body, returns to his boat-building, and finishes his boat (527–628).

VÄINÄMÖINEN, old and steadfast,
Had not found the words he wanted
In the dark abode of Tuoni,
In the eternal realms of Mana,
And for evermore he pondered,
In his head reflected ever,
Where the words he might discover,
And obtain the charms he needed.

Once a shepherd came to meet him,
And he spoke the words which follow :   10
"You can find a hundred phrases,
And a thousand words discover,
Known to Antero Vipunen only,
In his monstrous mouth and body,
And there is a path which leads there,
And a cross-road must be traversed,
Not the best among the pathways,
Nor the very worst of any.
Firstly you must leap along it
O'er the points of women's needles,   20
And another stage must traverse
O'er the points of heroes' sword-blades,
And a third course must be traversed
O'er the blades of heroes' axes."

Väinämöinen, old and steadfast,
Pondered deeply o'er the journey,

To the smithy then he hastened,
And he spoke the words which follow :
" O thou smith, O Ilmarinen,
Forge me straightway shoes of iron,   30
Forge me likewise iron gauntlets,
Make me, too, a shirt of iron,
And a mighty stake of iron,
All of steel, which I will pay for,
Lined within with steel the strongest,
And o'erlaid with softer iron,
For I go some words to seek for,
And to snatch the words of power,
From the giant's mighty body,
Mouth of Antero Vipunen wisest."   40
    Then the smith, e'en Ilmarinen,
Answered in the words which follow :
" Vipunen has long since perished,
Long has Antero departed
From the nets he has constructed,
And the snares that he has fashioned.
Words from him you cannot hope for ;
Half a word you could not look for."
    Väinämöinen, old and steadfast,
Started on his way, unheeding,   50
And the first day speeded lightly
O'er the points of women's needles,
And the second day sprang nimbly
O'er the points of heroes' sword-blades,
And upon the third day speeded
O'er the blades of heroes' axes.
    Vipunen in songs was famous,
Full of craft the aged hero ;
With his songs he lay extended,
Outstretched with his spells of magic.   60
On his shoulders grew a poplar,
From his temples sprang a birch-tree,
On his chin-tip grew an alder,
On his beard a willow-thicket,
On his brow were firs with squirrels,
From his teeth sprang branching pine-trees.

Then at once did Väinämöinen,
Draw his sword and free the iron
From the scabbard formed of leather,
From his belt of lambskin fashioned;   70
Fell the poplar from his shoulders,
Fell the birch-trees from his temples,
From his chin the spreading alders,
From his beard the willow-bushes,
From his brow the firs with squirrels,
From his teeth the branching pine-trees.

Then he thrust his stake of iron
Into Vipunen's mouth he thrust it,
In his gnashing gums he thrust it,
In his clashing jaws he thrust it,   80
And he spoke the words which follow:
" Rouse thyself, O slave of mortals,
Where beneath the earth thou restest,
In a sleep that long has lasted."

Vipunen, in songs most famous,
Suddenly awoke from slumber,
Feeling he was roughly treated,
And with pain severe tormented.
Then he bit the stake of iron,
Bit the outer softer iron,   90
But the steel he could not sever,
Could not eat the inner iron.

Then the aged Väinämöinen,
Just above his mouth was standing,
And his right foot slipped beneath him,
And his left foot glided onward.
Into Vipunen's mouth he stumbled,
And within his jaws he glided.

Vipunen, in songs most famous,
Opened then his mouth yet wider,   100
And his jaws he wide extended,
Gulped the well-beloved hero,
With a shout the hero swallowed,
Him the aged Väinämöinen.

Vipunen, in songs most famous,
Spoke the very words which follow:

"I have eaten much already,
And on ewes and goats have feasted,
And have barren heifers eaten,
And have also swine devoured,   110
But I ne'er had such a dinner,
Such a morsel never tasted."

But the aged Väinämöinen,
Uttered then the words which follow :
"Now destruction falls upon me,
And an evil day o'ertakes me,
Prisoned here in Hiisi's stable,
Here in Kalma's narrow dungeon."

So he pondered and reflected
How to live and how to struggle.   120
In his belt a knife had Väinö,
And the haft was formed of maple,
And from this a boat he fashioned,
And a boat he thus constructed,
And he rowed the boat, and urged it
Back and forth throughout the entrails,
Rowing through the narrow channels,
And exploring every passage.

Vipunen the old musician
Was not thus much incommoded ;   130
Then the aged Väinämöinen
As a smith began to labour,
And began to work with iron.
With his shirt he made a smithy,
With his shirt-sleeves made his bellows,
With the fur he made the wind-bag,
With his trousers made the air-pipe,
And the opening with his stockings,
And he used his knee for anvil,
And his elbow for a hammer.   140

Then he quick began to hammer,
Actively he plied his hammer,
Through the livelong night, unresting,
Through the day without cessation
In the stomach of the wise one,
In the entrails of the mighty.

Vipunen, in songs most famous,
Spoke aloud the words which follow :
"Who among mankind can this be,
Who among the roll of heroes ?   150
I have gulped a hundred heroes,
And a thousand men devoured,
But his like I never swallowed.
In my mouth the coals are rising,
On my tongue are firebrands resting,
In my throat is slag of iron.

"Go thou forth to wander, strange one,
Pest of earth, at once depart thou,
Ere I go to seek thy mother,
Seek thy very aged mother.   160
If I told it to thy mother,
Told the aged one the story,
Great would be thy mother's trouble,
Great the aged woman's sorrow,
That her son should work such evil,
And her child should act so basely.

"Still I hardly comprehend it,
Do not comprehend the reason,
How thou, Hiisi, here hast wandered,
Why thou cam'st, thou evil creature,   170
Thus to bite, and thus to torture,
Thus to eat, and thus to gnaw me.
Art thou some disease-created
Death that Jumala ordains me,
Or art thou another creature,
Fashioned and unloosed by others,
Hired beforehand to torment me,
Or hast thou been bribed with money?

"If thou art disease-created,
Death by Jumala ordained me,   180
Then I trust in my Creator,
And to Jumala resign me ;
For the good the Lord rejects not,
Nor does he destroy the righteous.

"If thou art another creature,
And an evil wrought by others,

Then thy race would I discover,
And the place where thou wast nurtured.
  "Once before have ills assailed me,
Plagues from somewhere have attacked me,   190
From the realms of mighty sorcerers,
From the meadows of the soothsayers,
And the homes of evil spirits,
And the plains where dwell the wizards,
From the dreary heaths of Kalma,
From beneath the firm earth's surface,
From the dwellings of the dead men,
From the realms of the departed,
From the loose earth heaped in hillocks,
From the regions of the landslips,   200
From the loose and gravelly districts,
From the shaking sandy regions,
From the valleys deeply sunken,
From the moss-grown swampy districts,
From the marshes all unfrozen,
From the billows ever tossing,
From the stalls in Hiisi's forest,
From five gorges in the mountains,
From the slopes of copper mountains,
From their summits all of copper,   210
From the ever-rustling pine-trees,
And the rustling of the fir-trees,
From the crowns of rotten pine-trees,
And the tops of rotten fir-trees,
From those spots where yelp the foxes,
Heaths where elk are chased on snowshoes,
From the bear's own rocky caverns,
From the caves where bears are lurking,
From the furthest bounds of Pohja,
From the distant realms of Lapland,   220
From the wastes where grow no bushes,
From the lands unploughed for ever,
From the battle-fields extended,
From the slaughter-place of heroes,
From the fields where grass is rustling,
From the blood that there is smoking,

From the blue sea's watery surface,
From the open sea's broad surface,
From the black mud of the ocean,
From the depth of thousand fathoms, 230
From the fiercely rushing torrents,
From the seething of the whirlpool,
And from Rutja's mighty cataract,
Where the waters rush most wildly,
From the further side of heaven,
Where the rainless clouds stretch furthest,
From the pathway of the spring-wind,
From the cradle of the tempests.

"From such regions hast thou journeyed
Thence hast thou proceeded, Torment, 240
To my heart of evil guiltless,
To my belly likewise sinless,
To devour and to torment me,
And to bite me and to tear me?

"Pine away, O hound of Hiisi,
Dog of Manala the vilest,
O thou demon, quit my body,
Pest of earth, O quit my liver,
Let my heart be undevoured,
Leave thou, too, my spleen uninjured, 250
Make no stoppage in my belly,
And my lungs forbear to traverse,
Do not pierce me through the navel,
And my loins forbear to injure,
And my backbone do not shatter,
Nor upon my sides torment me.

"If my strength as man should fail me,
Then will I invoke a greater,
Which shall rid me of the evil,
And shall drive away the horror. 260
"From the earth I call the Earth-Queen,
From the fields, the Lord primeval,
From the earth I call all swordsmen,
From the sands the hero-horsemen,
Call them to my aid and succour,
To my help and aid I call them,

In the tortures that o'erwhelm me,
And amid this dreadful torment.

"If you do not heed their presence,
And you will not shrink before them,   270
Come, O forest, with thy people,
Junipers, bring all your army,
Come, O pine-woods, with your household,
And thou pond with all thy children,
With their swords a hundred swordsmen,
And a thousand mail-clad heroes,
That they may assail this Hiisi,
And may overwhelm this Juutas!

"If you do not heed their presence,
And you will not shrink before them,   280
Rise thou up, O Water-Mother,
Raise thy blue cap from the billows,
And thy soft robe from the waters,
From the ooze thy form of beauty,
For a powerless hero's rescue,
For a weakly man's protection,
Lest I should be eaten guiltless,
And without disease be slaughtered.

"If you will not heed their presence,
And you will not shrink before them,   290
Ancient Daughter of Creation,
Come in all thy golden beauty,
Thou the oldest of all women,
Thou the first of all the mothers,
Come to see the pains that rack me,
And the evil days drive from me,
That thy strength may overcome them,
And perchance may free me from them.

"But if this not yet should move you,
And you will not yet draw backwards,   300
Ukko, in the vault of heaven,
On the thundercloud's wide border,
Come thou here, where thou art needed,
Hasten here, where I implore thee,
To dispel the works of evil,
And destroy this vile enchantment,

With thy sword of flame dispel it,
With thy flashing sword-blade smite it.
    "Go thou horror, forth to wander,
Curse of earth, depart thou quickly,   310
Here no more shall be thy dwelling,
And if thou such dwelling needest,
Elsewhere shalt thou seek thy dwelling,
Far from here a home shalt find thee,
In the household of thy master,
In the footsteps of thy mistress.
    "When you reach your destination,
And your journey you have finished,
In the realms of him who made you,
In the country of your master,   320
Give a signal of your coming,
Let a lightning flash announce it,
Let them hear the roll of thunder,
Let them see the lightning flashing,
And the yard-gate kick to pieces,
Pull a shutter from the window,
Then the house thou soon canst enter,
Rush into the room like whirlwind,
Plant thy foot within it firmly,
And thy heel where space is narrow,   330
Push the men into the corner,
And the women to the doorposts,
Scratch the eyes from out the masters,
Smash the heads of all the women,
Curve thou then to hooks thy fingers,
Twist thou then their heads all crooked.
    "Or if this is not sufficient,
Fly as cock upon the pathway,
Or as chicken in the farmyard,
With thy breast upon the dunghill,   340
Drive the horses from the stable,
From the stalls the horned cattle,
Push their horns into the dungheap,
On the ground their tails all scatter,
Twist thou then their eyes all crooked,
And their necks in haste then break thou.

"Art thou Sickness, tempest-carried,
Tempest-carried, wind-conducted,
And a gift from wind of springtime,
By the frosty air led hither,⁣   350
On the path of air conducted,
On the sledge-way of the spring-wind,
Then upon the trees repose not,
Rest thou not upon the alders,
Hasten to the copper mountain,
Hasten to its copper summit,
Let the wind convey thee thither,
Guarded by the wind of springtide.

"But if thou from heaven descended,
From the rainless clouds' broad margins,⁣   360
Then again ascend to heaven,
Once again in air arise thou,
To the clouds where rain is falling,
To the stars that ever twinkle,
That thou there mayst burn like fire,
And that thou mayst shine and sparkle
On the sun's own path of splendour,
And around the moon's bright circle.

"If thou art some pest of water,
Hither drifted by the sea-waves,⁣   370
Let the pest return to water,
Journey back amid the sea-waves,
To the walls of muddy castles,
To the crests of waves like mountains,
There amid the waves to welter,
Rocking on the darkling billows.

"Cam'st thou from the heaths of Kalma,
From the realms of the departed,
To thy home return thou quickly,
To the dark abodes of Kalma,⁣   380
To the land upheaved in hillocks,
To the land that quakes for ever,
Where the people fall in battle,
And a mighty host has perished.

"If thou foolishly hast wandered
From the depths of Hiisi's forest,

From the nest amid the pine-trees,
From thy home among the fir-trees,
Then I drive thee forth and ban thee,
To the depths of Hiisi's forest,   390
To thy home among the fir-trees,
To thy nest among the pine-trees.
There thou mayst remain for ever,
Till the flooring-planks have rotted,
And the wooden walls are mildewed,
And the roof shall fall upon you.

"I will drive thee forth and ban thee,
Drive thee forth, O evil creature,
Forth unto the old bear's dwelling,
To the lair of aged she-bear,   400
To the deep and swampy valleys,
To the ever-frozen marshes,
To the swamps for ever quaking,
Quaking underneath the footsteps,
To the ponds where sport no fishes,
Where no perch are ever noticed.

"But if there thou find'st no refuge,
Further yet will I then ban thee,
To the furthest bounds of Pohja,
To the distant plains of Lapland,   410
To the barren treeless tundras,
To the country where they plough not,
Where is neither moon nor sunlight,
Where the sun is never shining.
There a charming life awaits thee,
There to roam about at pleasure.
In the woods the elks are lurking.
In the woods men hunt the reindeer,
That a man may still his hunger,
And may satisfy his craving.   420

"Even further yet I ban thee,
Banish thee, and drive thee onward,
To the mighty falls of Rutja,
To the fiercely raging whirlpool,
Thither where the trees have fallen,
And the fallen pines are rolling,

Tossing trunks of mighty fir-trees,
Wide-extended crowns of pine-trees.
Swim thou there, thou wicked heathen,
In the cataract's foaming torrent, 430
Round to drive 'mid boundless waters,
Resting in the narrow waters.

" But if there you find no refuge,
Further yet will I then ban you,
To the river black of Tuoni,
To the eternal stream of Mana,
Never in thy life escaping,
Never while thy life endureth,
Should I not consent to free thee,
Nor to ransom thee be able, 440
Come with nine sheep thee to ransom,
Which a single ewe has farrowed,
And with bullocks, nine in number,
From a single cow proceeding,
And with stallions, nine in number,
From a single mare proceeding.

" Need you horses for your journey,
Or there's aught you need for driving,
Horses I will give in plenty,
Plenty I can give for riding. 450
Hiisi has a horse of beauty,
With a red mane, on the mountain.
Fire is flashing from his muzzle,
And his nostrils brightly shining,
And his hoofs are all of iron,
And of steel are they constructed.
He can climb upon a mountain,
Climb the sloping sides of valleys,
If his rider mounts him boldly,
Urges him to show his mettle. 460

" But if this is not sufficient,
Then may Hiisi make thee snowshoes.
Take the alder-shoes of Lempo,
Where the thick smoke is the foulest,
Skate thou to the land of Hiisi,
Rushing through the woods of Lempo,

Dashing through the land of Hiisi,
Gliding through the evil country.
If a stone impedes thy pathway,
Crash and scatter it asunder;   470
Lies a branch across thy pathway,
Break the branch in twain when passing;
If a hero bar thy passage,
Drive him boldly from thy pathway.
Go thy way, thou lazy creature,
Go thou forth, thou man of evil,
Now, before the day is dawning,
Or the morning twilight glimmer,
Or as yet the sun has risen,
Or thou yet hast heard the cockcrow!   480
Thou delay'st too long to leave me,
Take thy flight, O evil creature,
Fare thee forth into the moonlight,
Wander forth amid its brightness.

"If thou wilt not leave me quickly,
O thou dog without a mother,
I will take the eagles' talons
And the claws of the blood-suckers,
And of birds of prey the talons,
And of hawks the talons likewise,   490
That I thus may seize the demons,
Utterly o'ercome these wretches,
That my head may ache no longer,
Nor my breathing more oppress me.

"Once did Lempo's self flee from me,
When he wandered from his mother,
When was aid from Jumala granted,
Gave his aid, the Great Creator.
Wander forth without thy mother,
O thou uncreated creature,   500
Wretched dog without a master,
Forth, O whelp without a mother,
Even while the time is passing,
Even while the moon is waning."

Väinämöinen, old and steadfast,
Answered in the words which follow:

" Here I find a pleasant dwelling,
Here I dwell in much contentment,
And for bread the liver serves me,
And the fat with drink supplies me,
And the lungs are good for cooking,
And the fat is best for eating.

" Therefore will I sink my smithy
In thy heart for ever deeper,
And will strike my hammer harder,
Pounding on the tenderest places,
That in all thy life thou never
Freedom from the ill may'st hope for,
If thy spells thou dost not teach me,
All thy magic spells shalt teach me,
Till thy spells I learn in fulness,
And a thousand spells have gathered ;
Till no spells are hidden from me,
Nor the spells of magic hidden,
That in caves their power is lost not,
Even though the wizards perish."

Vipunen, in songs so famous,
He the sage so old in wisdom,
In whose mouth was mighty magic,
Power unbounded in his bosom,
Opened then his mouth of wisdom,
Of his spells the casket opened,
Sang his mighty spells of magic,
Chanted forth of all the greatest,
Magic songs of the Creation,
From the very earliest ages,
Songs that all the children sing not,
Even heroes understand not,
In these dreary days of evil,
In the days that now are passing.

Words of origin he chanted,
All his spells he sang in order,
At the will of the Creator,
At behest of the Almighty,
How himself the air he fashioned,
And from air the water parted,
And the earth was formed from water,

510

520

530

540

And from earth all herbage sprouted.
Then he sang the moon's creation,
Likewise how the sun was fashioned,   550
How the air was raised on pillars,
How the stars were placed in heaven.
   Vipunen, in songs the wisest,
Sang in part, and sang in fulness.
Never yet was heard or witnessed,
Never while the world existed,
One who was a better singer,
One who was a wiser wizard.
From his mouth the words were flowing,
And his tongue sent forth his sayings,   560
Quick as legs of foals are moving,
Or the feet of rapid courser.
   Through the days he sang unceasing,
Through the nights without cessation.
To his songs the sun gave hearing,
And the golden moon stayed listening,
Waves stood still on ocean's surface,
Billows sank upon its margin,
Rivers halted in their courses,
Rutja's furious cataract halted,   570
Vuoksi's cataract ceased its flowing,
Likewise, too, the river Jordan.
   When the aged Väinämöinen
Unto all the spells had listened,
And had learned the charms in fulness,
All the magic spells creative,
He prepared himself to travel
From the wide-spread jaws of Vipunen ;
From the belly of the wise one,
From within his monstrous body.   580
   Said the aged Väinämöinen,
" O thou Antero Vipunen hugest,
Open thou thy mouth gigantic,
And thy jaws extend more widely.
I would quit for earth thy body,
And would take my journey homeward."
   Vipunen then, in songs the wisest,
Answered in the words which follow :

"Much I've drunk, and much have eaten,
And consumed a thousand dainties,   590
But before I never swallowed
Aught like aged Väinämöinen.
Good indeed has been thy coming,
Better 'tis when thou departest."

Then did Antero Vipunen open
Wide expanding gums grimacing,
Open wide his mouth gigantic,
And his jaws extended widely,
While the aged Väinämöinen
To his mouth made lengthened journey,   600
From the belly of the wise one,
From within his monstrous body.
From his mouth he glided swiftly,
O'er the heath he bounded swiftly,
Very like a golden squirrel,
Or a golden-breasted marten.

Further on his path he journeyed,
Till at length he reached the smithy.
Said the smith, e'en Ilmarinen,
"Have you found the words you wanted,   610
Have you learned the spells creative,
That the boat-sides you can fashion,
Spells to fix the stern together,
And the bows to deftly fashion?"

Väinämöinen, old and steadfast,
Answered in the words which follow:
"Spells a hundred have I gathered,
And a thousand spells of magic,
Secret spells were opened to me,
Hidden charms were all laid open."   620

To his boat he hastened quickly,
And he set to work most wisely,
Set to work the boat to finish,
And he fixed the sides together,
And the stern he fixed together,
And the bows he deftly fashioned,
But the boat he built unhammerea,
Nor a chip he severed from it.

RUNO XVIII.—VÄINÄMÖINEN AND ILMARINEN TRAVEL TO POHJOLA

Argument

Väinämöinen sets sail in his new boat to woo the Maiden of Pohja (1–40). Ilmarinen's sister sees him, calls to him from the shore, learns the object of his journey, and hastens to warn her brother that a rival has set forth to Pohjola to claim the bride (41–266). Ilmarinen makes ready, and rides on horseback to Pohjola along the shore (267–470). The Mistress of Pohjola sees the suitors approaching, and advises her daughter to choose Väinämöinen (471–634). But the daughter herself prefers Ilmarinen, the forger of the Sampo, and tells Väinämöinen, who is first to arrive, that she will not marry him (635–706).

VÄINÄMÖINEN, old and steadfast,
Pondered deeply and reflected
How he best should woo the maiden,
Hasten to the long-haired maiden,
In the gloomy land of Pohja,
Sariola, for ever misty,
She the far-famed Maid of Pohja,
She the peerless Bride of Pohja.

There the pale-grey boat was lying,
And the boat with red he painted,　　　　　　　10
And adorned the prow with gilding,
And with silver overlaid it ;
Then upon the morning after,
Very early in the morning,
Pushed his boat into the water,
In the waves the hundred-boarded,
Pushed it from the barkless rollers,
From the rounded logs of pine-tree
Then he raised a mast upon it,
On the masts the sails he hoisted,　　　　　　　20
Raised a red sail on the vessel,
And another blue in colour,
Then the boat himself he boarded,
And he walked upon the planking,
And upon the sea he steered it,
O'er the blue and plashing billows.

I—*G 259

Then he spoke the words which follow,
And in words like these expressed him:
"Enter, Jumala, my vessel,
Enter here, O thou most gracious,   30
Strengthen thou the hero's weakness,
And the weakling do thou cherish,
On these far-extending waters,
On the wide expanse of billows.

"Breathe, O wind, upon the vessel,
Drive, O wave, the boat before thee,
That I need not row with fingers,
Nor may thus disturb the waters,
On the wide expanse of ocean,
Out upon the open ocean."   40

Annikki, the ever-famous,
Night's fair daughter, maid of twilight,
Long before the day had risen,
Early in the morn had wakened,
And had washed her clothes and spread them,
And had rinsed and wrung the clothing,
Where the red steps reach the furthest,
Where the planking is the broadest,
Out upon the misty headland,
On the shady island's ending.   50

Then she turned and gazed around her,
In the cloudless air surrounding,
And she gazed aloft to heaven,
And from shore across the water,
And above the sun was shining,
And below the waves were gleaming.

O'er the waves her eyes were glancing,
To the south her head was turning,
To the mouth of Suomi's river,
Where the stream of Väinölä opens.   60
On the sea a blotch she sighted,
Something blue among the billows.

Then she spoke the words which follow,
And in terms like these expressed her:
"What's this speck upon the ocean,
What this blue upon the billows?

If it be a flock of wild geese,
Or of other beauteous birdies,
Let them on their rushing pinions
Soar aloft amid the heavens. 70
  " If it be a shoal of salmon,
Or a shoal of other fishes,
Let them leap as thcy are swimming,
Plunging then beneath the water.
  "If it be a rocky island,
Or a stump amid the water,
Let the billows rise above it,
Or the waters drive it forward."
  Now the boat came gliding onward,
And the new boat sailed on swiftly 80
Forward to the misty headland,
And the shady island's ending.
  Annikki, the ever famous,
Saw the vessel fast approaching,
Saw the hundred-boarded passing,
And she spoke the words which follow :
" If thou art my brother's vessel,
Or the vessel of my father,
Then direct thy journey homeward,
To the shore the prow directing, 90
Where the landing-stage is stationed,
While the stern is pointing from it.
If thou art a stranger vessel,
May'st thou swim at greater distance,
Towards another stage then hasten,
With the stern to this directed."
  'Twas no vessel of her household,
Nor a boat from foreign regions,
But the boat of Väinämöinen,
Built by him, the bard primeval, 100
And the boat approached quite closely,
Onward sailed in hailing distance,
Till a word, and then a second,
And a third were heard distinctly.
  Annikki, the ever-famous,
Night's fair daughter, maid of twilight,

Hailed the boat as it approached her:
"Whither goest thou, Väinämöinen,
Whither, hero of the waters,
Wherefore, pride of all the country?"   110
     Then the aged Väinämöinen
From the boat made ready answer:
"I am going salmon-fishing,
Where the salmon-trout are spawning,
In the gloomy stream of Tuoni,
In the deep reed-bordered river."
     Annikki, the ever-famous,
Answered in the words which follow:
"Tell me not such idle falsehoods!
Well I know the spawning season,   120
For aforetime oft my father
And my grandsire, too, before him,
Often went a salmon-fishing,
And the salmon-trout to capture.
In the boats the nets were lying,
And the boats were full of tackle,
Here lay nets, here lines were resting,
And the beating-poles beside them;
And beneath the seats were tridents,
In the stern, long staves were lying.   130
Whither goest thou, Väinämöinen,
Wherefore, O Uvantolainen?"
     Said the aged Väinämöinen,
"Forth in search of geese I wander,
Where the bright-winged birds are sporting,
And the slimy fish are catching,
In the deep sound of the Saxons,
Where the sea is wide and open."
     Annikki, the ever-famous,
Answered in the words which follow: 140
"Well I know who speaks me truly,
And can soon detect the liar,
For aforetime oft my father,
And my grandsire, too, before him,
Went abroad the geese to capture,
And to chase the red-beaked quarry,

And his bow was great, and tight-strung,
And the bow he drew was splendid,
And a black dog leashed securely,
In the stern was tightly tethered,   150
On the strand the hounds were running,
And the whelps across the shingle ;
Speak the truth, O Väinämöinen,
Whither do you take your journey ? "
    Said the aged Väinämöinen,
" Wherefore take I not my journey,
Where a mighty fight is raging,
There to fight among my equals,
Where the greaves with blood are spattered,
Even to the knees all crimsoned ? "   160
    Annikki again insisted,
Loudly cried the tin-adorned one :
" Well I know the ways of battle,
For aforetime went my father
Where a mighty fight was raging,
There to fight among his equals,
And a hundred men were rowing,
And a thousand men were standing.
In the prow their bows were lying,
And beneath the seats their sword-blades.   170
Speak the truth, and tell me truly,
Cease to lie, and speak sincerely.
Whither goest thou, Väinämöinen,
Wherefore, O Suvantolainen ? "
    Then the aged Väinämöinen
Answered in the words which follow :
" Come thou in my boat, O maiden,
In my boat, O maiden, seat thee,
And the truth I then will tell thee,
Cease to lie, and speak sincerely."   180
    Annikki, the tin-adorned one,
Cried aloud in indignation :
" May the wind assail thy vessel,
And the east wind fall upon it,
May thy boat capsize beneath thee,
And the prow sink down beneath thee,

If you will not tell me truly
Where you mean to take your journey,
If the truth you will not tell me,
And at last will end your lying!"   190
      Then the aged Väinämöinen,
Answered in the words which follow:
"All the truth I now will tell you,
Though at first I lied a little.
Forth I fare to woo a maiden,
Seek the favour of a maiden,
In the gloomy land of Pohja,
Sariola, for ever misty,
In the land where men are eaten,
Where they even drown the heroes."   200
      Annikki, the ever-famous,
Night's fair daughter, maid of twilight,
When she knew the truth for certain,
All the truth, without evasion,
Down she threw her caps unwashen,
And unrinsed she left the clothing,
On the bench she left them lying,
Where the red bridge has its ending,
In her hand her gown she gathered,
In her hand the folds collecting,   210
And began from thence to hasten,
And with rapid pace she hurried,
Till at length she reached the smithy.
To the forge at once she hastened.
      There she found smith Ilmarinen,
He the great primeval craftsman,
And he forged a bench of iron,
And adorned it all with silver.
Cubit-high his head was sooted,
On his shoulders ash by fathoms.   220
      Annikki the door then entered,
And she spoke the words which follow:
"Smith and brother Ilmarinen,
Thou the great primeval craftsman,
Forge me now a weaver's shuttle,
Pretty rings to deck my fingers,

Golden earrings, two or three pairs,
Five or six linked girdles make me,
For most weighty truth I'll tell you,
All the truth without evasion."   230
    Said the smith, said Ilmarinen,
"If you tell me news important,
Then a shuttle will I forge you,
Pretty rings to deck your fingers,
And a cross upon your bosom,
And the finest head-dress forge you.
If the words you speak are evil,
All your ornaments I'll shatter,
Tear them off to feed the furnace,
And beneath the forge will thrust them."   240
    Annikki, the ever-famous,
Answered in the words which follow:
"O thou smith, O Ilmarinen,
Do you still propose to marry
Her, the bride who once was promised,
And as wife was pledged unto you?
    "While you weld and hammer always,
Ever working with your hammer,
Making horseshoes in the summer,
Iron horseshoes for the winter,   250
Working at your sledge at night-time,
And its frame in daytime shaping,
Forth to journey to your wooing,
And to Pohjola to travel,
One more cunning goes before you,
And another speeds beyond you,
And your own will capture from you,
And your love will ravish from you,
Whom two years ago thou sawest,
Whom two years agone thou wooed'st.   260
Know that Väinämöinen journeys
O'er the blue waves of the ocean,
In a boat with prow all golden,
Steering with his copper rudder,
To the gloomy land of Pohja,
Sariola, for ever misty."

To the smith came grievous trouble,
To the iron-worker sorrow.
From his grasp the tongs slid downward,
From his hand he dropped the hammer.   270
    Said the smith, said Ilmarinen,
" Annikki, my little sister,
I will forge you now a shuttle,
Pretty rings to deck your fingers,
Golden earrings, two or three pairs,
Five or six linked girdles make you.
Warm for me the pleasant bathroom,
Fill the room with fragrant vapour,
Let the logs you burn be small ones,
And the fire with chips be kindled,   280
And prepare me too some ashes,
And some soap in haste provide me,
That I wash my head and cleanse it,
And I may make white my body
From the coal-dust of the autumn,
From the forge throughout the winter."
    Annikki, whose name was famous,
Heated secretly the bathroom,
With the boughs the wind had broken.
And the thunderbolt had shattered.   290
Stones she gathered from the river,
Heated them till they were ready,
Cheerfully she fetched the water,
From the holy well she brought it,
Broke some bath-whisks from the bushes,
Charming bath-whisks from the thickets,
And she warmed the honeyed bath-whisks,
On the honeyed stones she warmed them,
Then with milk she mixed the ashes,
And she made him soap of marrow,   300
And she worked the soap to lather,
Kneaded then the soap to lather,
That his head might cleanse the bridegroom,
And might cleanse himself completely.
    Then the smith, e'en Ilmarinen,
He the great primeval craftsman,

Wrought the maiden what she wished for,
And he wrought a splendid head-dress,
While she made the bathroom ready,
And she put the bath in order.   310
In her hands he placed the trinkets,
And the maiden thus addressed him :
"Now the bathroom's filled with vapour,
And the vapour-bath I've heated,
And have steeped the bath-whisks nicely,
Choosing out the best among them.
Bathe, O brother, at your pleasure,
Pouring water as you need it,
Wash your head to flaxen colour,
Till your eyes shine out like snowflakes."   320
    Then the smith, e'en Ilmarinen,
Went to take the bath he needed,
There he bathed himself at pleasure,
And he washed himself to whiteness,
Washed his eyes until they sparkled,
And his temples till they glistened,
And his neck to hen's-egg whiteness,
And his body all was shining.
From the bath the room he entered,
Changed so much they scarcely knew him,   330
For his face it shone with beauty,
And his cheeks were cleansed and rosy.
    Then he spoke the words which follow :
"Annikki, my little sister,
Bring me now a shirt of linen,
And the best of raiment bring me,
That I robe myself completely,
And may deck me like a bridegroom."
    Annikki, the ever-famous,
Brought him then a shirt of linen,   340
For his limbs no longer sweating,
For his body all uncovered.
Then she brought well-fitting trousers,
Which his mother had been sewing,
For his hips, no longer sooty,
And his legs were fully covered.

Then she brought him finest stockings,
Which, as maid, had wove his mother,
And with these his shins he covered,
And his calves were hidden by them.   350
Then she brought him shoes that fitted,
Best of Saxon boots she brought him,
And with these the stockings covered
Which his mother sewed as maiden ;
Then a coat of blue she chose him,
With a liver-coloured lining,
Covering thus the shirt of linen,
Which of finest flax was fashioned,
Then an overcoat of woollen,
Of four kinds of cloth constructed,   360
O'er the coat of bluish colour,
Of the very latest fashion,
And a new fur, thousand-buttoned,
And a hundred-fold more splendid,
O'er the overcoat of woollen,
And the cloth completely hiding ;
Round his waist a belt she fastened,
And the belt was gold-embroidered,
Which his mother wrought as maiden,
Wrought it when a fair-haired maiden,   370
Brightly-coloured gloves she brought him,
Gold-embroidered, for his fingers,
Which the Lapland children fashioned ;
On his handsome hands he drew them,
Then a high-crowned hat she brought him
(On his golden locks she placed it)
Which his father once had purchased,
When as bridegroom he adorned him.
    Thus the smith, e'en Ilmarinen,
Clothed himself, and made him ready,   380
Robed himself, and made him handsome,
And his servant he commanded :
"Yoke me now a rapid courser,
In the sledge adorned so finely,
That I start upon my journey,
And to Pohjola may travel."

Thereupon the servant answered,
" Horses six are in the stable,
Horses six, on oats that fatten ;
Which among them shall I yoke you ? "   390
    Said the smith, e'en Ilmarinen,
" Take the best of all the stallions,
Put the foal into the harness,
Yoke before the sledge the chestnut,
Then provide me with six cuckoos,
Seven blue birds at once provide me,
That upon the frame they perch them,
And may sing their cheerful music,
That the fair ones may behold them,
And the maidens be delighted.   400
Then provide me with a bearskin,
That I seat myself upon it,
And a second hide of walrus,
That the bright-hued sledge is covered."
    Thereupon the skilful servant,
He the servant paid with wages,
Put the colt into the harness,
Yoked before the sledge the chestnut,
And provided six fine cuckoos,
Seven blue birds at once provided,   410
That upon the frame should perch them,
And should sing their cheerful music ;
And a bearskin next provided,
That his lord should sit upon it,
And another hide of walrus,
And with this the sledge he covered.
    Then the smith, e'en Ilmarinen,
He the great primeval craftsman,
Sent aloft his prayer to Ukko,
And he thus besought the Thunderer :   420
" Scatter forth thy snow, O Ukko,
Let the snowflakes soft be drifted,
That the sledge may glide o'er snowfields,
O'er the snow-drifts gliding swiftly."
    Then the snow did Ukko scatter,
And the snowflakes soft were drifted,

Till the heath-stems all were covered,
On the ground the berry-bushes.

Then the smith, e'en Ilmarinen,
In his sledge of iron sat him,　　430
And he spoke the words which follow,
And in words like these expressed him :
"On my reins attend good fortune,
Jumala my sledge protecting,
That my reins good fortune fail not,
Nor my sledge may break, O Jumala !"

In one hand the reins he gathered,
And the whip he grasped with other,
O'er the horse the whip he brandished,
And he spoke the words which follow :　　440
"Whitebrow, speed thou quickly onward,
Haste away, O flaxen-maned one."

On the way the horse sprang forward,
On the water's sandy margin,
By the shores of Sound of Sima,
Past the hills with alders covered.
On the shore the sledge went rattling,
On the beach the shingle clattered.
In his eyes the sand was flying,
To his breast splashed up the water.　　450
Thus he drove one day, a second,
Drove upon the third day likewise,
And at length upon the third day,
Overtook old Väinämöinen,
And he spoke the words which follow,
And in words like these expressed him :
"O thou aged Väinämöinen,
Let us make a friendly compact,
That although we both are seeking,
And we both would woo the maiden,　　460
Yet by force we will not seize her,
Nor against her will shall wed her."

Said the aged Väinämöinen,
"I will make a friendly compact,
That we will not seize the maiden,
Nor against her will shall wed her.

Let the maiden now be given
To the husband whom she chooses,
That we nurse not long vexation,
Nor a lasting feud be fostered."   470

   Further on their way they travelled,
On the path that each had chosen ;
Sped the boat, the shore re-echoed,
Ran the horse, the earth resounded.

   But a short time passed thereafter,
Very short the time elapsing,
Ere the grey-brown dog was barking,
And the house-dog loudly baying,
In the gloomy land of Pohja,
Sariola, for ever cloudy,   480
Sooner still the dog was growling,
But with less-continued growling,
By the borders of the cornfield,
'Gainst the ground his tail was wagging.

   Then exclaimed the Lord of Pohja,
'Go, my daughter, to discover
Why the grey-brown dog is barking,
And the long-eared dog is baying."

   But the daughter made him answer:
" I have not the time, my father,   490
I must clean the largest cowshed,
Tend our herd of many cattle,
Grind the corn between the millstones,
Through the sieve must sift the flour,
Grind the corn to finest flour,
And the grinder is but feeble."

   Gently barked the castle's Hiisi,
And again the dog was growling,
And again said Pohja's Master :
" Go, old dame, and look about you,   500
See why barks the grey-brown house-dog,
Why the castle-dog is growling."

   But the old dame made him answer:
"This is not a time for talking,
For my household cares are heavy,
And I must prepare the dinner,

And must bake a loaf enormous,
And for this the dough be kneading,
Bake the loaf of finest flour,
And the baker is but feeble."   510
　　Thereupon said Pohja's Master :
" Women they are always hurried,
And the maidens always busy,
When before the stove they roast them,
When they in their beds are lying ;
Son, go you, and look around you."
　　Thereupon the son made answer :
" I've no time to look about me ;
I must grind the blunted hatchet,
Chop a log of wood to pieces,   520
Chop to bits the largest wood-pile,
And to faggots small reduce it.
Large the pile, and small the faggots,
And the workman of the weakest."
　　Still the castle-dog was barking,
And the yard-dog still was barking,
And the furious whelp was baying,
And the island watch-dog howling,
Sitting by the furthest cornfield,
And his tail was briskly wagging.   530
　　Then again said Pohja's Master,
" Not for nought the dog is barking,
Never has he barked for nothing,
Never growls he at the fir-trees."
　　So he went to reconnoitre,
And he walked across the courtyard,
To the cornfield's furthest borders,
To the path beyond the ploughed land.
Gazed he where the dog's snout pointed,
Where he saw his muzzle pointing,   540
To the hill where storms are raging,
To the hills where grow the alders,
Then he saw the truth most clearly,
Why the grey-brown dog was barking,
And the pride of earth was baying,
And the woolly-tailed one howling,

For he saw a red boat sailing
Out amid the Bay of Lempi,
And a handsome sledge was driving
On the shore of Sound of Sima.   550
    After this the Lord of Pohja
To the house returned directly,
And beneath the roof he hastened,
And he spoke the words which follow :
" There are strangers swiftly sailing
O'er the blue lake's watery surface,
And a gaudy sledge is gliding
On the shore of Sound of Sima ;
And a large boat is approaching
To the shore of Bay of Lempi."   560
    Then said Pohjola's old Mistress,
" Whence shall we obtain an omen
Why these strangers here are coming ?
O my little waiting-maiden,
On the fire lay rowan-faggots,
And the best log in its glowing.
If the log with blood is flowing,
Then the strangers come for battle,
If the log exudes clear water,
Then is peace abiding with us."   570
    Then the little maid of Pohja,
She, the modest waiting-maiden,
On the fire laid rowan-faggots,
Placed the best log in its glowing.
From the log no blood was trickling,
Nor did water trickle from it ;
From the log there oozed forth honey,
From the log dripped down the nectar.
    From the corner spoke Suovakko,
Spoke the old dame 'neath the blankets :   580
" From the log if oozes honey,
From the log if drips the nectar,
Then the strangers who are coming,
May be ranked as noble suitors."
    Then did Pohja's aged Mistress,
Pohja's old dame, Pohja's daughter,

To the courtyard fencing hasten,
Hurry quick across the courtyard,
And they gazed across the water,
To the south their heads then turning,   590
And they saw from thence approaching,
Swift a ship of novel fashion,
Of a hundred planks constructed,
Out upon the Bay of Lempi.
Underneath the boat looked bluish,
But the sails of crimson colour.
In the stern there sat a hero,
At the copper rudder's handle,
And they saw a stallion trotting
With a red sledge strange of aspect,   600
And the gaudy sledge was speeding
On the shore of Sound of Sima,
And they saw six golden cuckoos,
Perching on the frame, and calling,
Seven blue birds were likewise perching
On the reins, and these were singing;
And a stalwart hero, sitting
In the sledge, the reins was holding.

Then said Pohjola's old Mistress,
And she spoke the words which follow :   610
"Whom will you accept as husband,
If they really come to woo you,
As a life-companion woo you,
Dove-like in his arms to nestle?

"He who in the boat is sailing,
In the red boat fast approaching,
Out upon the Bay of Lempi,
Is the aged Väinämöinen.
In the boat he brings provisions,
And of treasures brings a cargo.   620

"He who in the sledge is driving,
In the gaudy sledge is speeding,
On the shore of Sound of Sima,
Is the smith named Ilmarinen.
He with empty hands is coming ;
Filled his sledge with spells of magic.

"Therefore if the room they enter,
Bring them then the mead in tankard,
In the two-eared tankard bring it,
And in his hands place the tankard   630
Whom thou dost desire to follow;
Choose thou Väinölä's great hero,
He whose boat with wealth is loaded,
And of treasures brings a cargo."

But the lovely maid of Pohja,
Thus made answer to her mother:
"O my mother who hast borne me,
O my mother who hast reared me,
Nothing do I care for riches,
Nor a man profound in wisdom,   640
But a man of lofty forehead,
One whose every limb is handsome.
Never once in former ages,
Gave a maid her life in thiswise.
I, a maid undowered, will follow
Ilmarinen, skilful craftsman,
He it was who forged the Sampo,
And the coloured cover welded."

Then said Pohja's aged Mistress,
"O indeed, my child, my lambkin,   650
If you go with Ilmarinen,
From whose brow the sweat falls freely,
You must wash the blacksmith's aprons,
And the blacksmith's head wash likewise."

But the daughter gave her answer,
In the very words which follow:
"Him from Väinölä I choose not,
Nor an aged man will care for,
For an old man is a nuisance,
And an aged man would vex me."   660
Then did aged Väinämöinen
Reach his journey's end the soonest,
And he steered his crimson vessel,
Brought his boat of bluish colour
To the rollers steel-constructed,
To the landing-stage of copper.

After this the house he entered,
Underneath the roof he hastened,
And upon the floor spoke loudly,
Near the door beneath the rafters,   670
And he spoke the words which follow,
And expressed himself in thiswise :
"Wilt thou come with me, O maiden,
Evermore as my companion,
Wife-like on my knees to seat thee,
In my arms as dove to nestle?"

Then the lovely maid of Pohja,
Answered in the words which follow :
"Have you then the boat constructed,
Built the large and handsome vessel,   680
From the splinters of my spindle,
From the fragments of my shuttle?"

Then the aged Väinämöinen
Answered in the words which follow :
"I have built a noble vessel
And a splendid boat constructed,
Strongly built to face the tempests,
And the winds its course opposing,
As it cleaves the tossing billows,
O'er the surface of the water,   690
Bladder-like amid the surges,
As a leaf, by current drifted,
Over Pohjola's wide waters,
And across the foaming billows."

Then the lovely maid of Pohja,
Answered in the words which follow :
"Nothing do I reck of seamen,
Heroes boasting of the billows !
Drives the wind their minds to ocean,
And their thoughts the east wind saddens :   700
Therefore thee I cannot follow,
Never pledge myself unto thee,
Evermore as thy companion,
In thy arms as dove to nestle,
Spread the couch whereon thou sleepest,
For thy head arrange the pillows."

Runo XIX.—The Exploits and Betrothal
of Ilmarinen

Argument

Ilmarinen arrives at the homestead of Pohjola, woos the daughter of the house, and perilous tasks are assigned to him (1–32). Aided by the advice of the Maiden of Pohja he succeeds in performing the tasks successfully. Firstly, he ploughs a field of serpents, secondly, he captures the Bear of Tuoni and the Wolf of Manala, and thirdly, he captures a large and terrible pike in the river of Tuonela (33–344). The Mistress of Pohjola promises and betroths her daughter to Ilmarinen (345–498). Väinämöinen returns from Pohjola in low spirits, and warns every one against going wooing in company with a younger man (499–518).

THEN the smith, e'en Ilmarinen,
He the great primeval craftsman,
Came himself into the chamber,
And beneath the roof he hastened.
    Brought the maid of mead a beaker,
Placed a can of drink of honey
In the hands of Ilmarinen,
And the smith spoke out as follows:
"Never while my life is left me,
Long as shines the golden moonlight,   10
Will I taste the drink before me,
Till my own is granted to me,
She for whom so long I waited,
She for whom so long I pined for."
    Then said Pohjola's old Mistress,
In the very words which follow:
"Trouble great befalls the suitor,
Comes to her for whom he waiteth;
One shoe still remains unfitted,
And unfitted is the other;   20
But the bride is waiting for you,
And you may indeed receive her,
If you plough the field of vipers,
Where the writhing snakes are swarming,

But without a plough employing,
And without a ploughshare guiding.
Once the field was ploughed by Hiisi,
Lempo seamed it next with furrows,
With the ploughshare formed of copper,
With the plough in furnace smelted ;   30
But my own son, most unhappy,
Left the half untilled behind him."

   Then the smith, e'en Ilmarinen,
Sought the maiden in her chamber,
And he spoke the words which follow :
" Night's own daughter, twilight maiden,
Do you not the time remember,
When I forged the Sampo for you,
And the brilliant cover welded,
And a binding oath thou sweared'st,   40
By the God whom all men worship,
'Fore the face of Him Almighty,
And you gave a certain promise
Unto me, the mighty hero,
You would be my friend for ever,
Dove-like in my arms to nestle ?
Nothing will your mother grant me,
Nor will she her daughter give me,
Till I plough the field of vipers,
Where the writhing snakes are swarming."   50

   Then his bride assistance lent him,
And advice the maiden gave him :
" O thou smith, O Ilmarinen,
Thou the great primeval craftsman !
Forge thyself a plough all golden,
Cunningly bedecked with silver,
Then go plough the field of serpents,
Where the writhing snakes are swarming."

   Then the smith, e'en Ilmarinen,
Laid the gold upon the anvil,   60
Worked the bellows on the silver,
And he forged the plough he needed,
And he forged him shoes of iron ;
Greaves of steel he next constructed,

And with these his feet he covered,
Those upon his shins he fastened ;
And he donned an iron mail-coat,
With a belt of steel he girt him,
Took a pair of iron gauntlets,
Gauntlets like to stone for hardness ;   70
Then he chose a horse of mettle,
And he yoked the steed so noble,
And he went to plough the acre,
And the open field to furrow.
There he saw the heads all rearing,
Saw the heads that hissed unceasing,
And he spoke the words which follow :
"O thou snake, whom God created,
You who lift your head so proudly,
Who is friendly and will hearken,   80
Rearing up your head so proudly,
And your neck so proudly lifting ;
From my path at once remove you,
Creep, thou wretch, among the stubble,
Creeping down among the bushes,
Or where greenest grass is growing !
If you lift your head from out it,
Ukko then your head shall shatter,
With his sharp and steel-tipped arrows,
With a mighty hail of iron."   90
    Then he ploughed the field of vipers,
Furrowed all the land of serpents,
From the furrows raised the vipers,
Drove the serpents all before him,
And he said, returning homeward :
" I have ploughed the field of vipers,
Furrowed all the land of serpents,
Driven before me all the serpents :
Will you give me now your daughter,
And unite me with my darling ? "   100
    Then did Pohjola's old Mistress,
Answer in the words which follow :
" I will only give the maiden,
And unite you with my daughter,

If you catch the Bear of Tuoni,
Bridle, too, the Wolf of Mana,
Far in Tuonela's great forest,
In the distant realms of Mana.
Hundreds have gone forth to yoke them;
Never one returned in safety."　　　　　　110
　　Then the smith, e'en Ilmarinen,
Sought the maiden in her chamber,
And he spoke the words which follow:
"Now the task is laid upon me,
Manala's fierce wolves to bridle,
And to hunt the bears of Tuoni,
Far in Tuonela's great forest,
In the distant realms of Mana."
　　Then his bride assistance lent him,
And advice the maiden gave him.　　　　　120
"O thou smith, O Ilmarinen,
Thou the great primeval craftsman!
Forge thee bits, of steel the hardest,
Forge thee muzzles wrought of iron,
Sitting on a rock in water,
Where the cataracts fall all foaming.
Hunt thou then the Bears of Tuoni,
And the Wolves of Mana bridle."
　　Then the smith, e'en Ilmarinen,
He the great primeval craftsman,　　　　　130
Forged him bits, of steel the hardest,
Forged him muzzles wrought of iron,
Sitting on a rock in water,
Where the cataracts fall all foaming.
　　Then he went the beasts to fetter,
And he spoke the words which follow:
"Terhenetär, Cloudland's daughter!
With the cloud-sieve sift thou quickly,
And disperse thy mists around me,
Where the beasts I seek are lurking,　　　140
That they may not hear me moving,
That they may not flee before me."
　　Then the Wolf's great jaws he muzzled,
And with iron the Bear he fettered,

On the barren heaths of Tuoni,
In the blue depths of the forest.
And he said, returning homeward:
"Give me now your daughter, old one.
Here I bring the Bear of Tuoni,
And the Wolf of Mana muzzled."   150
     Then did Pohjola's old Mistress
Answer in the words which follow:
"I will give you first the duckling,
And the blue-winged duck will give you,
When the pike, so huge and scaly,
He the fish so plump and floundering,
You shall bring from Tuoni's river,
And from Manala's abysses;
But without a net to lift it,
Using not a hand to grasp it.   160
Hundreds have gone forth to seek it,
Never one returned in safety."
     Then there came distress upon him,
And affliction overwhelmed him,
As he sought the maiden's chamber,
And he spoke the words which follow:
"Now a task is laid upon me,
Greater still than all the former;
For the pike, so huge and scaly,
He the fish so plump and floundering,   170
I must bring from Tuoni's river,
From the eternal stream of Mana,
But with neither snare nor drag-net,
Nor with help of other tackle."
     Then his bride assistance lent him,
And advice the maiden gave him.
"O thou smith, O Ilmarinen,
Do thou not be so despondent!
Forge thee now a fiery eagle,
Forge a bird of fire all flaming!   180
This the mighty pike shall capture,
Drag the fish so plump and floundering,
From the murky stream of Tuoni,
And from Manala's abysses."

Then the smith, e'en Ilmarinen,
Deathless artist of the smithy,
Forged himself a fiery eagle,
Forged a bird of fire all flaming,
And of iron he forged the talons,
Forged the claws of steel the hardest,   190
Wings like sides of boat constructed ;
Then upon the wings he mounted,
On the eagle's back he sat him,
On the wing-bones of the eagle.

Then he spoke unto the eagle,
And the mighty bird instructed :
"O my eagle, bird I fashioned,
Fly thou forth, where I shall order,
To the turbid stream of Tuoni,
And to Manala's abysses :   200
Seize the pike, so huge and scaly,
He the fish so plump and floundering."

Then the bird, that noble eagle,
Took his flight, and upward soaring,
Forth he flew the pike to capture,
Fish with teeth of size terrific,
In the river-depths of Tuoni,
Down in Manala's abysses :
To the water stretched a pinion,
And the other touched the heavens ;   210
In the sea he dipped his talons,
On the cliffs his beak he whetted.

Thus the smith, e'en Ilmarinen,
Journeyed forth to seek his booty
In the depths of Tuoni's river,
While the eagle watched beside him.
From the water rose a kelpie
And it clutched at Ilmarinen,
By the neck the eagle seized it,
And the kelpie's head he twisted.   220
To the bottom down he forced it,
To the black mud at the bottom.

Then came forth the pike of Tuoni,
And the water-dog came onward.

Not a small pike of the smallest,
Nor a large pike of the largest;
Long his tongue as twain of axe-shafts,
Long his teeth as rake-shaft measures,
Wide his gorge as three great rivers,
Seven boats' length his back extended,   230
And the smith he sought to scize on,
And to swallow Ilmarinen.

But the eagle rushed against him,
And the bird of air attacked him ;
Not an eagle of the small ones,
Nor an eagle of the large ones.
Long his beak as hundred fathoms,
Wide his gorge as six great rivers,
Six spears' length his tongue extended,
Five scythes' length his talons measured   240
And he saw the pike so scaly,
Saw the fish so plump and floundering.
Fiercely on the fish he darted,
Rushed against the fish so scaly.

Then the pike so large and scaly,
He the fish so plump and floundering,
Tried to drag the eagle's pinions
Underneath the sparkling waters,
But the eagle swift ascended,
Up into the air he raised him,   250
From the grimy ooze he raised him,
To the sparkling water o'er it.

Back and forth the eagle hovered,
And again he made an effort,
And he struck one talon fiercely
In the pike's terrific shoulders,
In the water-dog's great backbone,
And he fixed the other talon
Firmly in the steel-hard mountain,
In the rocks as hard as iron.   260
From the stone slipped off the talon,
Slipped from off the rocky mountain,
And the pike again dived downward,
In the water slid the monster,

I—H 259

Slipped from off the eagle's talons,
From the great bird's claws terrific,
But his sides were scored most deeply,
And his shoulders cleft asunder.

Once again, with iron talons,
Swooped again the furious eagle,   270
With his wings all fiery glowing,
And his eyes like flame that sparkled,
Seized the pike with mighty talons,
Grasped the water-dog securely,
Dragged the huge and scaly monster,
Raised him from the tossing water,
From the depths beneath the billows,
To the water's sparkling surface.

Then the bird with claws of iron
Made a third and final effort,   280
Brought the mighty pike of Tuoni,
He the fish so plump and floundering,
From the river dark of Tuoni,
And from Manala's abysses.
Scarce like water flowed the water
From the great pike's scales stupendous;
Nor like air the air extended
When the great bird flapped his pinions.

Thus the iron-taloned eagle
Bore the pike so huge and scaly,   290
To the branches of an oak-tree,
To a pine-tree's crown, wide spreading.
There he feasted on the booty,
Open ripped the fish's belly,
Tore away the fish's breastbone,
And the head and neck he sundered.

Said the smith, said Ilmarinen,
"O thou wicked, wicked eagle,
What a faithless bird I find you,
You have seized upon the quarry,   300
And have feasted on the booty,
Open ripped the fish's belly,
Torn away the fish's breastbone,
And the head and neck have sundered."

But the iron-taloned eagle
Rose and soared away in fury,
High aloft in air he raised him,
To the borders of the cloudland.
Fled the clouds, the heavens were thundering,
And the props of air bowed downward :   310
Ukko's bow in twain was broken,
In the moon the horns sharp-pointed.

Then the smith, e'en Ilmarinen,
Took the pike's head, which he carried,
To the old crone as a present,
And he spoke the words which follow :
"Make of this a chair for ever,
In the halls of lofty Pohja."

Then he spoke the words which follow,
And in words like these expressed him :   320
"I have ploughed the field of serpents,
Furrowed all the land of serpents ;
Bridled, too, the wolves of Mana,
And have chained the bears of Tuoni ;
Brought the pike so huge and scaly,
He the fish so plump and floundering,
From the river deep of Tuoni,
And from Manala's abysses.
Will you give me now the maiden,
And bestow your daughter on me ? "   330

Then said Pohjola's old Mistress,
"Badly have you done your errand,
Thus the head in twain to sever,
Open rip the fish's belly,
Tear away the fish's breastbone,
Feasting thus upon the booty."

Then the smith, e'en Ilmarinen,
Answered in the words that follow :
"Never can you bring, undamaged,
Quarry from the best of regions.   340
This is brought from Tuoni's river,
And from Manala's abysses.
Is not yet the maiden ready,
She for whom I longed and laboured ? "

Then did Pohjola's old Mistress
Answer in the words which follow :
" Yes, the maiden now is ready,
She for whom you longed and laboured.
I will give my tender duckling,
And prepare the duck I cherished,　　　　350
For the smith, for Ilmarinen,
At his side to sit for ever,
On his knee as wife to seat her,
Dove-like in his arms to nestle."

On the floor a child was sitting,
On the floor a child was singing :
" To our room there came already,
Came a bird into our castle ;
From the north-east flew an eagle,
Through the sky a hawk came flying,　　　360
In the air one wing was flapping,
On the sea the other rested,
With his tail he swept the ocean,
And to heaven his head he lifted ;
And he gazed around, and turned him,
Back and forth the eagle hovered,
Perched upon the heroes' castle,
And his beak he whetted on it,
But the roof was formed of iron,
And he could not pierce within it.　　　370
" So he gazed around and turned him,
Back and forth the eagle hovered,
Perched upon the women's castle,
And his beak he whetted on it,
But the roof was formed of copper,
And he could not pierce within it.
" So he gazed around and turned him,
Back and forth the eagle hovered,
Perched upon the maidens' castle,
And his beak he whetted on it,　　　380
And the roof was formed of linen,
And he forced his way within it.
"Then he perched upon the chimney,
Then upon the floor descended,

Pushed aside the castle's shutter,
Sat him at the castle window,
Near the wall, all green his feathers,
In the room, his plumes a hundred.
  "Then he scanned the braidless maidens,
Gazing on the long-haired maiden,   390
On the best of all the maidens,
Fairest maid with hair unbraided,
And her head with beads was shining,
And her head with beauteous blossoms.
  "In his claws the eagle seized her,
And the hawk with talons grasped her,
Seized the best of all the party,
Of the flock of ducks the fairest,
She the sweetest-voiced and tenderest,
She the rosiest and the whitest,   400
She the bird of air selected,
In his talons far he bore her,
She who held her head the highest,
And her form of all the shapeliest,
And her feathers of the finest,
And her plumage of the softest."
  Then did Pohjola's old Mistress
Answer in the words that follow :
"Wherefore dost thou know, my darling,
Or hast heard, my golden apple,   410
How the maiden grew amongst us,
And her flaxen hair waved round her?
Perhaps the maiden shone with silver,
Or the maiden's gold was famous.
Has our sun been shining on you,
Or the moon afar been shining?"
  From the floor the child made answer,
And the growing child responded :
"Therefore did your darling know it,
And your fostling learned to know it.   420
In the far-famed maidens' dwelling,
In the home where dwells the fair one ;
Good report rejoiced the father,
When he launched his largest vessel ;

But rejoices more the mother,
When the largest loaf is baking,
And the wheaten bread is baking,
That the guests may feast profusely.
"Thus it was your darling knew it,
Far around the strangers knew it,   430
How the young maid grew in stature,
And how tall grew up the maiden.
Once I went into the courtyard,
And I wandered to the storehouse,
Very early in the morning,
In the earliest morning hours,
And the soot in streaks ascended,
And the smoke in clouds rose upward,
From the far-famed maiden's dwelling,
From the blooming maiden's homestead,   440
And the maid herself was grinding,
Busy working at the handmill;
Rung the mill like call of cuckoo,
And the pestle quacked like wild geese,
And the sieve like bird was singing,
And the stones like beads were rattling.
"Forth a second time I wandered,
And into the field I wandered,
In the meadow was the maiden,
Stooping o'er the yellow heather;   450
Working at the red-stained dye-pots,
Boiling up the yellow kettles.
"When I wandered forth a third time
Sat the maid beneath the window,
There I heard the maiden weaving,
In her hands the comb was sounding,
And I heard the shuttle flying,
As in cleft of rock the ermine,
And the comb-teeth heard I sounding,
As the wooden shaft was moving,   460
And the weaver's beam was turning,
Like a squirrel in the tree-tops."
Then did Pohjola's old Mistress
Answer in the words which follow:

"Bravo, bravo, dearest maiden,
Have I not for ever told thee,
Not to sing among the pine-trees,
Not to sing amid the valleys,
Not to arch thy neck too proudly,
Nor thy white arms leave uncovered,   470
Nor thy young and beauteous bosom,
Nor thy shape so round and graceful?
    "I have warned thee all the autumn,
And besought thee all the summer,
Likewise in the spring have cautioned,
At the second springtide sowing,
To construct a secret dwelling,
With the windows small and hidden,
Where the maids may do their weaving,
And may work their looms in safety,   480
All unheard by Suomi's gallants,
Suomi's gallants, country lovers."
    From the floor the child made answer,
And the fortnight-old responded:
"Easily a horse is hidden
In the stall, with fine-tailed horses;
Hard it is to hide a maiden,
And to keep her long locks hidden.
Though you build of stone a castle,
And amid the sea shall rear it,   490
Though you keep your maidens in it,
And should rear your darlings in it,
Still the girls cannot be hidden,
Nor attain their perfect stature,
Undisturbed by lusty gallants,
Lusty gallants, country lovers.
Mighty men, with lofty helmets,
Men who shoe with steel their horses."
    Then the aged Väinämöinen
Head bowed down, and deeply grieving: 500
Wandered on his journey homeward,
And he spoke the words which follow:
"Woe is me, a wretched creature,
That I did not learn it sooner,

That in youthful days one weddeth,
And must choose a life-companion.
All thing else a man may grieve for,
Save indeed an early marriage,
When in youth already children,
And a household he must care for."   510

Thus did warn old Väinämöinen,
Cautioned thus Suvantolainen,
That old men against the younger,
Should not struggle for a fair one :
Warned them not to swim too proudly,
Neither try to race in rowing,
Nor to seek to woo a maiden,
With a younger man contending.

Runo XX.—The Great Ox, and the Brewing of the Ale

Argument

An enormous ox is slaughtered in Pohjola (1–118). They brew ale and prepare a feast (119–516). They dispatch messengers to invite the heroes to the wedding, but Lemminkainen is expressly passed over (517–614).

How shall we our song continue,
And what legends shall we tell you?
Thus will we pursue our story ;
These the legends we will tell you ;
How in Pohjola they feasted,
And the drinking-bout was Godlike.

Long prepared they for the wedding,
For the feast provided all things,
In the household famed of Pohja,
Halls of Sariola the misty.   10

What provisions were provided,
What did they collect together,
For a lengthy feast at Pohja,
For the multitude of drinkers,

For the feasting of the people,
For the multitude of feasters?
　In Carelia grew a bullock,
Fat the ox they reared in Suomi,
Not a large one, not a small one,
But a calf of middle stature.　　　　　　　20
While he switched his tail in Häme
Stooped his head to Kemi's river,
Long his horns one hundred fathoms,
Muzzle broad as half a hundred,
For a week there ran an ermine
All along the yoke he carried,
All day long there flew a swallow
'Twixt the mighty ox's horn-tips,
Striving through the space to hasten,
Nor found resting-place between them;　　30
Month-long ran a summer-squirrel
From his neck unto his tail-end,
Nor did he attain the tail-tip,
Till a month had quite passed over.
　'Twas this calf of size stupendous,
'Twas this mighty bull of Suomi,
Whom they led forth from Carelia
Till they reached the fields of Pohja.
By his horns, a hundred led him,
And a thousand dragged his muzzle,　　40
And they led the ox still further,
Till to Pohjola they brought him.
　On his road the ox proceeded,
By the Sound of Sariola strayed;
Browsed the grass in marshy places,
While his back the clouds were touching;
But they could not find a butcher
Who could fell the country's marvel
On the list of Suomi's children,
'Mid the mighty host of people,　　　　50
Not among the youthful people,
Nor among the very aged.
　From afar an old man journeyed,
Virokannas from Carelia;

And he spoke the words which follow:
"Wait thou, wait, thou ox unhappy,
While I go and fetch my mallet.
If I strike you with my mallet
On the skull, unhappy creature,
Never in another summer, 60
Would you turn about your muzzle,
Or your tail would jerk around you,
Here among the fields of Pohja,
By the Sound of Sariola stray."

Then the old man went to strike him,
Virokannas moved against him,
Went to slay the ox unhappy;
But his head the ox was turning,
And his black eyes he was blinking.
To a pine-tree sprang the old man, 70
Virokannas in the bushes,
In the scrubby willow-thicket.

After this they sought a butcher,
Who the mighty ox could slaughter,
From Carelia's lovely country,
From the vast expanse of Suomi,
From the peaceful land of Russia,
From the hardy land of Sweden,
From the regions wide of Lapland,
From the mighty land of Turja, 80
And they sought through Tuoni's regions,
In the depths of Mana's kingdom,
And they sought, but no one found they,
Long they searched, but vainly searched they.

Yet again they sought a butcher,
Sought again to find a slaughterer,
On the ocean's shining surface,
On the wide-extending billows.
From the dark sea rose a hero,
Rose a hero from the sea-swell, 90
From the shining surface rising,
From the wide expanse of water.
He was not among the greatest,
But in nowise of the smallest.

In a bowl would he lie sleeping,
And beneath a sieve stand upright.
   'Twas an old man, iron-fisted,
Iron-coloured, too, to gaze on ;
On his head a stony helmet ;
Shoes of stone his feet protected ;   100
In his hand a knife, gold-bladed,
And the haft o'erlaid with copper.
   Thus the people found a butcher,
And at length they found a slaughterer,
Who should fell the bull of Suomi,
And should fell the country's marvel.
Scarce had he beheld the quarry,
Than at once his neck he shattered,
On his knees he forced the bullock,
And upon his side he threw him.   110
Did he yield them much provisions ?
Not so very much he yielded.
Of his flesh a hundred barrels,
And a hundred fathoms sausage ;
Seven boat-loads of blood they gathered,
Six large casks with fat were loaded,
All for Pohjola's great banquet,
Feast of Sariola the misty.
   Then they built a house in Pohja,
Built a house with hall enormous,   120
Fathoms nine its sides extended,
And the breadth thereof was seven.
If a cock crowed at the smoke-hole,
Underneath they could not hear it,
If a dog at end was barking,
At the door they did not hear it.
   Then did Pohjola's old Mistress
Walk across the flooring's planking,
To the middle of the chamber,
And she pondered and reflected :   130
" How shall I get ale sufficient,
And shall brew the beer most wisely,
To prepare it for the wedding,
When the beer will much be needed ?

How to brew the beer I know not,
Nor how ale was first concocted."
    By the stove there sat an old man,
From the stove spoke up the old man:
"Ale of barley is concocted,
And the drink with hops is flavoured,   140
Yet they brew not save with water,
And the aid of furious fire.
    "Hop is called the son of Revel;
Planted in the ground when little,
With a plough they ploughed the region,
Like an ant, away they cast him
Close to Kaleva's great well-spring,
There where Osmo's field is sloping;
There the tender plant sprang upward,
And the green shoot mounted quickly.   150
Up a little tree it mounted,
Rising to the leafy summit.
    "Sowed, by chance, an old man barley,
In the fresh-ploughed field of Osmo,
And the barley sprouted bravely,
And it grew and flourished greatly,
On the new-ploughed field of Osmo,
Kaleva's descendant's cornland.
    "But a little time passed over,
When the hops exclaimed from tree-top,   160
And upon the field the barley,
And in Kaleva's well-water,
'When shall we be yoked together,
Each with other be united?
Life in solitude is weary;
Better two or three together.'
    "Osmotar, the ale-constructer
She, the maid who beer concocted,
Took, on this, the grains of barley,
Gathered six of grains of barley,   170
Seven hop-tassels next she gathered,
And eight ladles took of water,
Then upon the fire she placed it,
And allowed it there to simmer,

And she boiled the ale of barley
Through the fleeting days of summer,
Out upon the cloudy headland,
Cape upon the shady island;
Poured it then in wooden barrels,
And in tubs of birchwood stored it.   180
   "Thus she brewed the ale and stored it,
But the ale was not fermented,
And she pondered and reflected,
And she spoke the words which follow:
'What must now be added to it,
What is needful to provide for,
That the ale may be fermented,
And the beer be brought to foaming?'
   "Kalevatar, beauteous maiden,
She the maid with slender fingers,   190
Which she ever moves so deftly,
She whose feet are shod so lightly,
Felt about the seams of staving,
Groping all about the bottom,
Trying one and then the other,
In the midst of both the kettles;
Found a splinter at the bottom,
From the bottom took a splinter.
   "Then she turned it and reflected:
'What might perhaps be fashioned from it,   200
In the hands of lovely maiden,
In the noble damsel's fingers,
Brought into the hands of maiden,
To the noble damsel's fingers?'
   "In her hands the maiden took it,
In the noble damsel's fingers,
And she clapped her hands together,
Both her hands she rubbed together,
Rubbed them on her thighs together,
And a squirrel white created.   210
   "Then she gave her son directions,
And instructed thus the squirrel:
'O thou squirrel, gold of woodlands,
Flower of woodlands, charm of country,

Speed thou forth where I shall bid thee,
Where I bid thee and direct thee,
Forth to Metsola's bright regions,
And to Tapiola's great wisdom.
There a little tree upclimbing,
Heedful to the leafy summit,   220
That the eagle may not seize thee,
Nor the bird of air may grasp thee.
From the pine-tree bring me pine-cones,
From the fir bring shoots of fir-tree,
Bring them to the hands of maiden,
For the beer of Osmo's daughter.'

" Knew the squirrel now his pathway,
Trailed his bushy tail behind him,
And his journey soon accomplished,
Quickly through the open spaces,   230
Past one wood, and then a second,
And a third he crossed obliquely,
Into Metsola's bright regions,
And to Tapiola's great wisdom.

" There he saw three lofty pine-trees,
There he saw four slender fir-trees,
Climbed a pine-tree in the valley,
On the heath he climbed a fir-tree,
And the eagle did not seize him,
Nor the bird of air did grasp him.   240

" From the pine he broke the pine-cones,
From the fir the leafy tassels,
In his claws he hid the pine-cones,
And within his paws he rolled them,
To the maiden's hands he brought them,
To the noble damsel's fingers.

" In the beer the maiden laid them,
In the ale she placed them likewise,
But the ale was not fermented,
Nor the fresh drink yet was working.   250

" Osmotar, the ale-preparer,
She, the maid who beer concocted,
Pondered yet again the matter.
'What must now be added to it,

That the ale shall be fermented,
And the beer be brought to foaming?'
　"Kalevatar, beauteous maiden,
She, the maid with slender fingers,
Which she ever moves so deftly,
She whose feet are shod so lightly,　　　　260
Felt about the seams of staving,
Groping all about the bottom,
Trying one, and then the other,
In the midst of both the kettles,
Found a chip upon the bottom,
Took the chip from off the bottom.
　"Then she turned it and reflected,
'What might perhaps be fashioned from it,
In the hands of lovely maiden,
In the noble damsel's fingers,　　　　270
Brought into the hands of maiden,
To the noble damsel's fingers?'
　"In her hands the maiden took it
In the noble damsel's fingers,
And she clapped her hands together,
Both her hands she rubbed together,
Rubbed them on her thighs together,
And she made a gold-breast marten.
　"Thus the marten she instructed,
Thus the orphan child directed:　　　　280
'O my marten, O my birdling,
O my fair one, beauteous-hided!
Thither go, where I shall bid thee,
Where I bid thee, and direct thee,
To the Bear's own rocky cavern,
Where the forest bears are prowling,
Where the bears are always fighting,
Where they lurk in all their fierceness.
With thy hands scrape foam together,
In thy paws the foam then carry,　　　　290
To the maiden's hands convey it,
And to Osmo's daughter's shoulders.'
　"Understood the way the marten,
Forth the golden-breasted hastened,

And his journey soon accomplished,
Quickly through the open spaces,
Past one wood, and then a second,
And a third he crossed obliquely,
To the Bear's own rocky cavern,
To the caverns bear-frequented,   300
Where the bears are always fighting,
Where they lurk in all their fierceness,
In the rocks as hard as iron,
And among the steel-hard mountains.
  "From the bears' mouths foam was dropping,
From their furious jaws exuding;
In his hands the foam he gathered,
With his paws the foam collected,
To the maiden's hands he brought it,
To the noble damsel's fingers.   310
  "In the ale the maiden poured it,
In the beer she poured it likewise,
But the ale was not fermented,
Nor the drink of men foamed over.
  "Osmotar, the ale-preparer,
She the maid who beer concocted,
Pondered yet again the matter,
'What must now be added to it,
That the ale shall be fermented,
And the beer be brought to foaming?   320
  "Kalevatar, beauteous maiden,
She the maid with slender fingers,
Which she ever moves so deftly,
She whose feet are shod so lightly
Felt about the seams of staving,
Groping all about the bottom,
Trying one and then the other,
Then the space between the kettles,
And a mustard-pod she saw there;
From the ground the pod she lifted.   330
  "Then she turned it, and surveyed it,
'What might perhaps be fashioned from it,
In the hands of lovely maiden,
In the noble damsel's fingers,

Brought into the hands of maiden,
To the noble damsel's fingers?'
　" In her hands the maiden took it,
In the noble damsel's fingers,
And she clapped her hands together,
Both her hands she rubbed together,   340
Rubbed them on her thighs together,
And a bee she thus created.
　" And the bee she thus instructed,
And the bee she thus directed :
' O thou bee, thou bird so nimble,
King of all the flowery meadows,
Thither fly, where I shall bid thee,
Where I bid thee and direct thee,
To an isle on ocean's surface,
Where the reefs arise from ocean.   350
There a maiden lies in slumber,
With her belt of copper loosened ;
By her side springs sweetest herbage,
On her lap rest honey grasses.
On thy wings bring sweetest honey,
Bring thou honey on thy clothing,
From the fairest of the herbage,
From the bloom of golden flowerets,
To the maiden's hands convey it,
And to Osmo's daughter's shoulders.'   360
　" Then the bee, that bird so nimble,
Flew away, and hastened onward,
And his journey soon accomplished,
Speeding o'er the open spaces,
First across the sea, along it,
Then in an oblique direction,
To an isle on ocean's surface,
Where the reefs arise from ocean.
There he saw the maiden sleeping,
With a tin brooch on her bosom,   370
Resting in an unmowed meadow,
All among the fields of honey ;
By her side grew golden grasses,
At her belt sprang silver grasses.

" Then he soaked his wings with honey,
Plunged his plumes in liquid honey,
From the brightest of the herbage,
From the tips of golden flowerets ;
To the maiden's hands he brought it,
To the noble damsel's fingers.   380

" In the ale the maiden cast it,
In the beer she poured it likewise,
And the beer at length fermented,
And the fresh drink now foamed upward,
From within the new-made barrels,
From within the tubs of birchwood,
Foaming upward to the handles,
Rushing over all the edges ;
To the ground it wished to trickle,
And upon the floor ran downward.   390

" But a little time passed over,
Very little time passed over,
When the heroes flocked to drink it,
Chief among them Lemminkainen.
Drunk was Ahti, drunk was Kauko,
Drunken was the ruddy rascal,
With the ale of Osmo's daughter,
And the beer of Kalevatar.

" Osmotar, the ale-preparer,
She, the maid who beer concocted,   400
Uttered then the words which follow :
' Woe is me, my day is wretched,
For I brewed the ale so badly
And the beer so ill concocted,
That from out the tubs 'tis flowing,
And upon the floor is gushing.'

" From a tree there sang a bullfinch,
From the roof-tree sang a throstle,
' No, the ale is not so worthless ;
'Tis the best of ale for drinking ;   410
If into the casks you pour it,
And should store it in the cellar,
Store it in the casks of oakwood,
And within the hoops of copper.

"Thus was ale at first created,
Beer of Kaleva concocted,
Therefore is it praised so highly,
Therefore held in greatest honour,
For the ale is of the finest,
Best of drinks for prudent people;　　420
Women soon it brings to laughter,
Men it warms into good humour,
And it makes the prudent merry,
But it brings the fools to raving."

Then did Pohjola's old Mistress,
When she heard how ale was fashioned,
Water pour in tubs the largest,
Half she filled the new-made barrels,
Adding barley as 'twas needed,
Shoots of hop enough she added,　　430
And the ale began she brewing,
And the beer began its working,
In the new tubs that contained it,
And within the tubs of birchwood.

'Twas for months the stones were glowing,
And for summers water boiling,
Trees were burning on the islands,
Water from the wells was carried.
Bare of trees they left the islands,
And the lakes were greatly shrunken,　　440
For the ale was in the barrels,
And the beer was stored securely
For the mighty feast of Pohja,
For carousing at the mansion.

From the island smoke was rising,
On the headland fire was glowing;
Thick the clouds of smoke were rising,
In the air there rose the vapour.
For the fire was burning fiercely,
And the fire was brightly glowing,　　450
Half it filled the land of Pohja,
Over all Carelia spreading.

All the people gazed upon it,
Gazed, and then they asked each other,

" Wherefore is the smoke arising,
In the air the vapour rising?
'Tis too small for smoke of battle,
'Tis too large for herdsman's bonfire."
Then rose Lemminkainen's mother,
At the earliest dawn of morning,   460
And she went to fetch some water.
Clouds of smoke she saw arising,
Up from Pohjola's dominions,
And she spoke the words which follow :
" Perhaps it is the smoke of combat,
Perhaps it is the fire of battle."
Ahti, dweller on the island,
He the handsome Kaukomieli,
Wandered round and gazed about him,
And he pondered and reflected,   470
" I must go and look upon it,
From a nearer spot examine,
Whence the smoke is thus ascending
Filling all the air with vapour,
If it be the smoke of combat,
If it be the fire of battle."
Kauko went to gaze about him,
And to learn whence smoke was rising,
But it was not fire of battle,
Neither was it fire of combat,   480
But 'twas fire where ale was brewing,
Likewise where the beer was brewing,
Near where Sound of Sariola spreads,
Out upon the jutting headland.
Then did Kauko gaze around him,
And one eye he rolled obliquely,
And he squinted with the other,
And his mouth he pursed up slowly,
And at last he spoke, while gazing,
And across the sound he shouted,   490
" O my dearest foster-mother,
Pohjola's most gracious Mistress !
Brew thou ale of extra goodness,
Brew thou beer the best of any,

For carousing at the mansion,
Specially for Lemminkainen,
At my wedding, now preparing,
With thy young and lovely daughter."
Now the ale was quite fermented,
And the drink of men was ripened,   500
And the red ale stored they safely,
And the good beer stored securely.
Underneath the ground they stored it,
Stored it in the rocky cellars,
In the casks of oak constructed,
And behind the taps of copper.
Then did Pohjola's old Mistress
All the food provide for feasting,
And the kettles all were singing,
And the stewpans all were hissing,   510
And large loaves of bread were baking,
And she stirred great pots of porridge,
Thus to feed the crowds of people,
At the banquet at the mansion,
At the mighty feast of Pohja,
The carouse at Sariola dim.
Now the bread they baked was ready,
And were stirred the pots of porridge,
And a little time passed over,
Very little time passed over,   520
When the ale worked in the barrels,
And the beer foamed in the cellars,
" Now must some one come to drink me,
Now must some one come to taste me,
That my fame may be reported,
And that they may sing my praises."
Then they went to seek a minstrel,
Went to seek a famous singer,
One whose voice was of the strongest,
One who knew the finest legends.   530
First to sing they tried a salmon,
If the voice of trout was strongest ;
Singing is not work for salmon,
And the pike recites no legends.

Crooked are the jaws of salmon,
And the teeth of pike spread widely.
    Yet again they sought a singer,
Went to seek a famous singer,
One whose voice was of the strongest,
One who knew the finest legends,   540
And they took a child for singer,
Thought a boy might sing the strongest.
Singing is not work for children,
Nor are splutterers fit for shouting.
Crooked are the tongues of children,
And the roots thereof are crooked.
    Then the red ale grew indignant,
And the fresh drink fell to cursing,
Pent within the oaken barrels,
And behind the taps of copper.   550
"If you do not find a minstrel,
Do not find a famous singer,
One whose voice is of the strongest,
One who knows the finest legends,
Then the hoops I'll burst asunder,
And among the dust will trickle."
    Then did Pohjola's old Mistress
Send the guests their invitations,
Sent her messengers to journey,
And she spoke the words which follow :   560
"O my maid, of all the smallest,
O my waiting-maid obedient,
Call the people all together,
To the great carouse invite them,
Call the poor, and call the needy,
Call the blind, and call the wretched,
Call the lame, and call the cripples ;
In the boat row thou the blind men ;
Bring the lame ones here on horseback,
And in sledges bring the cripples.   570
    "Ask thou all the folk of Pohja,
And of Kaleva the people :
Ask the aged Väinämöinen,
Greatest he of all the minstrels,

Only ask not Lemminkainen,
Ask not Ahti Saarelainen."
    Then the maid, of all the smallest,
Answered in the words which follow:
"Wherefore ask not Lemminkainen,
Only Ahti Saarelainen?"   580
    Then did Pohjola's old Mistress,
In these very words make answer:
"Therefore ask not Kaukomieli,
Not the reckless Lemminkainen.
He is always quick to quarrel,
And to fight is always ready.
And at weddings works he mischief,
And at banquets grievous scandal,
Brings to shame the modest maidens,
Clad in all their festive garments."   590
    Then the maid, of all the smallest,
Answered in the words which follow:
"How shall I know Kaukomieli
That I leave him uninvited?
For I know not Ahti's dwelling,
Nor the house of Kaukomieli."
    Then did Pohjola's old Mistress,
Answer in the words which follow:
"Easy may you hear of Kauko,
Learn of Ahti Saarelainen.   600
Ahti dwells upon an island,
Dwells the rascal near the water,
Where the bay outspreads the broadest,
At the curve of Kauko's headland."
    Then the maid, of all the smallest,
She the handmaid hired for money,
Bid the guests from six directions,
And in eight the news she carried;
All she asked of Pohja's people,
And of Kaleva the people,   610
Of the householders the poorest,
And the poorest clad amongst them,
Only not the youth named Ahti,
For she left him uninvited.

RUNO XXI.—THE WEDDING FEAST AT POHJOLA

Argument

The bridegroom and his party are received at Pohjola (1-226). The guests are hospitably entertained with abundance of food and drink (227-252). Väinämöinen sings and praises the people of the house (253-438).

THEN did Pohjola's old Mistress,
Crone of Sariola the misty,
Sometimes out of doors employ her,
Sometimes in the house was busied ;
And she heard how whips were cracking,
On the shore heard sledges rattling,
And her eyes she turned to northward,
Towards the sun her head then turning,
And she pondered and reflected,
"Wherefore are these people coming   10
On my shore, to me unhappy ?
Is it perhaps a hostile army ? "
　　So she went to gaze around her,
And observe the portent nearer ;
It was not a hostile army,
But of guests a great assembly,
And her son-in-law amid them,
With a mighty host of people.
　　Then did Pohjola's old Mistress,
Crone of Sariola the misty,   20
When she saw the bridegroom's party,
Speak aloud the words which follow :
"As I thought, the wind was blowing
And a faggot-stack o'erthrowing,
On the beach the billows breaking,
On the strand the shingle rattling.
So I went to gaze around me,
And observe the portent nearer ;
But I found no wind was blowing,
Nor the faggot-stack was falling,   30

On the beach no waves were breaking,
On the strand no shingle rattling.
'Twas my son-in-law's assemblage,
Twice a hundred men in number.
  " How shall I detect the bridegroom
In the concourse of the people?
He is known among the people,
As in clumps of trees the cherry,
Like an oak-tree in the thickets,
Or the moon, 'mid stars in heaven.   40
  " Black the steed that he is driving;
Which a ravenous wolf resembles;
Or a raven, keen for quarry,
Or a lark, with fluttering pinions.
Six there are of golden song-birds,
On his shafts all sweetly singing,
And of blue birds, seven are singing
Sitting on the sledge's traces."
  From the road was heard a clatter,
Past the well the runners rattled,   50
In the court arrived the bridegroom,
In the yard the people with him,
In the midst appeared the bridegroom,
With the greatest of the party.
He was not the first among them,
But by no means last among them.
  " Off, ye youths, and out, ye heroes,
To the court, O ye who loiter,
That ye may remove the breastbands,
And the traces ye may loosen,   60
That the shafts may quick be lowered:
Lead into the house the bridegroom."
  Then the bridegroom's horse sped onward,
And the bright-hued sledge drew forward
Through the courtyard of the Master,
When said Pohjola's old Mistress:
" O my man, whom I have hired,
Best among the village servants,
Take the horse that brought the bridegroom,
With the white mark on his frontlet,   70

From the copper-plated harness,
From the tin-decked breastband likewise,
From the best of reins of leather,
And from harness of the finest.
Lead the courser of the bridegroom,
And with greatest care conduct him
By the reins, of silken fabric,
By the bridle, decked with silver,
To the softest place for rolling,
Where the meadow is the smoothest,   80
Where the drifted snow is finest,
And the land of milky whiteness.

"Lead the bridegroom's horse to water,
To the spring that flows the nearest,
Where the water all unfrozen,
Gushes forth, like milk the sweetest,
'Neath the roots of golden pine-trees,
Underneath the bushy fir-trees.

"Fodder thou the bridegroom's courser,
From the golden bowl of fodder,   90
From the bowl adorned with copper,
With the choicest meal of barley,
And with well-boiled wheat of summer,
And with pounded rye of summer.

"Then conduct the bridegroom's courser
To the best of all the stables,
To the best of resting-places,
To the hindmost of the stables.
Tether there the bridegroom's courser,
To the ring of gold constructed,   100
To the smaller ring of iron,
To the post of curving birchwood,
Place before the bridegroom's courser,
Next a tray with oats o'erloaded,
And with softest hay another,
And a third with chaff the finest.

"Curry then the bridegroom's courser,
With the comb of bones of walrus,
That the hair remain uninjured,
Nor his handsome tail be twisted;   110

Cover then the bridegroom's courser
With a cloth of silver fabric,
And a mat of golden texture,
And a horse-wrap decked with copper.
  "Now my little village laddies,
To the house conduct the bridegroom,
Gently lift his hat from off him,
From his hands his gloves take likewise.
  "I would fain see if the bridegroom
Presently the house can enter,   120
Ere the doors are lifted from it,
And they have removed the doorposts,
And have lifted up the crossbars,
And the threshold has been sunken,
And the nearer walls are broken,
And the floor-planks have been shifted.
  "But the house suits not the bridegroom,
Nor the great gift suits the dwelling,
Till the doors are lifted from it,
And they have removed the doorposts,   130
And have lifted up the crossbars,
And the threshold has been sunken,
And the nearer walls been broken,
And the flooring-planks been shifted,
For the bridegroom's head is longer,
And the bridegroom's ears are higher.
  "Let the crossbars then be lifted,
That his head the roof may touch not,
Let the threshold now be sunken,
That his footsoles may not touch it,   140
Let them now set back the doorposts,
That the doors may open widely,
When at length the bridegroom enters,
When the noble youth approaches.
  "Praise, O Jumala most gracious,
For the bridegroom now has entered.
I would now the house examine,
Cast my gaze around within it,
See that washed are all the tables,
And the benches swabbed with water,   150

Scoured the smooth planks of the boarding,
And the flooring swept and polished.
  " Now that I the house examine,
'Tis so changed I scarcely know it,
From what wood the room was fashioned,
How the roof has been constructed,
And the walls have been erected,
And the flooring been constructed.

  " Side-walls are of bones of hedgehog,
Hinder-walls of bones of reindeer,   160
Front-walls of the bones of glutton,
And of bones of lamb the crossbar.
All the beams are wood of apple,
And the posts of curving birchwood,
Round the stove rest water-lilies,
Scales of bream compose the ceiling.

  " And one bench is formed of iron,
Others made from Saxon timber,
Gold-inlaid are all the tables ;
Floor o'erspread with silken carpets.   170

  " And the stove is bright with copper,
And the stove-bench stone-constructed,
And the hearth composed of boulders,
And with Kaleva's tree is boarded."

  Then the house the bridegroom entered,
Hastened on beneath the roof-tree,
And he spoke the words which follow :
"Grant, O Jumala, thy blessing
Underneath this noble roof-tree,
Underneath this roof so splendid."   180

  Then said Pohjola's old Mistress,
" Hail, all hail, to thee, who enters
In this room of small dimensions,
In this very lowly cottage,
In this wretched house of firwood,
In this house of pine constructed.

  " O my little waiting-maiden,
Thou the village maid I hired,
Bring a piece of lighted birchbark,
To a tarry torch apply it,   190

That I may behold the bridegroom,
And the bridegroom's eyes examine,
Whether they are blue or reddish;
Whether they are white as linen."
    Then the little waiting-maiden,
She, the little village maiden,
Brought a piece of lighted birchbark,
To a tarry torch applied it.
"From the bark the flame springs spluttering,
From the tar black smoke's ascending,   200
So his eyes might perhaps be sooted,
And his handsome face be blackened,
Therefore bring a torch all flaming,
Of the whitest wax constructed."
    Then the little waiting-maiden,
She the little village maiden,
Lit a torch, and brought it flaming,
Of the whitest wax constructed.
    White like wax the smoke was rising,
And the flame ascended brightly,   210
And the bridegroom's eyes were shining,
And his face was all illumined.
"Now the bridegroom's eyes I gaze on!
They are neither blue nor reddish,
Neither are they white like linen,
But his eyes they shine like lake-foam,
Like the lake-reed are they brownish,
And as lovely as the bulrush.
    "Now my little village laddies,
Hasten to conduct the bridegroom   220
To a seat among the highest,
To a place the most distinguished,
With his back towards the blue wall,
With his face towards the red board,
There among the guests invited,
Facing all the shouting people."
    Then did Pohjola's old Mistress,
Feast her guests in noble fashion,
Feast them on the best of butter,
And with cream-cakes in abundance;   230

Thus she served the guests invited,
And among them first the bridegroom.
　On the plates was placed the salmon,
At the sides the pork was stationed,
Dishes filled to overflowing,
Laden to the very utmost,
Thus to feast the guests invited ;
And among them first the bridegroom.
　Then said Pohjola's old Mistress,
"O my little waiting-maiden,　　　　　　　　　240
Bring me now the ale in measures,
Bring it in the jugs two-handled,
For the guests we have invited,
And the bridegroom chief among them."
　Then the little waiting-maiden,
She, the servant hired for money,
Brought the measures as directed,
Handed round the five-hooped tankards,
Till, with ale from hops concocted,
All the beards with foam were whitened ;　　250
All the beards of guests invited ;
And among them most the bridegroom's.
　What about the ale was spoken,
Of the ale in five-hooped tankards,
When at length it reached the minstrel,
Reached the greatest of the singers,
He the aged Väinämöinen,
First and oldest of the singers,
He the minstrel most illustrious,
He the greatest of the Sages ?　　　　　　　260
　First of all the ale he lifted,
Then he spoke the words which follow :
"O thou ale, thou drink delicious,
Let the drinkers not be moody !
Urge the people on to singing,
Let them shout, with mouth all golden,
Till our lords shall wonder at it,
And our ladies ponder o'er it,
For the songs already falter,
And the joyous tongues are silenced.　　　　270

When the ale is ill-concocted,
And bad drink is set before us,
Then the minstrels fail in singing,
And the best of songs they sing not,
And our cherished guests are silent,
And the cuckoos call no longer.

"Therefore who shall chant unto us,
And whose tongue shall sing unto us,
At the wedding feast of Pohja,
This carouse at Sariola held?　　　　　　280
Benches will not sing unto us,
Save when people sit upon them,
Nor will floors hold cheerful converse,
Save when people walk upon them,
Neither are the windows joyful,
If the lords should gaze not from them,
Nor resound the table's edges,
If men sit not round the tables,
Neither do the smoke-holes echo,
If men sit not 'neath the smoke-holes."　　290

On the floor a child was sitting,
On the stove-bench sat a milkbeard,
From the floor exclaimed the infant,
And the boy spoke from the stove-bench:
"I am not in years a father,
Undeveloped yet my body,
But however small I may be,
If the other big ones sing not,
And the stouter men will shout not,
And the rosier cheeked will sing not,　　300
Then I'll sing, although a lean boy,
Though a thin boy, I will whistle,
I will sing, though weak and meagre,
Though my stomach is not rounded,
That the evening may be cheerful,
And the day may be more honoured."

By the stove there sat an old man,
And he spoke the words which follow:
"That the children sing befits not,
Nor these feeble folk should carol.　　　310

Children's songs are only falsehoods,
And the songs of girls are foolish.
Let the wisest sing among us,
Who upon the bench is seated."

Then the aged Väinämöinen,
Answered in the words which follow:
"Are there any who are youthful,
Of the noblest of the people,
Who will clasp their hands together,
Hook their hands in one another, 320
And begin to speak unto us,
Swaying back and forth in singing,
That the day may be more joyful,
And the evening be more blessed?

From the stove there spoke the old man,
"Never was it heard among us,
Never heard or seen among us,
Nor so long as time existed,
That there lived a better minstrel,
One more skilled in all enchantment, 330
Than myself when I was warbling,
As a child when I was singing,
Singing sweetly by the water,
Making all the heath re-echo,
Chanting loudly in the firwood,
Talking likewise in the forest.

"Then my voice was loud and tuneful,
And its tones were most melodious,
Like the flowing of a river,
Or the murmur of a streamlet, 340
Gliding as o'er snow the snowshoes,
Like a yacht across the billows;
But 'tis hard for me to tell you
How my wisdom has departed,
How my voice so strong has failed me,
And its sweetness has departed.
Now it flows no more like river,
Rising like the tossing billows,
But it halts like rake in stubble,
Like the hoe among the pine-roots, 350

Like a sledge in sand embedded,
Or a boat on rocks when stranded."
　　Then the aged Väinämöinen
In such words as these expressed him:
"If no other bard comes forward
To accompany my singing,
Then alone my songs I'll carol,
And will now commence my singing,
For to sing was I created,
As an orator was fashioned;　　　　　　　　360
How, I ask not in the village,
Nor I learn my songs from strangers."
　　Then the aged Väinämöinen
Of the song the lifelong pillar,
Set him to the pleasant labour,
Girt him for the toil of singing,
Loud he sang his songs so pleasing,
Loud he spoke his words of wisdom.
　　Sang the aged Väinämöinen,
Sang by turns, and spoke his wisdom,　　　370
Nor did words that suited fail him,
Neither were his songs exhausted,
Sooner stones in rocks were missing,
Or a pond lacked water-lilies.
　　Therefore thus sang Väinämöinen
Through the evening for their pleasure,
And the women all were laughing,
And the men in high good-humour,
While they listened and they wondered
At the chants of Väinämöinen,　　　　　　380
For amazement filled the hearers,
Wonder those who heard him singing.
　　Said the aged Väinämöinen,
When at length his song he ended,
"This is what I have accomplished
As a singer and magician,
Little can I thus accomplish,
And my efforts lead me nowhere:
But, if sang the great Creator,
Speaking with his mouth of sweetness,　　390

He would sing his songs unto you,
As a singer and magician.

" He would sing the sea to honey,
And to peas would sing the gravel,
And to malt would sing the seasand,
And to salt would sing the gravel,
Forest broad would sing to cornland,
And the wastes would sing to wheatfields,
Into cakes would sing the mountains,
And to hens' eggs change the mountains.   400

" As a singer and magician,
He would speak, and he would order,
And would sing unto this homestead,
Cowsheds ever filled with cattle,
Lanes o'erfilled with beauteous blossoms,
And the plains o'erfilled with milch-kine,
Full a hundred horned cattle,
And with udders full, a thousand.

" As a singer and magician,
He would speak and he would order   410
For our host a coat of lynxskin,
For our mistress cloth-wrought dresses,
For her daughters boots with laces,
And her sons with red shirts furnish.

" Grant, O Jumala, thy blessing,
Evermore, O great Creator,
Unto those we see around us,
And again in all their doings,
Here, at Pohjola's great banquet,
This carouse at Sariola held,   420
That the ale may stream in rivers,
And the mead may flow in torrents,
Here in Pohjola's great household,
In the halls at Sariola built,
That by day we may be singing,
And may still rejoice at evening
Long as our good host is living,
In the lifetime of our hostess.

" Jumala, do thou grant thy blessing,
O Creator, shed thy blessing,   430

On our host at head of table,
On our hostess in her storehouse,
On their sons, the nets when casting,
On their daughters at their weaving.
May they have no cause for trouble,
Nor lament the year that follows,
After their protracted banquet,
This carousal at the mansion!"

RUNO XXII.—THE TORMENTING OF THE BRIDE

Argument

The bride is prepared for her journey and is reminded of her past
life and of the altered life that now lies before her (1–124). She
becomes very sorrowful (125–184). They bring her to weeping (185–
382). She weeps (383–448). They comfort her (449–522).

WHEN the drinking-bout was ended,
And the feast at length was over,
At the festival at Pohja,
Bridal feast held at Pimentola,
Then said Pohjola's old Mistress,
To the bridegroom, Ilmarinen,
"Wherefore sit'st thou, highly-born one,
Waitest thou, O pride of country?
Sit'st thou here to please the father,
Or for love of mother waitest,   10
Or our dwelling to illumine,
Or the wedding guests to honour?
   "Not for father's pleasure wait'st thou,
Nor for love thou bear'st the mother,
Nor the dwelling to illumine,
Nor the wedding guests to honour;
Here thou sit'st for maiden's pleasure,
For a young girl's love delaying,
For the fair one whom thou long'st for,
Fair one with unbraided tresses.   20

"Bridegroom, dearest of my brothers,
Wait a week, and yet another;
For thy loved one is not ready,
And her toilet is not finished.
Only half her hair is plaited,
And a half is still unplaited.

"Bridegroom, dearest of my brothers,
Wait a week, and yet another,
For thy loved one is not ready,
And her toilet is not finished;   30
One sleeve only is adjusted,
And unfitted still the other.

"Bridegroom, dearest of my brothers,
Wait a week, and yet another,
For thy loved one is not ready,
And her toilet is not finished.
For one foot is shod already,
But unshod remains the other.

"Bridegroom, dearest of my brothers,
Wait a week, and yet another,   40
For thy loved one is not ready,
And her toilet is not finished.
For one hand is gloved already,
And ungloved is still the other.

"Bridegroom, dearest of my brothers,
Thou hast waited long unwearied;
For thy love at length is ready,
And thy duck has made her toilet.

"Go thou forth, O plighted maiden,
Follow thou, O dove new-purchased!   50
Near to thee is now thy union,
Nearer still is thy departure,
He who leads thee forth is with thee,
At the door is thy conductor,
And his horse the bit is champing,
And his sledge awaits the maiden.

"Thou wast fond of bridegroom's money
Reaching forth thy hands most greedy
Glad to take the chain he offered,
And to fit the rings upon thee.   60

Now the longed-for sledge is ready,
Eager mount the sledge so gaudy,
Travel quickly to the village,
Quickly speeding on thy journey.
 "Hast thou never, youthful maiden,
On both sides surveyed the question,
Looked beyond the present moment,
When the bargain was concluded?
All thy life must thou be weeping,
And for many years lamenting,   70
How thou left'st thy father's household,
And thy native land abandoned,
From beside thy tender mother,
From the home of she who bore thee.
 "O the happy life thou leddest,
In this household of thy father!
Like a wayside flower thou grewest,
Or upon the heath a strawberry,
Waking up to feast on butter,
Milk, when from thy bed arising,   80
Wheaten-bread, from couch upstanding,
From thy straw, the fresh-made butter,
Or, if thou could eat no butter,
Strips of pork thou then could'st cut thee.
 "Never yet wast thou in trouble,
Never hadst thou cause to worry,
To the fir-trees tossed thou trouble,
Worry to the stumps abandoned,
Care to pine-trees in the marshlands,
And upon the heaths the birch-trees.   90
Like a leaflet thou wast fluttering,
As a butterfly wast fluttering,
Berry-like in native soil,
Or on open ground a raspberry.
 "But thy home thou now art leaving,
To another home thou goest,
To another mother's orders,
To the household of a stranger.
Different there from here thou'lt find it
In another house 'tis different;   100

Other tunes the horns are blowing,
Other doors thou hearest jarring,
Other gates thou hearest creaking,
Other voices at the fishlines.
  "There the doors thou hardly findest,
Strange unto thee are the gateways,
Not like household daughter art thou,
May not dare to blow the fire,
Nor the stove canst rightly heaten,
So that thou canst please the master.   110
  "Didst thou think, O youthful maiden,
Didst thou think, or didst imagine,
Only for a night to wander,
In the morn again returning?
'Tis not for one night thou goest,
Not for one night, not for two nights,
For a longer time thou goest.
Thou for months and days hast vanished,
Lifelong from thy father's dwelling,
For the lifetime of thy mother,   120
And the yard will then be longer,
And the threshold lifted higher,
If again thou ever comest,
To thy former home returning."
  Now the hapless girl was sighing,
Piteously she sighed and panted,
And her heart was filled with trouble,
In her eyes the tears were standing,
And at length she spoke as follows:
"Thus I thought, and thus imagined,   130
And throughout my life imagined,
Said throughout my years of childhood,
Thou art not as maid a lady
In the wardship of thy parents,
In the meadows of thy father,
In thy aged mother's dwelling.
Thou wilt only be a lady
When thy husband's home thou seekest,
Resting one foot on the threshold,
In his sledge the other placing,   140

Then thy head thou liftest higher,
And thy ears thou liftest higher.
    "This throughout my life I wished for,
All my youthful days I hoped for,
And throughout the year I wished it,
Like the coming of the summer.
Now my hope has found fulfilment ;
Near the time of my departure ;
One foot resting on the threshold,
In my husband's sledge the other,   150
But I do not yet know rightly,
If my mind has not been altered.
Not with joyful thoughts I wander
Nor do I depart with pleasure
From the golden home beloved,
Where I passed my life in childhood,
Where I passed my days of girlhood,
Where my father lived before me.
Sadly I depart in sorrow,
Forth I go, most sadly longing,   160
As into the night of autumn,
As on slippery ice in springtime,
When on ice no track remaineth,
On its smoothness rests no footprint.
    "What may be the thoughts of others,
And of other brides the feelings ?
Do not other brides encounter,
Bear within their hearts the trouble,
Such as I, unhappy, carry ?
Blackest trouble rests upon me,   170
Black as coal my heart within me,
Coal-black trouble weighs upon me.
    "Such the feelings of the blessed,
Such the feelings of the happy ;
As the spring day at its dawning,
Or the sunny spring-day morning ;
But what thoughts do now torment me,
And what thoughts arise within me ?
Like unto a pond's flat margin,
Or of clouds the murky border ;   180

Like the gloomy nights of autumn,
Or the dusky day of winter,
Or, as I might better say it,
Darker than the nights of autumn!"
Then an old crone of the household,
In the house for long abiding,
Answered in the words which follow:
"Quiet, quiet, youthful maiden!
Dost remember, how I told thee,
And a hundred times repeated,   190
Take no pleasure in a lover,
In a lover's mouth rejoice not,
Do not let his eyes bewitch thee,
Nor his handsome feet admire?
Though his mouth speaks charming converse,
And his eyes are fair to gaze on,
Yet upon his chin is Lempo;
In his mouth there lurks destruction.

"Thus I always counsel maidens,
And to all their kind I counsel,   200
Though great people come as suitors,
Mighty men should come as wooers,
Yet return them all this answer;
And on thy side speak unto them,
In such words as these address them,
And in thiswise speak unto them:
'Not the least would it beseem me,
Not beseem me, or become me,
As a daughter-in-law to yield me,
As a slave to yield my freedom.   210
Such a pretty girl as I am,
Suits it not to live as slave-girl,
To depart consent I never,
To submit to rule of others.
If another word you utter,
I will give you two in answer,
If you by my hair would pull me,
And you by my locks would drag me,
From my hair I'd quickly shake you,
From my locks dishevelled drive you.'   220

"But to this thou hast not hearkened,
To my words thou hast not listened,
Wilfully thou sought'st the fire,
In the boiling tar hast cast thee.
Now the fox's sledge awaits thee,
To the bear's hug art thou going,
And the fox's sledge will take thee,
Far away the bear convey thee,
Ever slave to other masters,
Ever slave of husband's mother.   230

"From thy home to school thou goest,
From thy father's house to suffering.
Hard the school to which thou goest,
Long the pain to which thou goest.
Reins for thee are bought already,
Iron fetters all in order,
Not for others are they destined,
But alas, for thee, unhappy.

"Shortly wilt thou feel their harshness,
Helpless feel, and unprotected,   240
For the father's chin is wagging,
And the mother's tongue is stormy ;
And the brother's words are coldness,
And the sister's harsh reproaches.

"Hear, O maiden, what I tell thee,
What I speak, and what I tell thee,
In thy home thou wast a floweret,
And the joy of father's household,
And thy father called thee Moonlight,
And thy mother called thee Sunshine,   250
And thy brother Sparkling Water,
And thy sister called thee Blue-cloth.
To another home thou goest,
There to find a stranger mother.
Never is a stranger mother
Like the mother who has borne thee :
Seldom does she give good counsel,
Seldom gives the right instructions.
Sprig the father shouts against thee,
Slut the mother calls unto thee,   260

And the brother calls thee Doorstep,
And the sister, Nasty Creature.
    "Now the best that could await thee,
Best the fate that could await thee,
If as fog thou wert dispersing,
From the house like smoke departing,
Blown like leaf away that flutters,
As a spark away is drifted.
    "But a bird that flies thou art not,
Nor a leaf away that flutters,   270
Nor a spark in drafts that's drifting,
Nor the smoke from house ascending.
    "Lack-a-day, O maid, my sister!
Changed hast thou, and what art changing!
Thou hast changed thy much-loved father
For a father-in-law, a bad one;
Thou hast changed thy tender mother
For a mother-in-law most stringent;
Thou hast changed thy noble brother
For a brother-in-law so crook-necked,   280
And exchanged thy gentle sister
For a sister-in-law all cross-eyed;
And hast changed thy couch of linen
For a sooty hearth to rest on;
And exchanged the clearest water
For the muddy margin-water,
And the sandy shore hast bartered
For the black mud at the bottom;
And thy pleasant meadow bartered
For a dreary waste of heathland;   290
And thy hills of berries bartered
For the hard stumps of a clearing.
    "Didst thou think, O youthful maiden,
Think, O dove, full-fledged at present,
Care would end and toil be lessened,
With the party of this evening,
When to rest thou shalt betake thee,
And to sleep thou art conducted?
    "But to rest they will not lead thee,
Nor to sleep will they conduct thee;   300

Nought awaits thee now but watching,
Nought awaits thee now save trouble,
Heavy thoughts will come upon thee,
Saddened thoughts will overwhelm thee.
  " Long as thou didst wear no head-dress,
Wert thou also free from trouble ;
When no linen veil waved round thee,
Thou wast also free from sorrow.
Now the head-dress brings thee trouble,
Heavy thoughts the linen fabric,   310
And the linen veil brings sorrow,
And the flax brings endless trouble.
  " How may live at home a maiden ?
Maid in father's house abiding ;
Like a monarch in his palace,
Only that the sword is wanting,
But a son's wife's fate is dismal !
With her husband she is living
As a prisoner lives in Russia,
Only that the jailor's wanting.   320
  "Work she must in working season,
And her shoulders stoop with weakness,
And her body faints with weakness,
And with sweat her face is shining.
Then there comes another hour
When there's need to make the fire,
And to put the hearth in order,
She must force her hands to do it.
  " Long must seek, this girl unhappy,
Long the hapless one must seek for,   330
Salmon's mind, and tongue of perchling,
And her thoughts from perch in fishpond,
Mouth of bream, of chub the belly,
And from water-hen learn wisdom.
  "'Tis beyond my comprehension,
Nine times can I not imagine,
To the mother's much-loved daughters,
Best beloved of all her treasures,
Whence should come to them the spoiler,
Where the greedy one was nurtured,   340

Eating flesh, and bones devouring,
To the wind their hair abandoning,
And their tresses wildly tossing,
To the wind of springtime gives them.
  " Weep thou, weep thou, youthful maiden,
When thou weepest, weep thou sorely.
Weep thyself of tears a handful,
Fill thy fists with tears of longing,
Drop them in thy father's dwelling,
Pools of tears upon the flooring,   350
Till the room itself is flooded,
And above the floor in billows !
If thou weepest yet not freely
Thou shalt weep when thou returnest,
When to father's house thou comest,
And shalt find thy aged father
Suffocated in the bathroom,
'Neath his arm a dried-up bath-whisk.
  " Weep thou, weep thou, youthful maiden,
When thou weepest, weep thou sorely ;   360
If thou weepest not yet freely,
Thou shalt weep when thou returnest,
When to mother's house thou comest,
And thou find'st thy aged mother
Suffocated in the cowshed,
In her dying lap a straw-sheaf.
  " Weep thou, weep thou, youthful maiden,
When thou weepest, weep thou sorely.
If thou weepest yet not freely,
Thou shalt weep when thou returnest,   370
When to this same house thou comest,
And thou find'st thy rosy brother
Fallen in the porch before it,
In the courtyard helpless fallen.
  " Weep thou, weep thou, youthful maiden,
When thou weepest, weep thou sorely.
If thou weepest yet not freely,
Thou shalt weep when thou returnest,
When to this same house thou comest,
And thou find'st thy gentle sister   380

Fallen down upon the pathway,
And beneath her arm a mallet."
　　Then the poor girl broke out sobbing,
And awhile she sobbed and panted,
And she soon commenced her weeping,
Pouring forth her tears in torrents.
　　Then she wept of tears a handful,
Filled her fists with tears of longing,
Wet she wept her father's dwelling,
Pools of tears upon the flooring,　　　　　　　390
And she spoke the words which follow,
And expressed herself in thiswise :
" O my sisters, dearest to me,
Of my life the dear companions,
All companions of my childhood,
Listen now to what I tell you.
'Tis beyond my comprehension
Why I feel such deep oppression,
Making now my life so heavy,
Why this trouble weighs upon me,　　　　　　400
Why this darkness rests upon me ;
How I should express my sorrow.
　　" Otherwise I thought and fancied,
Wished it different, all my lifetime,
Thought to go as goes the cuckoo,
Crying 'Cuckoo' from the hill-tops,
Now the day I have attained to,
Come the time that I had wished for ;
But I go not like the cuckoo,
Crying 'Cuckoo' from the hill-tops,　　　　　410
More as duck amid the billows,
On the wide bay's open waters,
Swimming in the freezing water,
Shivering in the icy water.
　　" Woe, my father and my mother,
Woe, alas, my aged parents !
Whither would you now dismiss me,
Drive a wretched maid to sorrow,
Make me thus to weep for sorrow,
Overburdened thus with trouble,　　　　　　420

With distress so heavy-burdened,
And with care so overloaded?
  " Better, O unhappy mother,
Better, dearest who hast borne me,
O thou dear one, who hast suckled,
Nurtured me throughout my lifetime,
Hadst thou swaddled up a tree-stump,
And hadst bathed a little pebble,
Rather than have washed thy daughter,
And have swaddled up thy darling,   430
For this time of great affliction,
And of this so grievous sorrow.
  " Many speak unto me elsewise,
Many counsel me in thiswise:
' Do not, fool, give way to sorrow,
Let not gloomy thoughts oppress thee.'
Do not, O ye noble people,
Do not speak to me in thiswise!
Far more troubles weigh upon me,
Than in a cascade are pebbles,   440
Than in swampy ground the willows,
Or the heath upon the marshland.
Never can a horse pull forward,
And a shod horse struggle onward,
And the sledge sway not behind him,
And the collar shall not tremble.
Even thus I feel my trouble,
And oppressed by dark forebodings."
  From the floor there sang an infant,
From the hearth a growing infant.   450
" Wherefore dost thou weep, O maiden,
Yielding to such grievous sorrow?
Cast thy troubles to the horses,
Sorrow to the sable gelding.
Leave complaints to mouths of iron,
Lamentations to the thick-heads,
Better heads indeed have horses,
Better heads, and bones much harder,
For their arching necks are firmer,
All their frame is greatly stronger.   460

"No, thou hast no cause for weeping,
Nor to yield to grievous sorrow ;
To the marsh they do not lead thee,
Push thee not into the ditches.
Leavest thou these fertile cornfields,
Yet to richer fields thou goest,
Though they take thee from the brewery,
'Tis to where the ale's abundant.

"If around thee now thou gazest,
Just beside thee where thou standest,   470
There thy bridegroom stands to guard thee,
By thy side thy ruddy husband.
Good thy husband, good his horses,
All things needful fill his cellars,
And the grouse are loudly chirping,
On the sledge, as glides it onwards,
And the thrushes make rejoicing,
As they sing upon the traces,
And six golden cuckoos likewise
Flutter on the horse's collar,   480
Seven blue birds are also perching,
On the sledge's frame, and singing.

"Do not yield thee thus to trouble,
O thou darling of thy mother !
For no evil fate awaits thee,
But in better case thou comest,
Sitting by thy farmer husband,
Underneath the ploughman's mantle,
'Neath the chin of the bread-winner,
In the arms of skilful fisher,   490
Warm from chasing elk on snowshoes,
And from bathing after bear-hunt.

"Thou hast found the best of husbands,
And hast won a mighty hero,
For his bow is never idle,
Neither on the pegs his quivers ;
And the dogs in house he leaves not,
Nor in hay lets rest the puppies.

"Three times in this spring already,
In the earliest hours of morning,   500

Has he stood before the fire,
Rising from his couch of bushes;
Three times in this spring already
On his eyes the dew has fallen,
And the shoots of pine-trees combed him,
And the branches brushed against him.
    " All his people he exhorted,
To increase his flocks in number,
For indeed the bridegroom owneth
Flocks that wander through the birchwoods,   510
Tramp their way among the sand-hills,
Seek for pasture in the valleys;
Hundreds of the horned cattle,
Thousands with their well-filled udders;
On the plains are stacks in plenty,
In the valley crops abundant,
Alder-woods for cornland suited,
Meadows where the barley's springing,
Stony land for oats that's suited,
Watered regions, fit for wheatfields.   520
All rich gifts in peace await thee,
Pennies plentiful as pebbles."

Runo XXIII.—The Instructing of the Bride

Argument

The bride is instructed and directed how to conduct herself in her husband's house (1–478). An old vagrant woman relates the experiences of her life as a daughter, as a wife, and after her separation from her husband (479–850).

Now the girl must be instructed,
And the bride be taught her duty,
Who shall now instruct the maiden,
And shall teach the girl her duty?
Osmotar, experienced woman,
Kaleva's most beauteous maiden;

She shall give the maid instruction,
And shall teach the unprotected
How to bear herself with prudence,
And with wisdom to conduct her,   10
In her husband's house with prudence,
To his mother most obedient.

So she spoke the words which follow,
And in terms like these addressed her:
"O thou bride, my dearest sister,
Thou my darling, best-beloved,
Listen now to what I tell thee,
For a second time repeated.
Now thou goest, a flower transplanted,
Like a strawberry forward creeping,   20
Whisked, like shred of cloth, to distance,
Satin-robed, to distance hurried,
From thy home, renowned so greatly,
From thy dwelling-place so beauteous.
To another home thou comest,
To a stranger household goest;
In another house 'tis different;
Otherwise in strangers' houses.
Walk thou there with circumspection,
And prepare thy duties wisely,   30
Not as on thy father's acres,
Or the lands of thine own mother,
Where they sing among the valleys,
And upon the pathways shouting.

"When from out this house thou goest,
All thy doings must be different;
Three things leave at home behind thee,
Sleep indulged in in the daytime,
Counsels of thy dearest mother,
And fresh butter from the barrels.   40

"All thy thoughts must now be altered;
Leave thy sleepiness behind thee,
Leave it for the household maiden,
By the stove so idly sitting.
To the bench-end cast thy singing,
Joyous carols to the windows,

Girlish ways unto the bath-whisks,
And thy pranks to blanket-edges,
Naughtinesses to the stove-bench,
On the floor thy lazy habits,
Or renounce them to thy bridesmaid,　50
And into her arms unload them,
That she take them to the bushes,
Out upon the heath convey them.

　"Other habits wait thy learning,
And the old must be forgotten.
Father's love you leave behind you;
Learn to love thy husband's father;
Deeper now must thou incline thee,
Fitting language must thou utter.　60

　"Other habits wait thy learning,
And the old must be forgotten.
Mother's love thou leav'st behind thee;
Learn to love thy husband's mother.
Deeper now must thou incline thee;
Fitting language must thou utter.

　"Other habits wait thy learning,
And the old must be forgotten.
Brother's love thou leav'st behind thee;
Learn to love thy husband's brother;　70
Deeper now must thou incline thee;
Fitting language must thou utter.

　"Other habits wait thy learning,
And the old must be forgotten.
Sister's love thou leav'st behind thee,
Learn to love thy husband's sister.
Deeper now must thou incline thee,
Fitting language must thou utter.

　"Never may'st thou in thy lifetime,
While the golden moon is shining,　80
Seek a house of doubtful morals,
With the worthless men consorting,
For a house must needs be moral,
And a house must needs be noble,
And for sense a husband wishes,
And desires the best behaviour.

Heedfulness will much be needed
In a house of doubtful morals;
Steadiness will much be wanting
In a man's of doubtful morals.   90
    "Is the old man a wolf in corner,
By the hearth the crone a she-bear,
Brother-in-law on step a viper,
In the yard like nail the sister,
Equal honour must thou give them,
Deeper must thou then incline thee,
Than thou bowed before thy mother,
In the house of thine own father,
Than thou bowed before thy father,
Or before thy dearest mother.   100
    "Thou wilt always need in future
Ready wit and clear perception,
And thy thoughts must all be prudent,
Firmly fixed thy understanding,
Eyes of keenness in the evening,
That the fire is always brilliant,
Ears of sharpness in the morning,
Thus to listen for the cockcrow.
If the cockcrow once has sounded,
Though the second has not sounded,   110
It becomes the young to rouse them,
Though the old folk still are resting.
    "If the cock should not be crowing,
Nor the master's bird be crowing,
Let the moon for cockcrow serve thee,
Take the Great Bear for thy guidance.
Often thou should'st seek the open,
Often go the moon to gaze on,
From the Great Bear seek instruction,
And the distant stars to gaze on.   120
    "If you see the Great Bear clearly,
With his front to south directed,
And his tail extending northward,
Then 'tis time for thee to rouse thee
From the side of thy young husband,
Leaving him asleep and ruddy,

Fire to seek among the ashes
Seeking for a spark in firebox,
Blowing then the fire discreetly,
That from carelessness it spread not.   130
    " If no fire is in the ashes,
And no spark is in the firebox,
Coax thou then thy dearest husband,
And cajole thy handsome husband :
' Light me now the fire, my dearest,
Just a spark, my darling berry !'
    " If you have a flint, a small one,
And a little piece of tinder,
Strike a light as quick as may be,
Light the pine-chip in the holder,   140
Then go out to clear the cowshed,
And the cattle do thou fodder,
For the mother's cow is lowing,
And the father's horse is neighing,
And her chain the son's cow rattles,
And the daughter's calf is lowing,
That the soft hay should be thrown them,
And the clover laid before them.
    " Go thou stooping on the pathway,
Bend thou down among the cattle,   150
Gently give the cows their fodder,
Give the sheep their food in quiet,
Spread it straight before the cattle,
Drink unto the calves so helpless,
To the foals give straw well-chosen,
To the lambkins hay the softest,
See that on the swine thou tread'st not,
Nor the hogs with foot thou spurnest,
Take thou to the swine the food-trough,
Set before the hogs the food-tray.   160
    " Do not rest thee in the cowshed,
Do not loiter with the sheep-flock ;
When thou'st visited the cowshed,
And hast looked to all the cattle,
Do thou quickly hasten homeward,
Home returning like a blizzard,

For the baby there is crying,
Crying underneath the blanket,
And the poor child still is speechless,
And its tongue no words can utter,   170
Whether it is cold or hungry,
Or if something else annoys it,
Ere its well-known friend is coming,
And the mother's voice it heareth.
    "When into the room thou comest,
Come thou fourth into the chamber;
In thy hand a water-bucket,
Underneath thy arm a besom,
And between thy teeth a pine-chip;
Thou art then the fourth among them.   180
    "Sweep thou then the floor to cleanness,
Sweep thou carefully the planking,
And upon the floor pour water,
Not upon the heads of babies.
If you see a child there lying,
Though thy sister-in-law's the infant,
Up upon the bench then lift it,
Wash its eyes, and smooth its hair down,
Put some bread into its handies,
And upon the bread spread butter,   190
But if bread perchance be wanting,
Put a chip into its handies.
    "Then the tables must be scoured,
At the week-end at the latest;
Wash them, and the sides remember,
Let the legs be not forgotten;
Then the benches wash with water,
Sweep thou too the walls to cleanness,
And the boards of all the benches,
And the walls with all their corners.   200
    "If there's dust upon the tables,
Or there's dust upon the windows,
Dust them carefully with feathers,
Wipe them with a wetted duster,
That the dust should not be scattered,
Nor should settle on the ceiling.

"From the stove scrape all the rust off,
From the ceiling wipe the soot off,
And the ceiling-props remember,
Nor should'st thou forget the rafters,   210
That the house be all in order,
And a fitting place to live in.

"Hear, O maiden, what I tell thee,
What I say, and what I tell thee,
Do not go without thy clothing,
Nor without thy shift disport thee,
Move about without thy linen,
Or without thy shoes go shuffling:
Greatly shocked would be thy bridegroom,
And thy youthful husband grumble.   220

"In the yard there grows a rowan,
Thou with reverent care should'st tend it,
Holy is the tree there growing,
Holy likewise are its branches,
On its boughs the leaves are holy,
And its berries yet more holy,
For a damsel may discover,
And an orphan thence learn teaching,
How to please her youthful husband,
To her bridegroom's heart draw nearer.   230

"Let thy ears be keen as mouse-ears,
Let thy feet as hare's be rapid,
And thy young neck proudly arching,
And thy fair neck proudly bending,
Like the juniper uprising,
Or the cherry's verdant summit.

"Likewise hold thyself discreetly,
Always ponder and consider;
Never venture thou to rest thee
On the bench at length extended,   240
Nor upon thy bed to rest thee,
There to yield thee to thy slumbers.

"Comes the brother from his ploughing,
Or the father from the storehouse,
Or thy husband from his labour,
He, thy fair one, from the clearing,

Haste to fetch the water-basin,
Hasten thou to bring a towel,
Bowing with respect before them,
Speaking words of fond affection.   250
  "Comes the mother from the storehouse,
In her arms the flour-filled basket,
Run across the yard to meet her,
Bowing with respect before her,
Take thou from her hands the basket,
Quickly to the house to bear it.
  "If you do not know your duty,
Do not comprehend it fully,
What the work that waits the doing,
Where you should begin your labours,   260
Ask the old crone then in thiswise :
'O my mother-in-law beloved,
How is this work to be managed,
And arranged these household matters ?'
  "And the old crone thus will answer,
And your mother-in-law will tell you :
'Thus this work is to be managed,
And arranged these household matters,
Pounding thus, and grinding thiswise,
And the handmill quickly turning.   270
Likewise do thou fetch the water,
That the dough be fitly kneaded,
Carry logs into the bakehouse,
And the oven heat thou fully,
Set thou then the loaves for baking,
And the large cakes bake thou likewise,
Wash thou then the plates and dishes,
Likewise washing clean the meal-tubs.'
  "When thy work she thus has told thee,
And thy mother-in-law has taught thee,   280
From the stones the parched corn taking,
Hasten to the room for grinding ;
But when you at length have reached it,
And the room for grinding entered,
Do not carol as thou goest,
Do not shout thy very loudest,

Leave it to the stones to carol,
Talking through the handmill's opening,
Neither do thou groan too loudly,
Let the handmill groan unto thee; 290
Lest thy father-in-law should fancy
Or thy mother-in-law imagine
That with discontent thou groanest,
And art sighing from vexation.
Lift the meal, and sift it quickly,
To the room in dish convey it,
Bake thou there the loaves with pleasure,
After thou with care hast kneaded,
That the flour becomes not lumpy,
But throughout is mixed most smoothly. 300
    "If you see the bucket leaning,
Take the bucket on your shoulder,
On your arm the water-bucket.
Go thou then to fetch the water.
Carry thou the bucket nicely,
On the yoke-end do thou fix it,
Like the wind returning quickly,
Like the wind of springtime rushing,
By the water do not linger,
By the well forbear to rest thee, 310
Lest thy father-in-law should fancy,
Or thy mother-in-law imagine
That you wished to see your likeness,
And your beauty to admire,
Rosy cheeks in water painted,
In the well your charms reflected.
    "When you wander to the wood-pile,
Wander there to fetch the faggots,
Do not split them up at random,
Take some faggots of the aspen, 320
Lift thou up the faggots gently,
Make as little noise as may be,
Lest thy father-in-law should fancy,
Or thy mother-in-law imagine,
That you pitch them down in crossness,
And in temper make them clatter.

"When you wander to the storehouse,
Thither go to fetch the flour,
Do not linger in the storehouse,
Do not long remain within it,   330
Lest thy father-in-law should fancy,
Or thy mother-in-law imagine,
You were doling out the flour,
Sharing with the village women.

"When you go to wash the dishes,
And the pots and pans to scour,
Wash the jugs and wash the handles,
And the rims of mugs for drinking,
Sides of cups with circumspection,
Handles of the spoons remembering.   340
Mind thou, too, the spoons and count them,
Look thou to the dishes also,
Lest the dogs should steal them from you,
Or the cats should take them from you,
Or the birds away should take them,
Or the children should upset them :
For the village swarms with children,
Many little heads thou findest,
Who might carry off the dishes,
And the spoons about might scatter.   350

"When the evening bath is wanted,
Fetch the water and the bath-whisks,
Have the bath-whisks warm and ready,
Fill thou full with steam the bathroom.
Do not take too long about it,
Do not loiter in the bathroom,
Lest thy father-in-law should fancy,
Or thy mother-in-law imagine,
You were lying on the bath-boards,
On the bench your head reclining.   360

"When the room again you enter,
Then announce the bath is ready :
'O my father-in-law beloved,
Now the bath is fully ready :
Water brought, and likewise bath-whisks,
All the boards are cleanly scoured.

Go and bathe thee at thy pleasure,
Wash thou there as it shall please thee,
I myself will mind the steaming,
Standing underneath the boarding.'   370
 "When the time has come for spinning,
And the time has come for weaving,
In the village seek not counsel,
Do not cross the ditch for teaching,
Seek it not in other households,
Nor the weaver's comb from strangers.
 "Spin thyself the yarn thou needest,
With thy fingers do thou spin it,
Let the yarn be loosely twisted,
But the flaxen thread more closely.   380
Closely in a ball then wind it,
On the winch securely twist it,
Fix it then upon the warp-beam,
And upon the loom secure it,
Then the shuttle fling thou sharply,
But the yarn do thou draw gently.
Weave the thickest woollen garments,
Woollen gowns construct thou likewise,
From a single fleece prepare them,
From a winter fleece construct them,   390
From the wool of lamb of springtime,
And the fleece of ewe of summer.
 " Listen now to what I tell thee,
And to what again I tell thee.
Thou must brew the ale of barley,
From the malt the sweet drink fashion,
From a single grain of barley,
And by burning half a tree-trunk.
When the malt begins to sweeten,
Take thou up the malt and taste it.   400
With the rake disturb it never,
Do not use a stick to turn it,
Always use your hands to stir it,
And your open hands to turn it.
Go thou often to the malthouse,
Do not let the sprout be injured,

Let the cat not sit upon it,
Or the tomcat sleep upon it.
Of the wolves have thou no terror,
Fear thou not the forest monsters,　　　　410
When thou goest to the bath-house,
Or at midnight forth must wander.
　" When a stranger pays a visit,
Be not angry with the stranger,
For a well-appointed household,
Always has for guests provision :
Scraps of meat that are not needed,
Cakes of bread the very nicest.
　"Ask the guest to sit and rest him,
With the guest converse in friendship,　　　　420
With thy talk amuse the stranger,
Till the dinner shall be ready.
　"When the house the stranger's leaving,
And he's taking his departure,
Do not thou go with the stranger
Any further than the housedoor,
Lest the husband should be angry,
And thy darling should be gloomy.
　" If you e'er feel inclination
To the village forth to wander,　　　　430
Ask permission ere thou goest,
There to gossip with the strangers.
In the time that you are absent,
Speak thy words with heedful caution,
Do not grumble at your household,
Nor thy mother-in-law abuse thou.
　" If the village girls should ask you,
Any of the village women,
' Does your mother-in-law give butter,
As at home your mother gave you ? '　　　　440
Never do thou make the answer,
' No, she does not give me butter ; '
Tell thou always that she gives it,
Gives it to you by the spoonful,
Though 'twas only once in summer,
And another time in winter.

"List again to what I tell thee,
And again impress upon thee.
When at length this house thou leavest,
And thou comest to the other,　　　　　　450
Do thou not forget thy mother,
Or despise thy dearest mother,
For it was thy mother reared thee,
And her beauteous breasts that nursed thee,
From her own delightful body,
From her form of perfect whiteness.
Many nights has she lain sleepless,
Many meals has she forgotten,
While she rocked thee in thy cradle,
Watching fondly o'er her infant.　　　　　　460
"She who should forget her mother,
Or despise her dearest mother,
Ne'er to Manala should travel,
Nor to Tuonela go cheerful.
There in Manala is anguish,
Hard in Tuonela the reckoning,
If she has forgot her mother,
Or despised her dearest mother.
Tuoni's daughters come reproaching,
Mana's maidens all come mocking :　　　　　　470
'Why hast thou forgot thy mother,
Or despised thy dearest mother?
Great the sufferings of thy mother,
Great her sufferings when she bore thee,
Lying groaning in the bathroom,
On a couch of straw extended,
When she gave thee thy existence,
Giving birth to thee, the vile one!'"
On the ground there sat an old crone,
Sat an old dame 'neath her mantle,　　　　　　480
Wanderer o'er the village threshold,
Wanderer through the country's footpaths,
And she spoke the words which follow,
And in words like these expressed her :
"To his mate the cock was singing,
Sang the hen's child to his fair one,

And in March the crow was croaking,
And in days of spring was chattering;
Rather let my singing fail me,
Let me rather check my singing,   490
Chattering in a house all golden,
Always near to one who loves me;
But no love nor house is left me,
And all love departed from me.

" Hear, O sister, what I tell thee,
When thy husband's house thou seekest,
Follow not thy husband's notions,
As was done by me unhappy.
Larks have tongues, and husbands notions;
But a lover's heart is greater.   500

" I was as a flower that flourished,
As a wild rose in the thicket,
And I grew as grows a sapling,
Grew into a slender maiden.
I was beauteous as a berry,
Rustling in its golden beauty;
In my father's yard a duckling,
On my mother's floor a gosling,
Water-bird unto my brother,
And a goldfinch to my sister.   510
Flowerlike walked I on the pathway,
As upon the plain the raspberry,
Skipping on the sandy lakeshore,
Dancing on the flower-clad hillocks,
Singing loud in every valley,
Carolling on every hill-top,
Sporting in the leafy forests,
In the charming woods rejoicing.

" As the trap the fox-mouth seizes,
And the tongue entraps the ermine,   520
Towards a man inclines a maiden,
And the ways of other households.
So created is the maiden,
That the daughter's inclination
Leads her married, as step-daughter,
As the slave of husband's mother.

As a berry grows in marshland,
And in other waters, cherry,
Like a cranberry sought I sorrow,
Like a strawberry exhortation.   530
Every tree appeared to bite me,
Every alder seemed to tear me,
Every birch appeared to scold me,
Every aspen to devour me.

"As my husband's bride they brought me,
To my mother-in-law they led me.
Here there were, as they had told me,
Waiting for the wedded maiden,
Six large rooms of pine constructed,
And of bedrooms twice as many.   540
Barns along the forest-borders,
By the roadside flowery gardens,
By the ditches fields of barley,
And along the heaths were oatfields,
Chests of corn threshed out already,
Other chests awaiting threshing,
Hundred coins received already,
And a hundred more expected.

"Foolishly had I gone thither,
Recklessly my hand had given,   550
For six props the house supported,
Seven small poles the house supported,
And the woods were filled with harshness,
And with lovelessness the forests,
By the roadsides dreary deserts,
In the woodlands thoughts of evil,
Chests containing spoilt provisions,
Other chests beside them spoiling;
And a hundred words reproachful,
And a hundred more to look for.   560

"But I let it not distress me,
Hoping there to live in quiet,
Wishing there to dwell in honour,
And a peaceful life to live there;
But when first the room I entered,
Over chips of wood I stumbled,

On the door I knocked my forehead,
And my head against the doorposts.
At the door were eyes of strangers :
Darksome eyes were at the entrance,   570
Squinting eyes in midst of chamber,
In the background eyes most evil.
From the mouths the fire was flashing,
From beneath the tongues shot firebrands,
From the old man's mouth malicious,
From beneath his tongue unfriendly.

    " But I let it not distress me,
In the house I dwelt unheeding,
Hoping still to live in favour,
And I bore myself with meekness,   580
And with legs of hare went skipping,
With the step of ermine hurried,
Very late to rest retired,
Very early rose to suffering.
But, unhappy, won no honour,
Mildness brought me only sorrow,
Had I tossed away the torrents,
Or the rocks in twain had cloven.

    " Vainly did I grind coarse flour,
And with pain I crushed its hardness,   590
That my mother-in-law should eat it,
And her ravenous throat devour it,
At the table-end while sitting,
From a dish with golden borders.
But I ate, unhappy daughter,
Flour scraped up, to handmill cleaving,
With my ladle from the hearthstone,
With my spoon from off the pestle.

    " Oft I brought, O me unhappy,
I, the son's wife, to his dwelling,   600
Mosses from the swampy places,
And as bread for me I baked it.
Water from the well I carried,
And I drank it up in mouthfuls.
Fish I ate, O me unhappy,
Smelts I ate, O me unhappy,

As above the net I leaned me,
In the boat as I was swaying,
For no fish received I ever
From my mother-in-law neglectful,   610
Neither in a day of plenty,
Nor a day of double plenty.

"Fodder gathered I in summer,
Winter worked I with the pitchfork,
Even as a labourer toiling,
Even as a hired servant,
And my mother-in-law for ever,
Evermore for me selected,
Worst of all the flails for threshing,
Heaviest mallet from the bathroom,   620
From the beach the heaviest mallet,
In the stall the largest pitchfork.
Never did they think me weary,
Nor my weakness e'er considered,
Though my work had wearied heroes,
Or the strength of foals exhausted.

"Thus did I, a girl unhappy,
Work at proper time for working,
And my shoulders stooped with weakness;
And at other times they ordered   630
That the fire should now be kindled,
With my hands that I should stir it.

"To their hearts' desire they scolded,
With their tongues they heaped reproaches
On my spotless reputation,
On my character, though stainless.
Evil words they heaped upon me,
And abuse they showered upon me,
Like the sparks from furious fire,
Or a very hail of iron.   640

"Until then despaired I never,
And had spent my life as erstwhile
There to aid the harsh old woman,
To her fiery tongue submitting:
But 'twas this that brought me evil,
This that caused me greatest anguish,

When to wolf was changed my husband,
To a growling bear converted,
Turned his side to me when eating,
Turned his back asleep or working.   650
   "I myself broke out in weeping,
And I pondered in the storehouse,
And my former life remembering,
And my life in former seasons,
In the homestead of my father,
In my sweetest mother's dwelling.
   "Then in words I spoke my feelings,
And I spoke the words which follow:
'Well indeed my dearest mother
Understood to rear her apple,   660
And the tender shoot to cherish,
But she knew not where to plant it,
For the tender shoot is planted
In a very evil station,
In a very bad position,
'Mid the hard roots of a birch-tree,
There to weep while life remaineth,
And to spend the months lamenting.
   "'Surely, surely, I am worthy
Of a home than this much better,   670
Worthy of a larger homestead,
And a floor more wide-extended,
Worthy of a better partner,
And a husband far more handsome.
With a birchbark shoe I'm fitted,
With a slipshod shoe of birchbark,
Like a very crow's his body,
With a beak like any raven,
And his mouth like wolf's is greedy,
And his form a bear resembles.   680
   "'Such a one I might have found me,
If I'd wandered to the mountains,
Picked from off the road a pine-stump,
From the wood a stump of alder,
For his face the turf resembles,
And his beard the moss from tree-trunks,

Head of clay, and mouth all stony,
And his eyes like coals of fire,
Knobs of birch his ears resemble,
And his legs are forking willows.'   690
    "While my song I thus was singing,
Sighing in my grievous trouble,
He, my husband, chanced to hear it,
At the wall as he was standing.
When I heard him then approaching,
At the storehouse gate when standing,
I was conscious of his coming,
For I recognized his footstep.
And his hair in wind was tossing,
And his hair was all disordered,   700
And his gums with rage were grinning,
And his eyes with fury staring,
In his hand a stick of cherry,
'Neath his arm a club he carried,
And he hurried to attack me,
And upon the head he struck me.
    "When the evening came thereafter,
And there came the time for sleeping,
At his side a rod he carried,
Took from nail a whip of leather,   710
Not designed to flay another,
But alas, for me, unhappy.
    "Then when I myself retired,
To my resting-place at evening,
By my husband's side I stretched me,
By my side my husband rested,
When he seized me by the elbows,
With his wicked hands he grasped me,
And with willow rods he beat me,
And the haft of bone of walrus.   720
    "From his cold side then I raised me,
And I left the bed of coldness,
But behind me ran my husband,
From the door came wildly rushing.
In my hair his hands he twisted,
Grasping it in all his fury,

In the wind my hair he scattered,
To the winds of spring abandoned.
  " What advice should now be followed,
Where had I to look for counsel?   730
Shoes of steel I put upon me,
Bands of copper put upon me,
As I stood beyond the house-wall.
In the street for long I listened,
Till the wretch should calm his fury,
And his passion had subsided,
But his anger never slumbered,
Neither for a time abated.
  " At the last the cold o'ercame me,
In my hiding-place so dismal,   740
Where I stood beyond the house-wall,
And without the door I waited,
And I pondered and reflected :
' This I cannot bear for ever,
Nor can bear their hatred longer,
Longer can I not endure it,
In this dreadful house of Lempo,
In this lair of evil demons.'
  " From the handsome house I turned me,
And my pleasant home abandoned,   750
And commenced my weary wanderings,
Through the swamps and through the lowlands,
Past the open sheets of water,
Past the cornfields of my brother.
There the dry pines all were rustling,
And the crowns of fir-trees singing,
All the crows were croaking loudly,
And the magpies all were chattering,
  " ' Here for thee no home remaineth,
In the house thy birth which witnessed.'   760
  " But I let it not distress me,
As I neared my brother's homestead,
But the gates themselves addressed me,
And the cornfields all lamented :
  " ' Wherefore hast thou thus come homeward,
What sad news to hear, O wretched ?

Long ago has died thy father,
Perished has thy sweetest mother,
All estranged is now thy brother,
And his wife is like a Russian.'   770

"But I let it not distress me,
And at once the house I entered,
At the door I grasped the handle,
Cold within my hand I felt it.

"After, when the room I entered,
In the doorway I was standing,
And the mistress stood there proudly,
But she did not come to meet me,
Nor to me her hand she offered.
I myself was proud as she was,   780
And I would not go to meet her,
And my hand I would not offer.
On the stove my hand I rested.
Cold I felt the very hearthstones,
To the burning coals I reached it;
In the stove the coals were frozen.

"On the bench there lay my brother,
Lazy on the bench extended,
On his shoulders soot by fathoms,
And by spans upon his body,   790
On his head glowed coals a yard high,
And of hard-caked soot a quartful.

"Asked my brother of the stranger,
Of the guest he thus inquired:
'Stranger, why hast crossed the water?'

"And on this I gave him answer:
'Dost thou then not know thy sister,
Once the daughter of thy mother?
We are children of one mother,
Of one bird are we the nestlings: 800
By one goose have we been nurtured,
In one grouse's nest been fostered.'

"Then my brother broke out weeping,
From his eyes the tears were falling.

"To his wife then said my brother,
And he whispered to his darling,

'Bring some food to give my sister!'
But with mocking eyes she brought me
Cabbage-stalks from out the kitchen,
Whence the whelp the fat had eaten,   810
And the dog had licked the salt from,
And the black dog had his meal of.

   "To his wife then said my brother,
And he whispered to his darling,
'Fetch some ale to give the stranger!'
But with mocking eyes she carried
Water only for the stranger,
But, instead of drinking water,
Water she had washed her face in,
And her sister washed her hands in.   820

   "From my brother's house I wandered,
Left the house that I was born in,
Hurried forth, O me unhappy,
Wandered on, O me unhappy,
Wretched on the shores to wander,
Toiling on, for ever wretched,
Always to the doors of strangers,
Always to the gates of strangers,
On the beach, with poorest children,
Sufferers of the village poorhouse.   830

   "There were many of the people,
Many were there who abused me,
And with evil words attacked me,
And with sharpest words repulsed me.
Few there are among the people
Who have spoken to me kindly,
And with kindly words received me,
And before the stove who led me,
When I came from out the rainstorm,
Or from out the cold came shrinking,   840
With my dress with rime all covered,
While the snow my fur cloak covered.

   "In my youthful days I never,
I could never have believed it,
Though a hundred told me of it,
And a thousand tongues repeated

Such distress should fall upon me,
Such distress should overwhelm me,
As upon my head has fallen,
Laid upon my hands such burdens."

850

RUNO XXIV.—THE DEPARTURE OF THE BRIDE AND
BRIDEGROOM

Argument

The bridegroom is instructed how he should behave towards his bride, and is cautioned not to treat her badly (1–264). An old beggar relates how he once brought his wife to reason (265–296). The bride remembers with tears that she is now quitting her dear birthplace for the rest of her life, and says farewell to all (297–462). Ilmarinen lifts his bride into the sledge and reaches his home on the evening of the third day (463–528).

Now the girl had well been lectured,
And the bride had been instructed;
Let me now address my brother,
Let me lecture now the bridegroom.

"Bridegroom, dearest of my brothers,
Thou the best of all my brothers,
Dearest of my mother's children,
Gentlest of my father's children,
Listen now to what I tell thee,
What I speak and what I tell thee,   10
Of thy linnet who awaits thee,
And the dove that thou hast captured.

"Bridegroom, bless thy happy fortune,
For the fair one granted to thee,
When thou praisest, praise thou loudly,
Loudly praise the good that's granted,
Loudly praise thou thy Creator,
For the gracious gift He granted,
And her father praise thou also,
Even more her mother praise thou,   20

They who reared their lovely daughter
To the charming bride beside thee.
  "Stainless sits the maid beside thee,
Maiden bright to thee united,
Pledged to thee in all her beauty,
Fair one under thy protection,
Charming girl upon thy bosom,
At thy side so sweetly blushing,
Girl with strength to help in threshing,
Or to help thee in the hayfield,   30
Skilful, too, to do the washing,
Quick to bleach the clothes to whiteness,
Skilful, too, the thread in spinning,
Rapid, too, the cloth when weaving.
  "And I hear her loom resounding,
As upon the hill the cuckoo,
And I see her shuttle darting,
As the ermine through a thicket,
And the reel she twists as quickly
As the squirrel's mouth a fir-cone.   40
Never sound has slept the village,
Nor the country people slumbered,
For her loom's incessant clatter,
And the whizzing of the shuttle.
  "O thou loved and youthful bridegroom,
Handsomest of all the people,
Forge thou now a scythe of sharpness,
Fix the best of handles on it,
Carve it, sitting in the doorway,
Hammer it upon a tree-stump.   50
When there comes the time of sunshine,
Take thy young wife to the meadow,
Look thou where the grass is rustling,
And the harder grass is crackling,
And the reeds are gently murmuring,
And the sorrel gently rustling,
Also note where stand the hillocks,
And the shoots from stumps arising.
  "When another day is dawning,
Let her have a weaver's shuttle,   60

And a batten that shall suit it,
And a loom of best construction,
And a treadle of the finest.
Make the weaver's chair all ready,
For the damsel fix the treadle,
Lay her hand upon the batten.
Soon the shuttle shall be singing,
And the treadle shall be thumping,
Till the rattling fills the village,
And the noise is heard beyond it:　　　　70
And the crones will all perceive it,
And the village women question,
'Who is this we hear a-weaving?'
And you thus must make them answer:
''Tis my own, my darling, weaving,
'Tis my loved one makes the clatter,
Shall she loosen now the fabric,
And the shuttle cease from throwing?'
　　" 'Let her not the fabric loosen,
Nor the shuttle cease from throwing.　　　　80
Thus may weave the Moon's fair daughters,
Thus may spin the Sun's fair daughters,
Even thus the Great Bear's daughters.
Of the lovely stars the daughters.'
　　" O thou loved and youthful bridegroom,
Handsomest of all the people,
Set thou forth upon thy journey,
Hasten to commence thy journey,
Bear away thy youthful maiden,
Bear away thy dove so lovely.　　　　90
From thy finch depart thou never,
Nor desert thy darling linnet;
In the ditches do not drive her,
Nor against the hedge-stakes drive her,
Nor upset her on the tree-stumps,
Nor in stony places cast her.
In her father's house she never,
In her dearest mother's homestead,
In the ditches has been driven,
Nor against the hedge-stakes driven,　　　　100

Nor upset upon the tree-stumps,
Nor upset in stony places.
  "O thou loved and youthful bridegroom,
Handsomest of all the people,
Never may'st thou send the damsel,
Never may'st thou push the fair one
In the corner there to loiter,
Or to rummage in the corner.
In her father's house she never,
Never in her mother's household,   110
Went to loiter in the corner,
Or to rummage in the corner.
Always sat she at the window,
In the room she sat, and rocked her,
As her father's joy at evening,
And her mother's love at morning.

  "Never may'st thou, luckless husband,
Never may'st thou lead thy dovekin,
Where with arum-roots the mortar
Stands, the rind to pound from off them,   120
Or her bread from straw prepare her,
Neither from the shoots of fir-trees.
In her father's house she never,
In her tender mother's household,
Needed thus to use the mortar,
Pounding thus the rind from marsh-roots,
Nor from straw her bread prepare her,
Neither from the shoots of fir-tree.

  "May'st thou always lead this dovekin
To a slope with corn abundant,   130
Or to help her from the rye-bins,
From the barley-bins to gather,
Whence large loaves of bread to bake her,
And the best of ale to brew her,
Loaves of wheaten-bread to bake her,
Kneaded dough for cakes prepare her.

  "Bridegroom, dearest of my brothers,
Never may'st thou make this dovekin,
Nor may'st cause our tender gosling,
Down to sit, and weep in sadness.   140

If there comes an hour of evil,
And the damsel should be dreary,
Yoke thou in the sledge the chestnut,
Or the white horse do thou harness,
Drive her to her father's dwelling,
To her mother's home familiar.
"Never may'st thou treat this dovekin,
Never may this darling linnet,
Ever be like slave-girl treated,
Neither like a hired servant,   150
Neither be forbid the cellar,
Nor the storehouse closed against her.
Never in her father's dwelling,
In her tender mother's household,
Was she treated like a slave-girl,
Neither like a hired servant,
Neither was forbid the cellar,
Nor the storehouse closed against her.
Always did she cut the wheatbread,
And the hens' eggs also looked to,   160
And she looked to all the milk-tubs,
Looked within the ale-casks likewise,
In the morn the storehouse opened,
Locked it also in the evening.
"O thou loved and youthful bridegroom,
Handsomest of all the people,
If thou treatest well the damsel,
Thou wilt meet a good reception
When thou seek'st her father's dwelling,
Visiting her much loved mother.   170
Thou thyself wilt well be feasted,
Food and drink be set before thee,
And thy horse will be unharnessed,
And be led into the stable,
Drink and fodder set before him,
And a bowl of oats provided.
"Never surely, may our damsel,
May our well-beloved linnet,
Be in hissing tones upbraided,
That from no high race she springeth;   180

For in very truth our damsel
Comes of great and famous lineage.
If of beans you sow a measure
One bean each, it yields her kinsfolk;
If of flax you sow a measure,
But a thread it yields to each one.
"Never may'st thou, luckless husband,
Badly treat this beauteous damsel,
Nor chastise her with the slave-whip,
Weeping 'neath the thongs of leather,   190
'Neath the five-lashed whip lamenting,
Out beyond the barn lamenting.
Never was the maid aforetime,
Never in her father's dwelling,
With the slave-whip e'er corrected,
Weeping 'neath the thongs of leather,
'Neath the five-lashed whip lamenting,
Out beyond the barn lamenting.
"Stand thou like a wall before her,
Stand before her like a doorpost,   200
Do not let thy mother beat her,
Do not let thy father scold her,
Do not let the guests abuse her,
Do not let the neighbours blame her.
Drive the mob away with whipping,
Beat thou other people only,
Do thou not oppress thy darling,
Nor chastise thy heart's beloved,
Whom for three long years thou waitedst,
She whom thou alone hast longed for.   210
"Bridegroom, give thy bride instruction,
And do thou instruct thy apple,
In the bed do thou instruct her,
And behind the door advise her,
For a whole year thus instruct her,
Thus by word of mouth advise her,
With thine eyes the next year teach her,
And the third year teach by stamping.
"If to this she pays no heeding,
Nor concerns herself about it,   220

Choose a reed where reeds are growing,
From the heath fetch thou some horse-tail,
And with these correct the damsel,
In the fourth year thus correct her,
With the stalks then whip her lightly,
With the rough edge of the sedges,
But with whip-lash do not strike her,
Neither with the rod correct her.

"If to this she pays no heeding,
Nor concerns herself about it,   230
Bring a switch from out the thicket,
In the dell select a birch-rod,
Underneath thy fur cloak hide it,
That the neighbours may not know it,
Let the damsel only see it;
Threaten her, but do not touch her.

"If to this she pays no heeding,
Nor concerns herself about it,
With the switch correct the damsel,
With the birch-rod do thou teach her,   240
But within the room four-cornered,
Or within the hut moss-covered.
Do not beat her in the meadow,
Do not whip her in the cornfield,
Lest the noise should reach the village,
And to other homes the quarrel,
Neighbours' wives should hear the crying,
And the uproar in the forest.

"Always strike her on the shoulders,
On her soft cheeks do thou strike her,   250
On her eyes forbear to strike her,
On her ears forbear to touch her;
Lumps would rise upon her temples,
And her eyes with blue be bordered,
And the brother-in-law would question,
And the father-in-law perceive it,
And the village ploughmen see it,
And would laugh the village women:

"'Has she been among the spear-thrusts,
Has she marched into a battle,   260

Or the mouth of wolf attacked her,
Or the forest bear has mauled her,
Or was perhaps the wolf her husband,
Was the bear perchance her consort?'"
  By the stove there lay an old man,
By the hearth there sat a beggar;
From the stove there spoke the old man,
From the hearth there spoke the beggar.
  "Never may'st thou, luckless husband,
Listen to thy wife's opinion,   270
Tongue of lark, and whim of women,
Like myself, a youth unhappy,
For both bread and meat I bought her,
Bought her butter, ale I bought her,
Every sort of fish I bought her,
Bought her all sorts of provisions,
Home-brewed ale the best I bought her,
Likewise wheat from foreign countries.
  "But she let it not content her,
Nor did it improve her temper,   280
For one day the room she entered,
And she grasped my hair, and tore it,
And her face was quite distorted,
And her eyes were wildly rolling,
Always scolding in her fury,
To her heart's contentment scolding,
Heaping foul abuse upon me,
Roaring at me as a sluggard.
  "But I knew another method,
Knew another way to tame her,   290
So I peeled myself a birch-shoot,
When she came, and called me birdie;
But when juniper I gathered,
Then she stooped, and called me darling;
When I lifted rods of willow,
On my neck she fell embracing."
  Now the hapless girl was sighing,
Sighing much, and sobbing sadly;
Presently she broke out weeping,
And she spoke the words which follow: 300

"Soon must now depart the others,
And the time is fast approaching,
But my own departure's nearer,
Swiftly comes my time for parting.
Mournful is indeed my going,
Sad the hour of my departure,
From this far-renowned village,
And this ever-charming homestead,
Where my face was ever joyful,
And I grew to perfect stature,   310
All the days that I was growing,
While my childhood's years were passing.

    "Until now I never pondered,
Nor believed in all my lifetime,
Never thought on my departure,
Realized my separation,
From the precincts of this castle,
From the hill where it is builded.
Now I feel I am departing,
And I know that I am going.   320
Empty are the parting goblets,
And the ale of parting finished,
And the sledges all are waiting,
Front to fields, and back to homestead,
With one side towards the stables,
And the other to the cowhouse.

    "Whence comes now my separation,
Whence my sadness at departure,
How my mother's milk repay her,
Or the goodness of my father,   330
Or my brother's love repay him,
Or my sister's fond affection?

    "Thanks to thee, my dearest father,
For my former life so joyful,
For the food of days passed over,
For the best of all the dainties.
Thanks to thee, my dearest mother,
For my childhood's cradle-rocking,
For thy tending of the infant,
Whom thou at thy breast hast nurtured.   340

"Also thanks, my dearest brother,
Dearest brother, dearest sister,
Happiness to all the household,
All companions of my childhood,
Those with whom I lived and sported,
And who grew from childhood with me.

"May thou not, O noble father,
May thou not, O tender mother,
Or my other noble kindred,
Or my race, the most illustrious,   350
Ever fall into affliction,
Or oppressed by grievous trouble,
That I thus desert my country,
That I wander to a distance.
Shines the sun of the Creator,
Beams the moon of the Creator,
And the stars of heaven are shining,
And the Great Bear is extended
Ever in the distant heavens,
Evermore in other regions,   360
Not alone at father's homestead,
In the home where passed my childhood.

"Truly must I now be parted
From the home I loved so dearly,
From my father's halls be carried,
From among my mother's cellars,
Leave the swamps and fields behind me,
Leave behind me all the meadows,
Leave behind the sparkling waters,
Leave the sandy shore behind me,   370
Where the village women bathe them,
And the shepherd-boys are splashing.

"I must leave the quaking marshes,
And the wide-extending lowlands,
And the peaceful alder-thickets,
And the tramping through the heather,
And the strolling past the hedgerows,
And the loitering on the pathways,
And my dancing through the farmyards,
And my standing by the house-walls,   380

And the cleaning of the planking,
And the scrubbing of the flooring,
Leave the fields where leap the reindeer,
And the woods where run the lynxes,
And the wastes where flock the wild geese,
And the woods where birds are perching.
"Now indeed I am departing,
All the rest I leave behind me;
In the folds of nights of autumn,
On the thin ice of the springtime,   390
On the ice I leave no traces,
On the slippery ice no footprints,
From my dress no thread upon it,
Nor in snow my skirt's impression.
"If I should return in future,
And again my home revisit,
Mother hears my voice no longer,
Nor my father heeds my weeping,
Though I'm sobbing in the corner,
Or above their heads am speaking,   400
For the young grass springs already
And the juniper is sprouting
O'er the sweet face of my mother,
And the cheeks of her who bore me.
"If I should return in future
To the wide-extended homestead,
I shall be no more remembered,
Only by two little objects.
At the lowest hedge are hedge-bands,
At the furthest field are hedge-stakes,   410
These I fixed when I was little,
As a girl with twigs I bound them.
"But my mother's barren heifer,
Unto which I carried water,
And which as a calf I tended,
She will low to greet my coming,
From the dunghill of the farmyard,
Or the wintry fields around it;
She will know me, when returning,
As the daughter of the household.   420

"Then my father's splendid stallion,
Which I fed when I was little,
Which as girl I often foddered,
He will neigh to greet my coming,
From the dunghill of the farmyard,
Or the wintry fields around it ;
He will know me, when returning,
As the daughter of the household.

"Then the dog, my brother's favourite
Which as child I fed so often,   430
Which I trained when in my girlhood,
He will bark to greet my coming,
From the dunghill of the farmyard,
Or the wintry fields around it ;
He will know me, when returning,
As the daughter of the household.

"But the others will not know me,
To my former home returning,
Though my boats are still the old ones,
As when here I lived aforetime,   440
By the shores where swim the powans,
And the nets are spread as usual.

"Now farewell, thou room beloved,
Thou my room, with roof of boarding ;
Good it were for me returning,
That I once again should scrub thee.

"Now farewell, thou hall beloved,
Thou my hall, with floor of boarding ;
Good it were for me returning,
That I once again should scrub thee.   450

"Now farewell, thou yard beloved,
With my lovely mountain-ashtree ;
Good it were for me returning,
Once again to wander round thee.

"Now farewell to all things round me,
Berry-bearing fields and forests,
And the flower-bearing roadsides,
And the heaths o'ergrown with heather,
And the lakes with hundred islands,
And the depths where swim the powans,   460

And the fair hills with the fir-trees,
And the swampy ground with birch-trees."
Then the smith, e'en Ilmarinen,
In the sledge the maiden lifted,
With his whip he lashed the coursers,
And he spoke the words which follow :
" Now farewell to all the lakeshores,
Shores of lakes, and slopes of meadows,
All the pine-trees on the hill-sides,
And the tall trees in the firwoods,   470
And behind the house the alders,
And the junipers by well-sides,
In the plains, all berry-bushes,
Berry-bushes, stalks of grasses,
Willow-bushes, stumps of fir-trees,
Alder-leaves, and bark of birch-trees ! "
Thus at length, smith Ilmarinen
Forth from Pohjola departed,
With the children farewells singing,
And they sang the words which follow :   480
" Hither flew a bird of blackness,
Through the wood he speeded swiftly,
Well he knew to lure our duckling,
And entice from us our berry,
And he took from us our apple,
Drew the fish from out the water,
Lured her with a little money,
And enticed her with his silver.
Who will fetch us now the water,
Who will take us to the river?   490
"Now remain the buckets standing,
And the yoke is idly rattling,
And the floor unswept remaineth,
And unswept remains the planking,
Empty now are all the pitchers,
And the jugs two-handled dirty."
But the smith, e'en Ilmarinen,
With the young girl hastened homeward,
Driving rattling on his journey,
From the magic coast of Pohja,   500

By the shore of Sound of Sima.
On he drove across the sandhills,
Shingle crashed, and sand was shaking,
Swayed the sledge, the pathway rattled,
Loudly rang the iron runners,
And the frame of birch resounded,
And the curving laths were rattling,
Shaking was the cherry collar,
And the whiplash whistling loudly,
And the rings of copper shaking,   510
As the noble horse sprang forward,
As the White-front galloped onward.

Drove the smith one day, a second,
Driving likewise on the third day ;
With one hand the horse he guided,
And with one embraced the damsel,
One foot on the sledge-side rested,
Underneath the rug the other.
Quick they sped, and fast they journeyed,
And at length upon the third day   520
Just about the time of sunset,
Hove in sight the smith's fair dwelling
And they came to Ilma's homestead,
And the smoke in streaks ascended,
And the smoke rose thickly upward,
From the house in wreaths arising,
Up amid the clouds ascending.

RUNO XXV.—THE HOME-COMING OF THE BRIDE AND BRIDEGROOM

Argument

The bride, the bridegroom and their company are received at the home of Ilmarinen (1–382). The company are hospitably entertained with food and drink: and Väinämöinen sings the praises of the host, the hostess, the inviter, the bridesmaid, and the other wedding-guests (383–672). On the way back Väinämöinen's sledge breaks down, but he repairs it, and drives home (673–738).

LONG already 'twas expected,
Long expected and awaited,
That the new bride soon would enter
The abode of Ilmarinen ;
And the eyes with rheum were dripping
Of the old folks at the windows,
And the young folks' knees were failing
As about the door they waited,
And the children's feet were freezing,
By the wall as they were standing,　　　　　10
Mid-aged folks their shoes were spoiling,
As upon the beach they wandered.

And at length upon a morning,
Just about the time of sunrise,
From the wood they heard a rattling,
As the sledge came rushing onward.

Lokka then the kindest hostess,
Kaleva's most handsome matron,
Uttered then the words which follow :
" 'Tis my son's sledge now approaching,　　　　20
As from Pohjola he cometh,
And he brings the youthful damsel.
Straight he journeys to this country,
To the homestead hastens onward,
To the house his father gave him,
Which his parents had constructed."

Therefore thus did Ilmarinen
Hasten forward to the homestead,
To the house his father gave him,
Which his parents had constructed.   30
Hazel-grouse were twittering blithely
On the collar formed of saplings,
And the cuckoos all were calling,
On the sledge's sides while sitting,
And the squirrels leaped and frolicked
On the shafts of maple fashioned.

Lokka then the kindest hostess,
Kaleva's most beauteous matron,
Uttered then the words which follow,
And in words like these expressed her :   40
" For the new moon waits the village,
And the young await the sunrise,
Children search where grow the berries,
And the water waits the tarred boat ;
For no half-moon have I waited,
Nor the sun have I awaited,
But I waited for my brother,
For my brother and step daughter,
Gazed at morning, gazed at evening,
Knew not what had happened to them,   50
If a child he had been rearing,
Or a lean one he had fattened,
That he came not any sooner,
Though he faithfully had promised
Soon to turn his footsteps homeward,
Ere defaced had been his footprints.

" Ever gazed I forth at morning,
And throughout the day I pondered,
If my brother was not coming,
Nor his sledge was speeding onward   60
Swiftly to this little homestead,
To this very narrow dwelling.
Though the horse were but a straw one,
And the sledge were but two runners,
Yet a sledge I still would call it,
And a sledge would still esteem it,

If it homeward brought my brother,
And another fair one with him.

"Thus throughout my life I wished it,
This throughout the day I looked for,   70
Till my head bowed down with gazing,
And my hair bulged up in ridges,
And my bright eyes were contracted,
Hoping for my brother's coming
Swiftly to this little household,
To this very narrow dwelling,
And at length my son is coming,
And in truth is coming swiftly,
With a lovely form beside him,
And a rose-cheeked girl beside him.   80

"Bridegroom, O my dearest brother,
Now the white-front horse unharness,
Do thou lead the noble courser
To his own familiar pasture,
To the oats but lately garnered ;
Then bestow thy greetings on us,
Greet us here, and greet the others,
All the people of the village.

"When thou hast bestowed thy greetings,
Thou must tell us all thy story.   90
Did thy journey lack adventures,
Hadst thou health upon thy journey,
To thy mother-in-law when faring,
To thy father-in-law's dear homestead,
There to woo and win the maiden,
Beating down the gates of battle,
And the maiden's castle storming,
Breaking down the walls uplifted,
Stepping on her mother's threshold,
Sitting at her father's table ?   100

"But I see without my asking,
And perceive without inquiry,
He has prospered on his journey,
With his journey well contented.
He has wooed and won the gosling,
Beaten down the gates of battle,

Broken down the boarded castle,
And the walls of linden shattered,
When her mother's house he entered,
And her father's home he entered.   110
In his care is now the duckling,
In his arms behold the dovekin,
At his side the modest damsel,
Shining in her radiant beauty.

"Who has brought the lie unto us,
And the ill report invented,
That the bridegroom came back lonely,
And his horse had sped for nothing?
For the bridegroom comes not lonely,
Nor his horse has sped for nothing;   120
Perhaps the horse has brought back something,
For his white mane he is shaking,
For the noble horse is sweating,
And the foal with foam is whitened,
From his journey with the dovekin,
When he drew the blushing damsel.

"In the sledge stand up, O fair one,
On its floor, O gift most noble,
Do thou raise thyself unaided,
And do thou arise unlifted,   130
If the young man tries to lift thee,
And the proud one seeks to raise thee.

"From the sledge do thou upraise thee,
From the sledge do thou release thee,
Walk upon this flowery pathway,
On the path of liver-colour,
Which the swine have trod quite even,
And the hogs have trampled level,
Over which have passed the lambkins,
And the horses' manes swept over.   140

"Step thou with the step of gosling,
Strut thou with the feet of duckling,
In the yard that's washed so cleanly,
On the smooth and level grassplot,
Where the father rules the household,
And the mother holds dominion,

To the workplace of the brother,
And the sister's blue-flowered meadow.
　"Set thy foot upon the threshold,
Then upon the porch's flooring,　　　　　　150
On the honeyed floor advance thou,
Next the inner rooms to enter,
Underneath these famous rafters,
Underneath this roof so lovely.
　"It was in this very winter,
In the summer just passed over,
Sang the floor composed of duckbones,
That thyself should stand upon it,
And the golden roof resounded
That thou soon should'st walk beneath it,　　160
And the windows were rejoicing,
For thy sitting at the windows.
　"It was in this very winter,
In the summer just passed over,
Often rattled the door-handles,
For the ringed hands that should close them,
And the stairs were likewise creaking
For the fair one robed so grandly,
And the doors stood always open,
And their opener thus awaited.　　　　　　170
　"It was in this very winter,
In the summer just passed over,
That the room around has turned it,
Unto those the room who dusted,
And the hall has made it ready
For the sweepers, when they swept it,
And the very barns were chirping
To the sweepers as they swept them.
　"It was in this very winter,
In the summer just passed over,　　　　　　180
That the yard in secret turned it
To the gatherer of the splinters,
And the storehouses bowed downward,
For the wanderer who should enter,
Rafters bowed, and beams bent downward
To receive the young wife's wardrobe.

"It was in this very winter,
In the summer just passed over,
That the pathways had been sighing
For the sweeper of the pathways,   190
And the cowsheds nearer drawing
To the cleanser of the cowsheds ;
Songs and dances were abandoned,
Till should sing and dance our duckling.

"On this very day already,
And upon the day before it,
Early has the cow been lowing,
And her morning hay expecting,
And the foal has loud been neighing
That his truss of hay be cast him,   200
And the lamb of spring has bleated,
That its food its mistress bring it.

"On this very day already,
And upon the day before it,
Sat the old folks at the windows,
On the beach there ran the children,
By the wall there stood the women,
In the porch-door youths were waiting,
Waiting for the youthful mistress,
And the bride they all awaited.   210

"Hail to all within the household,
Likewise hail to all the heroes,
Hail, O barn, and all within thee,
Barn, and all the guests within thee,
Hail, O hall, and all within thee,
Birchbark roof, and all thy people,
Hail, O room, and all within thee,
Hundred-boards, with all thy children !
Hail, O moon, to thee, O monarch,
And the bridal train so youthful !   220
Never was there here aforetime,
Never yesterday nor ever,
Was a bridal train so splendid :
Never were such handsome people.

"Bridegroom, O my dearest brother,
Let the red cloths now be loosened,

Laid aside the veils all silken ;
Let us see thy cherished marten,
Whom for five long years thou wooed'st,
And for eight years thou hast longed for.   230
    " Hast thou brought whom thou hast wished for,
Hast thou brought with thee the cuckoo,
From the land a fair one chosen,
Or a rosy water-maiden ?
    " But I see without my asking,
Comprehend without inquiry,
Thou has really brought the cuckoo,
Hast the blue duck in thy keeping ;
Greenest of the topmost branches,
Thou hast brought from out the greenwood,   240
Freshest of the cherry-branches,
From the freshest cherry-thickets."
    On the floor there sat an infant,
From the floor spoke out the infant :
    " O my brother, what thou bringest,
Is a tar-stump void of beauty,
Half as long as a tar-barrel,
And as tall as is a bobbin.
    " Shame, O shame, unhappy bridegroom,
All thy life thou hast desired,   250
Vowed to choose from hundred maidens,
And among a thousand maidens,
Bring the noblest of the hundred,
From a thousand unattractive ;
From the swamp you bring a lapwing,
From the hedge you bring a magpie,
From the field you bring a scarecrow,
From the fallow field a blackbird.
    " What has she as yet accomplished,
In the summer just passed over,   260
If the gloves she was not weaving,
Nor begun to make the stockings ?
Empty to the house she cometh,
To our household brings no presents,
Mice are squeaking in the baskets,
Long-eared mice are in the coppers."

Lokka, most accomplished hostess,
Kaleva's most handsome matron,
Heard these wondrous observations,
And replied in words which follow :   270
    " Wretched child, what art thou saying?
To thy own disgrace thou speakest !
Thou may'st wonders hear of others,
Others may'st perchance disparage,
But thou may'st not shame this damsel,
Nor the people of this household.

    " Bad the words that thou hast uttered,
Bad the words that thou hast spoken,
With the mouth of calf of night-time,
With the head of day-old puppy.   280
Handsome is this noble damsel,
Noblest she of all the country,
Even like a ripening cranberry,
Or a strawberry on the mountain,
Like the cuckoo in the tree-top,
Little bird in mountain-ashtree,
In the birch a feathered songster,
White-breast bird upon the maple.

    " Ne'er from Saxony came ever,
Nor in Viro could they fashion   290
Such a girl of perfect beauty,
Such a duck without an equal,
With a countenance so lovely,
And so noble in her stature,
And with arms of such a whiteness,
And with slender neck so graceful.

    " Neither comes the damsel dowerless,
Furs enough she brought us hither,
Blankets, too, as gifts she brought us,
Cloths as well she carried with her.   300
    " Much already has this damsel
Wrought by working with her spindle,
On her own reel has she wound it,
With her fingers much has finished.
Cloths of very brilliant lustre
Has she folded up in winter,

In the spring days has she bleached them,
In the summer months has dried them;
Splendid sheets the beds to spread on,
Cushions soft for heads to rest on,   310
Silken neckcloths of the finest,
Woollen mantles of the brightest.

"Noble damsel, fairest damsel,
With thy beautiful complexion,
In the house wilt thou be honoured,
As in father's house the daughter,
All thy life shalt thou be honoured,
As in husband's house the mistress.

"Never will we cause thee trouble,
Never trouble bring upon thee.   320
To the swamp thou wast not carried,
Nor from the ditch-side they brought thee,
From the cornfields rich they brought thee,
But to better fields they led thee,
And they took thee from the ale-house,
To a home where ale is better.

"Noble girl, and fairest damsel,
One thing only will I ask thee,
Didst thou notice on thy journey
Shocks of corn that stood uplifted,   330
Ears of rye in shocks uplifted,
All belonging to this homestead,
From the ploughing of thy husband?
He has ploughed and he has sown it.

"Dearest girl, and youthful damsel,
This is what I now will tell thee,
Thou hast willed our house to enter:
Be contented with the household.
Here 'tis good to be the mistress,
Good to be a fair-faced daughter,   340
Sitting here among the milk-pans,
Butter-dishes at thy service.

"This is pleasant for a damsel,
Pleasant for a fair-faced dovekin.
Broad the planking of the bathroom,
Broad within the rooms the benches,

Here the master's like thy father,
And the mistress like thy mother,
And the sons are like thy brothers,
And the daughters like thy sisters.   350
  "If the longing e'er should seize thee,
And the wish should overtake thee,
For the fish thy father captured,
Or for grouse to ask thy brother,
From thy brother-in-law ask nothing,
From thy father-in-law ask nothing ;
Best it is to ask thy husband,
Ask him to obtain them for thee.
There are not within the forest
Any four-legged beasts that wander,   360
Neither birds in air that flutter
Two-winged birds with rushing pinions,
Neither in the shining waters
Swarm the best of all the fishes,
Which thy husband cannot capture ;
He can catch and bring them to thee.
  "Here 'tis good to be a damsel,
Here to be a fair-faced dovekin ;
Need is none to work the stone-mill ;
Need is none to work the mortar ;   370
Here the wheat is ground by water,
And the rye by foaming torrents,
And the stream cleans all utensils,
And the lake-foam cleanses all things.
  "O thou lovely little village,
Fairest spot in all the country !
Grass below, and cornfields over,
In the midst between the village.
Fair the shore below the village,
By the shore is gleaming water,   380
Where the ducks delight in swimming,
And the water-fowl are sporting."
  Drink they gave the bridal party,
Food and drink they gave in plenty,
Meat provided in abundance,
Loaves provided of the finest,

And they gave them ale of barley,
Spicy drink, from wheat concocted.
Roast they gave them in abundance,
Food and drink in all abundance, 390
In the dishes red they brought it,
In the handsomest of dishes.
Cakes were there, in pieces broken,
Likewise there were lumps of butter,
Powans too, to be divided,
Salmon too, to cut to pieces,
With the knives composed of silver,
And with smaller knives all golden.

Ale unpurchased there was flowing,
Mead for which you could not bargain ; 400
Ale flowed from the ends of rafters,
Honey from the taps was oozing,
Ale around the lips was foaming,
Mead the mood of all enlivened.
Who among them should be cuckoo,
Who should sing a strain most fitting ?
Väinämöinen, old and steadfast,
He the great primeval minstrel,
He himself commenced his singing,
Set about composing verses, 410
And he spoke the words which follow,
And expressed himself in thiswise :
" O my own beloved brethren,
O most eloquent companions,
O my comrades, ready talkers,
Listen now to what I tell you,
Rarely kiss the geese each other,
Rarely sisters gaze on sisters,
Rarely side by side stand brothers,
Side by side stand mother's children, 420
In these desert lands so barren,
In the wretched northern regions.
" Shall we give ourselves to singing,
Set about composing verses ?
None can sing except the singer,
None can call save vernal cuckoo,

None can paint, except Sinetär,
None can weave save Kankahatar.
    "Lapland's children, they are singing,
And the hay-shod ones are chanting,   430
As the elk's rare flesh they feast on,
Or the meat of smaller reindeer,
Wherefore then should I not carol,
Wherefore should our children sing not,
While upon the ryebread feasting,
Or when eating is concluded?
    "Lapland's children, they are singing,
And the hay-shod ones are chanting,
As they drink from water-pitchers,
While they chew the bark of fir-tree.   440
Wherefore then should I not carol,
Wherefore should our children sing not,
While the juice of corn we're drinking,
And the best-brewed ale of barley?
    "Lapland's children they are singing,
And the hay-shod ones are chanting,
Even by the sooty fire,
As they lay the coals upon it.
Wherefore then should I not carol,
Wherefore should our children sing not,   450
Underneath these famous rafters,
Underneath a roof so splendid?
    "Good it is for men to dwell here,
Good for women to reside here,
All among the barrels ale-filled,
Standing close beside the mead-tubs,
Near the sound where swarm the powans,
Near the place for netting salmon,
Where the food is never failing,
And the drink is never stinted.   460
    "Good it is for men to dwell here,
Good for women to reside here,
Here to eat by care untroubled,
Here to live without affliction,
Here to eat unvexed by trouble,
And to live without a sorrow.

Long as lives our host among us,
All the lifetime of our hostess.
  " Which shall I first praise in singing,
Shall it be the host or hostess? 470
Always first they praise the heroes,
Therefore first I praise the Master,
He who first prepared the marshland,
And along the shore who wandered,
And he brought great stumps of fir-trees,
And he trimmed the crowns of fir-trees,
Took them to a good position,
Firmly built them all together,
For his race a great house builded,
And he built a splendid homestead, 480
Walls constructed from the forest,
Rafters from the fearful mountains,
Laths from out the woods provided,
Boards from berry-bearing heathlands,
Bark from cherry-bearing uplands,
Moss from off the quaking marshes.
  " And the house is well-constructed,
And the roof securely fastened.
Here a hundred men were gathered,
On the house-roof stood a thousand, 490
When this house was first constructed,
And the flooring duly fitted.
  " Be assured our host so worthy,
In the building of this homestead,
Oft his hair exposed to tempest,
And his hair was much disordered.
Often has our host so noble,
On the rocks his gloves left lying,
Lost his hat among the fir-trees,
In the marsh has sunk his stockings. 500
  " Often has our host so noble
In the early morning hours,
When no others had arisen,
And unheard by all the village,
Left the cheerful fire behind him,
Watched for birds in wattled wigwam,

And the thorns his head were combing,
Dew his handsome eyes was washing.
"Thus receives our host so noble,
In his home his friends around him ;   510
Filled the benches are with singers,
And with joyous guests the windows,
And the floor with talking people,
Porches, too, with people shouting,
Near the walls with people standing,
Near the fence with people walking,
Through the yard are folks parading,
Children on the ground are creeping.
"Now I first have praised the master,
I will praise our gracious hostess,   520
She who has prepared the banquet,
And has filled the table for us.
"Large the loaves that she has baked us,
And she stirred us up thick porridge,
With her hands that move so quickly,
With her soft and tenfold fingers,
And she let the bread rise slowly,
And the guests with speed she feasted ;
Pork she gave them in abundance,
Gave them cakes piled up in dishes,   530
And the knives were duly sharpened,
And the pointed blades pressed downward,
As the salmon were divided,
And the pike were split asunder.
"Often has our noble mistress,
She the most accomplished housewife,
Risen up before the cockcrow,
And before the hen's son hastened,
That she might prepare the needful,
That the work might all be finished,   540
That the beer might be concocted,
And the ale be ready for us.
"Well indeed our noble hostess,
And this most accomplished housewife,
Best of ale for us concocted,
And the finest drink set flowing.

'Tis composed of malted barley,
And of malt the very sweetest,
And with wood she has not turned it,
With a stake she has not moved it, 550
Only with her hands has raised it,
Only with her arms has turned it,
In the bathroom filled with vapour,
On the boarding, scoured so cleanly.

"Nor did she, our noble hostess,
And this most accomplished mistress,
Let the germs mature them fully,
While on ground the malt was lying.
Oft she went into the bathroom,
Went alone, at dead of midnight, 560
Fearing not the wolf should harm her,
Nor the wild beasts of the forest.

"Now that we have praised the hostess,
Let us also praise the inviter;
Who was chosen as inviter,
And upon the road to guide us?
Best inviter of the village,
Best of guides in all the village.

"There we look on our inviter,
Clad in coat from foreign countries; 570
Round his arms 'tis tightly fitted,
Neatly round his waist 'tis fitted.

"There we look on our inviter,
In a narrow cloak attired;
On the sand the skirts are sweeping,
On the ground the train is sweeping.
Of his shirt we see a little,
Only see a very little,
As if Kuutar's self had wove it,
And the tin-adorned one wrought it. 580

"Here we look on our inviter,
Belted with a belt of woollen,
Woven by the Sun's fair daughter,
By her beauteous fingers broidered,
In the times ere fire existed,
And when all unknown was fire.

"Here we look on our inviter,
With his feet in silken stockings,
And with silk are bound his stockings,
And his garters are of satin,　　　　　590
And with gold are all embroidered,
And are all adorned with silver.
"Here we look on our inviter,
Best of Saxon shoes he's wearing,
Like the swans upon the river,
Or the ducks that swim beside them,
Or the geese among the thickets,
Birds of passage in the forests.

"Here we look on our inviter,
With his golden locks all curling,　　　600
And his golden beard is plaited,
On his head a lofty helmet:
Up among the clouds it rises,
Through the forest's glancing summit;
Such a one you could not purchase
For a hundred marks or thousand.

"Now that I have praised the inviter,
I will also praise the bridesmaid.
Whence has come to us the bridesmaid,
Whence was she, the happiest, chosen?　　　610

"Thence has come to us the bridesmaid,
Thence was she, the happiest, chosen,
Where is Tanikka's strong fortress,
From without the new-built castle.

"No, she came from other regions,
Not at all from such a region;
Thence has come to us the bridesmaid,
Thence was she, the happiest, chosen,
Brought to us across the water,
And across the open ocean.　　　620

"No, she came from other regions,
Not at all from such a region,
Grew like strawberry in the country,
On the heaths where cranberries flourish,
On the field of beauteous herbage,
On the heath of golden flowerets,

Thence has come to us the bridesmaid,
Thence was she, the happiest, chosen.
  "And the bridesmaid's mouth is pretty,
As the spindle used in Suomi,   630
And the bridesmaid's eyes are sparkling,
As the stars that shine in heaven,
Gleaming are the damsel's temples,
As upon the lake the moonlight.
  "Here we look upon our bridesmaid ;
Round her neck a chain all golden,
On her head a golden head-dress,
On her hands are golden bracelets,
Golden rings upon her fingers,
In her ears are golden earrings,   640
Loops of gold upon her temples,
And her brows are bead-adorned.
  "And I thought the moon was shining,
When her golden clasp was gleaming,
And I thought the sun was shining,
When I saw her collar gleaming,
And I thought a ship was sailing,
When I saw her head-dress moving.
  "Now that I have praised the bridesmaid,
I will glance at all the people ;   650
Very handsome are the people,
Stately are the aged people,
And the younger people pretty,
And the householders are handsome.
  "I have gazed at all the people,
And I knew them all already ;
But before it never happened,
Nor in future times will happen,
That we meet so fine a household,
Or we meet such handsome people,   660
Where the old folks are so stately,
And the younger people pretty.
Clothed in white are all the people,
Like the forest in the hoarfrost,
Under like the golden dawning :
Over like the morning twilight.

" Easy to obtain was silver,
Gold among the guests was scattered,
In the grass were littered purses,
In the lanes were bags of money,   670
For the guests who were invited,
For the guests most greatly honoured."
Väinämöinen, old and steadfast,
Of the song the mighty pillar,
After this his sledge ascended,
Homeward drove upon his journey,
And he sang his songs for ever,
Sang, and chanted spells of magic,
Sang a song, and sang a second,
But, as he the third was singing,   680
Clashed against a rock the runners,
Crashed the shafts against a tree-stump,
And the sledge broke off his chanting,
And the runners stopped his singing,
And the shafts in fragments shattered,
And the boards broke all asunder.
Spoke the aged Väinämöinen,
In the very words which follow:
" Are there none among the youthful,
Of the rising generation,   690
Or perchance among the aged,
Of the sinking generation,
Who to Tuonela can wander,
And can go to Mana's country,
Thence to fetch me Tuoni's auger,
Bring me Mana's mighty auger,
That a new sledge I may fashion,
Or repair my sledge that's broken?"
But said all the younger people,
And the aged people answered: 700
" There are none among the youthful,
None at all among the aged,
None of race so highly noble,
None is such a mighty hero,
As to Tuonela to travel,
Journey to the land of Mana,

Thence to bring you Tuoni's auger,
And from Mana's home to bring it,
That a new sledge you may fashion,
Or repair the sledge that's broken."   710

Then the aged Väinämöinen,
He the great primeval minstrel,
Went again to Tuoni's country,
Journeyed to the home of Mana,
Fetched from Tuonela the auger,
Brought from Mana's home the auger.

Then the aged Väinämöinen
Sang a blue wood up before him,
In the forest rose an oak-tree,
And a splendid mountain-ashtree,   720
And from these a sledge he fashioned,
And he shaped his runners from them,
And for shafts prepared them likewise,
And the frame he thus constructed,
Made a sledge to suit his purpose,
And a new sledge he constructed.

In the shafts the horse he harnessed,
Yoked before the sledge the chestnut,
In the sledge himself he seated,
And upon the seat he sat him,   730
And without the whip the courser,
Sped, by beaded whip unharassed,
To his long-accustomed fodder,
To the food that waited for him,
And he brought old Väinämöinen,
He the great primeval minstrel,
To his own door, widely open,
To the threshold brought him safely.

NOTES TO RUNOS I—XXV

(These are by the translator, when not otherwise stated. K. K. indicates Prof. Kaarle Krohn, and A. M. Madame Aino Malmberg. For proper names, refer to the Glossary at the end of Vol. II.)

RUNO I

11. Kulta, "golden," here rendered "dearest," is a term constantly applied in the *Kalevala* to anything dear or precious.

20. "Pohja, the North, or Pohjola, the North Land, is chiefly used for the dark North, where the sun is hidden. Poetically used for a homestead in the *Kalevala*. Occasionally it is used as synonymous with Lapland." (K. K.)

21. When singing to the accompaniment of a harp, two Finns clasp their hands together, and sway backwards and forwards, in the manner described in the text. Compare Acerbi's *Travels to the North Cape*, I., chaps. xx. and xxiii., and the illustration opposite his Vol. I., p. 226.

61. Probably the honey of humble-bees (*Bombus*) is here meant, or the expression may be merely figurative.

63, 64. The metre allows the translation of the names of the cows to be inserted here.

110. Ilmatar, the Daughter of the Air;—tar is the usual feminine suffix in Finnish, and is generally to be understood to mean " daughter of ——." In the following passages we have the combined Finnish version of the widespread cosmogonical myths of the Divine Spirit brooding over the waters of Chaos ; and the Mundane Egg. In the First Recension of the *Kalevala*, however, and in many Finnish ballads, an eagle is said to have built her nest on the knees of Väinämöinen after he was thrown into the sea by the Laplander, and the Creation-Myth is thus transferred to him.

229–244. In the Scandinavian Mythology the world was created in a similar manner by Othin and his brothers from the body of the giant Ymir.

289. Vaka vanha Väinämöinen—these are the usual epithets applied to Väinämöinen in the *Kalevala*. "Vanha" means old ; "vaka" is variously interpreted : I have used "steadfast" by Prof. Krohn's advice, though I think "lusty" might be a better rendering.

320. The ring-finger is usually called the "nameless finger" in Finnish.

RUNO II

27. The Bird Cherry (*Prunus Padus*).

29. The Mountain Ash, or Rowan Tree, is a sacred tree in Finland, as in Scotland.

83. The Great Oak-tree is a favourite subject in Finnish and Esthonian ballads.

117. Finnish and Esthonian water-heroes are sometimes described as entirely composed of copper.

211. Compare the account of the breaking up of the Sampo, and the dispersal of its fragments, in Runo XLIII.

245. The summer ermine is the stoat, which turns white in winter in the North, when it becomes the ermine. The squirrel also turns grey in the North in winter.

376. The cuckoo is regarded as a bird of good omen.

RUNO III

15. We here find Väinämöinen, the primeval minstrel and culture-hero, the first-born of mortals, living in an already populated world. There seems to be a similar discrepancy in Gen. iv. 14–17.

35. Women were held in great respect in heroic times in most Northern countries.

58. "I will bewitch him who tries to bewitch me." (K. K.)

72. A gold-adorned, or perhaps merely handsome, sledge.

154. Probably another epithet for the seal.

156. The powan, or fresh-water herring (*Coregonus*), of which there are several marine and fresh-water species. They are chiefly lake-fish of the Northern Hemisphere, and in the British Islands are better known in Scotland and Ireland, and in the North of England, than in the South.

168. The word used here may also mean the elk or ox.

230. The Arch of Heaven in the *Kalevala* means the rainbow.

231, 232. The Sun and Moon are male deities in Finnish, with sons and daughters.

233. The constellation of the Great Bear.

273. Most of the heroes of the *Kalevala*, except Kullervo, have black hair, and the heroines, except the wife of Ilmarinen, golden hair.

411, 412. A common ransom in Finnish and Esthonian stories.

459. The episode of Aino is a great favourite in Finland, and the name is in common use. The story often furnishes material to poets, sculptors, etc.

533. Different stories are told of the origin of both Väinämöinen and Ilmarinen, and they are often called brothers.

RUNO IV

4. Bath-whisks are used to heighten the circulation after bathing. "The leaves are left on the stems. The bath-whisks for the winter are all made early in the summer, when the leaves are softest. Of course they become quite dry, but before using, they are steeped in hot water till they become soft and fragrant." (A. M.)

75. "The store-houses where the peasant girls keep their clothes and

ornaments are sometimes very pretty, and the girls always sleep there in summer. There are other store-houses for food." (A. M.)

121. According to Speke, Central African women are compelled to drink large quantities of milk, to make them inordinately fat, which is considered a great beauty.

206. *Fuligala glacialis.*

295. Prof. Krohn thinks the sea and not a lake is here intended.

308. This passage is hardly intelligible. "I have heard some people suggest that Aino perhaps took a birch branch to be used as a bath-whisk." (A. M.)

377. There are many popular tales in Finnish relating to animals, especially the bear, wolf, and fox, but this is the only illustration of the true "beast-epos" in the *Kalevala.*

413. "The sauna, or bath-house, is always a separate building ; and there Finnish people take extremely hot baths almost every evening." (A. M.) It is also used for confinements.

RUNO V

220. Here a human mother, rather than Ilmatar, seems to be ascribed to Väinämöinen. Visits to parents' graves for advice and assistance are common in Scandinavian and Esthonian literature. Commentators have also quoted the story of Achilles and Thetis, but this is hardly a parallel case.

RUNO VI

120. This passage is again inconsistent with the legend of Väinämöinen being the son of Ilmatar.

RUNO VII

19. The word used here is "poika," which literally means a boy, or a son.

51, 52. The original admirably expresses the hovering motion of the bird :

Lenteleikse, liiteleikse,
Katseleikse, käänteleikse.

142. In the original "the song of a cock's child."

177, 178. Weeping appears no more disgraceful to the heroes of the *Kalevala* than to those of the *Iliad.* Still, Väinämöinen not unfrequently plays a very undignified part when in difficulties.

241. Louhi recognized him, though he would not mention his name.

286. "Virsu is a shoe made of birch bark." (A. M.)

311. It appears that the magic mill called a Sampo could only be forged by a competent smith from materials which Louhi alone possessed, and which, perhaps, she could not again procure. Otherwise

Ilmarinen could have forged another for himself, and it would have been unnecessary for the heroes to steal it. The chain forged by the dwarfs, according to the Prose Edda, for binding the wolf Fenrir, was also composed of materials which could not again be procured. " It was fashioned out of six things ; to wit, the noise made by the footfall of a cat, the beards of women, the roots of stones, the sinews of bears, the breath of fish, and the spittle of birds."

RUNO VIII

3, 4. The daughter of Louhi is never mentioned again in connection with the rainbow ; and it is quite incorrect to call her the Maiden of the Rainbow, as some writers have done, for no such title is ever applied to her in the poem.

35. There are so many instances of maidens being carried off, or enticed into sledges, in the *Kalevala*, that it seems almost to have been a recognized legal form of marriage by capture.

57. Finnish magicians profess to understand the language of birds ; but the passage in the text is probably intended only in jest.

152. In the Icelandic saga of Grettir, the hero mortally wounds himself in the leg while trying to chop up a piece of driftwood on which a witch had laid her curse.

179. The Finns supposed that if the origin of any hostile agent was known, and could be recited to it, its power for evil was at an end. In Denmark, the naming of any person or thing was an evil omen, and liable to bring about its destruction.

217, 218. Finnish hamlets are sometimes built on a hillside in the manner described.

RUNO IX

35, 36. Here we seem to have an allusion to the first chapter of Genesis.

44. The same epithet, Luonnotar, is sometimes applied to Ilmatar, and thus Väinämöinen might literally be called the brother of Iron.

111, 112. Pallas Athene sprang armed from the brain of Zeus ; Karna, in India, the son of the Sun, was born with armour and ear-rings ; and Mexitli in Mexico was born with a spear in his hand.

231. Hornets often build their nests under the eaves of houses.

242. Both frogs and toads exude a more or less poisonous secretion from the skin.

433. Honeydew seems to be meant here.

525, 526. An imaginary mountain to which the sorcerers professed to be able to banish pain and sickness.

RUNO X

306. Compare the account of the forging of the Gold and Silver Bride in Runo XXXVII.

311. "Ilmarinen first employs ordinary servants, and then calls the winds to his assistance." (K. K.)

331. In the Icelandic sagas, we read of the sword Tyrfing, forged by dwarfs, which, if ever drawn, could not again be sheathed till it had slain at least one victim.

332. Literally, "on best days."

414. In the story of Ala Ed-Deen Abush-Shamat, in the *1001 Nights*, we read of a magic bead with five facets, on which were engraved a camel, an armed horseman, a pavilion, a couch, etc., according to the use intended to be made of each facet.

RUNO XI

31–42. Salme and Linda are similarly wooed by the Sun, the Moon, and a Star in the Esthonian poem, Kalevipoeg (see Kirby's *Hero of Esthonia*, I., pp. 10–15).

264–266. These names mean respectively Blackies, Strawberries, Cranberries. "I think Lemminkainen means that he has no cows, and only calls these different berries his cows." (A. M.)

306. Lemminkainen appears to have been afraid that some one else might carry off his wife, if she showed herself in public (especially Untamo, says Prof. Krohn).

385. The Snow Bunting (*Plectrophanes nivalis*), a white bird more or less varied with black.

RUNO XII

25. The meaning is a little uncertain. Literally, "the only boy," as Madame Malmberg suggests. The commentary renders it, "the gallant youth."

93. The Finns and Lapps often hide money in the ground. The word used in l. 94 is "penningin," from "penni," a word common to most Teutonic and Northern languages.

211, 212. Such omens of death are common in fairy tales; as, for instance, the bleeding knives in the story of the Envious Sisters in the *1001 Nights*. The bleeding trees in mediæval romance belong to rather a different category of ideas.

233. Lemminkainen seems to have hidden himself to escape further remonstrances from his mother and Kyllikki.

262. Probably a creature like a kelpie or Phooka.

474. We are not told how Louhi escaped; but she seems to have come to no harm.

RUNO XIII

105. The part played by Hiisi in the *Kalevala* usually resembles that played by Loki in the Scandinavian Mythology.

109. Animals, etc., are often thus constructed in Finnish, Esthonian, and Siberian mythology by gods, demons, and magicians. They do not seem able to create from nothing, but to manufacture what they please or what they can from pre-existing materials, however incongruous.

111. I suppose rushes are here intended.

RUNO XIV

33. The word **here** translated "islands" properly means a wooded hill surrounded by marshland.

47, 48. Mielikki's gold and silver are the spoils of the chase.

69. Honey is sometimes used in the *Kalevala* for anything sweet and agreeable, just as golden is used for anything beautiful.

103, 104. It appears that the hunter's fortune in the chase was foretold by the rich or shabby garments worn by the forest-deities.

142. Finnish women often wear a blouse over their other garments.

216. Kuningas (king) is a Teutonic word, which rarely occurs in the *Kalevala*. The heroes are patriarchs, or chiefs of clans ; not kings, as in Homer.

248. There is often much confusion of terms in the *Kalevala*. The creature here mentioned is generally called an elk, but often a reindeer, and in this line a camel-foal.

304. When the inferior deities are deaf or too weak, the heroes appeal to the higher Gods.

308. The reference here seems to be to Gen. vii. 11. "The whole passage is of Christian origin." (K. K.)

RUNO XV

7. Compare Homer, *Iliad*, III., 311–314.

240. This episode slightly resembles the story of Isis and Osiris.

498. The constellation of Orion is variously called by the Finns, the Moonshine, the Sword of Kaleva, and the Scythe of Väinämöinen.

559–562. This conceit is common in fairy tales (especially in Russian ones) in the case of heroes wakened from the dead. Sometimes it takes a comic form ; and sometimes, as in the present case, a pathetic one.

617 "Dirty-nosed" is a common opprobrious expression in Esthonia.

RUNO XVI

27. The account of the boatbuilding in "Hiawatha's Sailing" is evidently imitated from this passage.

128. In Roman times divination from birds was chiefly taken from their flight or feeding.

RUNO XVII

20. Roads of this description are thoroughly Oriental in character.

86. In Icelandic sagas we often find heroes roused from their graves, but this is usually attempted in order to obtain a sword which has been buried with them.

93–104. Hiawatha was also swallowed by the sturgeon Nahma, but the circumstances were quite different.

211. Note the resonance of the line:

Kuusista kuhisevista.

237. Ahava, a dry cold wind that blows in March and April, probably corresponding to our cold spring east wind.

285, 286. Vipunen here refers to himself as a little man, which I presume is to be understood figuratively, as I have rendered it.

RUNO XVIII

379. Compare Cuchullain's wooing of Eimer in Irish story.

RUNO XIX

33. This episode is very like the story of Jason and Medea.

210. "The wolf Fenrir opens his enormous mouth; the lower jaw reaches to the earth, and the upper one to heaven, and would in fact reach still further were there space to admit of it." **(Prose** Edda.)

217. Vetehinen, a water-spirit.

311 "Ukko's bow" here means the rainbow, broken by the fiery eagle. It may be worth noting that in the Scandinavian Mythology, the sons of Fire (Muspell) are to ride over the rainbow, and break it to pieces, on their way to battle with the gods.

483. In the Danish Ballads there are several stories of children speaking in their cradles, but generally to vow vengeance against an enemy.

RUNO XX

17. The Great Ox is a stock subject in Finnish and Esthonian ballad literature.

RUNO XXI

161. The Glutton or wolverine, a well-known animal in sub-Arctic Europe, Asia, and America.

182–186. These civilities sound very Oriental.

393. This curious passage may have been partly suggested by the "coats of skin," and "the land flowing with milk and honey" of the Old Testament.

RUNO XXII

76. The word used here for father is taatto, which curiously recalls the Welsh tad. (English, dad.)

194. In the Scandinavian Mythology the giantess Skadi was required to choose a husband from among the gods by looking at their feet only.

RUNO XXIII

330. The usual word to express a long time is viikko, a week.

469, 470. These infernal damsels play various parts in the *Kalevala*, as boat-women, death-bringers, etc., and here we find them in the character of Furies.

487. The term "snowy month" is used for the period between Feb. 20 and March 20. I have rendered it March.

787–792. Perhaps this is only figurative, as in the case of the unpropitious forest-deities.

RUNO XXIV

119. The roots of the marsh arum (*Calla palustris*), not a British plant, though naturalized in a pond at Ripley. The most usual substitute for more wholesome food in times of famine is bread composed of a mixture of fir-bark and rye.

240. Slav peasant women are said sometimes to regard beating as a sign of affection on the part of their husbands, but this does not seem to be the case with the Finns. In the *Kalevala* we read a good deal about wife-beating in theory, but find very little of it in practice ; and even the licentious and violent Lemminkainen never thinks of beating his wife when he quarrels with her.

279–296. A similar story is told to the Princess by her confidante Olga, in the Russian opera *Rusalka* (water-nymph), Act III. scene i.

> "And now I'd better sing a little song :
> As they passed in our street,
> A man besought his wife,
> 'Why don't you look pleasant ?
> You are my delight,
> Darling Mashenka.'
> "But the woman was obstinate,
> And averted her little head ;
> 'Oh, I don't want your caresses,
> Nor your pretty speeches ;
> I'm not very well,
> And I've got a headache.'

> " But under a birch tree
> The man taught his wife ;
> 'Wait a bit, my darling,
> I'll beat that tune out of you,
> In my own way.'
> " Then the woman was sorry,
> Bowed low as the waistband.
> 'Don't frighten yourself, dearest,
> And do not be troubled,
> I find myself better,
> My headache has gone.' "

446, 450, 454. The commentary explains the word used here to mean ' wander round thee," an alteration which I consider unnecessary except in the last line.

467. From the sarcastic tone of this speech, Ilmarinen seems to have been quite tired and disgusted with all the fuss, in which most of our readers will probably sympathize with him.

RUNO XXV

47. According to popular usage, a son is ennobled by being called a brother.

97. In some of the legends of Sigurd and Brynhilda, Brynhilda is represented as lying asleep in a tower of glass, encompassed by a circle of fire, through which Sigurd had to ride to wake her. In this story she is the prototype of the Sleeping Beauty.

157. We often read in Russian folk-tales of revolving huts supported on fowls' legs.

159. The favourite weapon of the Icelander Skarphedin, the son of Njal, was a bell which rang out shortly before any person was to be killed by it.

169. In the dales of Yorkshire it used to be considered very inhospitable not to leave the door open at mealtimes.

289, 290. Saxony and Viro are Germany and Esthonia.

564. Apparently a sort of master of the ceremonies at Finnish weddings, corresponding to the Russian svat, or matchmaker.

596. The scoter duck, (*Oidemia nigra*).

642. Brows ; literally, eyelashes.

646. Her shift-collar.

665, 666. The beautiful Esthonian story of the Dawn, the Moon, and the Morning and Evening Twilight will be found in Jones and Kropf's *Folk-Tales of the Magyars*, pp. 326–328, and in Kirby's *Hero of Esthonia*, II., pp. 30–34.

END OF VOL. I

CONTENTS OF VOL. II